Doing Valu

Doing Valuable Time

The Present, the Future, and Meaningful Living

Cheshire Calhoun

OXFORD
UNIVERSITY PRESS

OXFORD
UNIVERSITY PRESS

Oxford University Press is a department of the University of Oxford. It furthers the University's objective of excellence in research, scholarship, and education by publishing worldwide. Oxford is a registered trade mark of Oxford University Press in the UK and certain other countries.

Published in the United States of America by Oxford University Press
198 Madison Avenue, New York, NY 10016, United States of America.

© Oxford University Press 2018

CIP data is on file at the Library of Congress
ISBN 978–0–19–085186–6

1 3 5 7 9 8 6 4 2

Printed by Sheridan Books, Inc., United States of America

Contents

Acknowledgments

Most of the essays in this book have undergone many incarnations as a result of probing questions and criticisms from audiences and anonymous reviewers. My special thanks to Susan Wolf who, when I first began thinking about meaningful living, graciously agreed to my visiting and consulting her. I have found her work on meaningful living especially inspiring. Special thanks, too, to Catriona Mackenzie for inviting me to present at the Practical Identity and Narrative Agency conference, thus giving me an opportunity to think about some of the ideas in chapter 3. And thanks to Glen Pettigrove, whose invitation to present a paper on a neglected virtue led to my reflections on contentment. I am grateful to my former mentor, Bob Solomon, and hope that he might have liked "Living with Boredom," a version of which was written for a special issue of *Sophia* honoring him after his death in 2007. Finally, thanks to Tyler Cook for meticulous editorial help in preparing this manuscript.

Chapter 2, "Geographies of Meaningful Living," originally appeared in *Journal of Applied Philosophy* 32, no. 1 (2015): 15–34. © 2015 John Wiley & Sons, Inc. Reprinted by permission of John Wiley & Sons, Inc. Some revisions, additions, and editorial changes have been made.

Portions of chapter 3, "Taking an Interest in One's Future," were taken from "Losing One's Self." Copyright 2008. From *Practical Identity and Narrative Agency* by Catriona MacKenzie and Kim Atkins. Reproduced by permission of Taylor and Francis Group, LLC, a division of Informa PLC.

Chapter 5, "What Good Is Commitment?," originally appeared in *Ethics* 119, no. 4 (July 2009): 613–641. © 2009 by The University of Chicago. All rights reserved. Some revisions, additions, and editorial changes have been made.

Chapter 6, "Living with Boredom," is a longer version of an essay that originally appeared in *Sophia*, "Living with Boredom, 2011, 269–279, Cheshire Calhoun (© Springer Science + Business Media B.V. 2011). With permission of Springer.

Chapter 7, "On Being Content with Imperfection," originally appeared in *Ethics* 127, no. 2 (January 2017): 327–352. © 2017 by The University of Chicago. All rights reserved. Some revisions, additions, and editorial changes have been made.

Doing Valuable Time

1

Introduction
Having a Future, Leading a Life, and Spending Time

We are *evaluators*. We evaluate the world and people around us, as well as the quality of our own lives. And we take up evaluative attitudes such as resentment and content-ment. Our capacity for evaluation makes possible our agency. We evaluate our options for action, engage in activities of our own choosing, select principles to live by, and in general, govern the course of our lives and our interactions with others. We are also *temporally oriented beings*. We anticipate particular future events, previsaging them in our imagination, and we live in the present under a general sense of what the future will be like. We can, and often do, imagine how the temporal unfolding of events might have proceeded otherwise, and thus how our past or present life might have been dif-ferent. We understand our own life's time as something to be spent and open to our choices of how to spend it; and we take steps in the present to determine our future.

This is a book about the connections between these two features of human persons. One connection is that our own present and future are a subject of evaluation and choice: we have views about what we should do in the present, as well as in the future; views about the goodness or badness of our present or future situation and what would have been, or would be, better or worse; and views about what sort of future would interest us in going on. Those views are often accompanied by evaluative attitudes—for example, hope, despair, disappointment, discontentment, interest, and boredom.

A second connection is that our pursuit of what we value typically takes place over time. So, as evaluators who also live through time, we have to decide not just what we value but also how committed we are to our future containing that value, and thus how much time we are willing to invest in pursuing our aims in the face of obstacles and setbacks that push the realization of our aims into a remoter future. Moreover, one of our aims as temporal evaluators is to spend time with what we value. So, we also have to decide which value qualities we want to spend time with (think, for example, about how you select books to read) and how much time to spend with a particular kind of value quality (two hours? an entire afternoon?). More generally, we have to decide how to manage the pursuit of what we value, given that the future includes the immediate, mediate, and long-range future and is ultimately limited by our own mortality.

What I have to say in this book about the connection between being an evaluator and being temporally oriented has been inspired by a set of important philosophical conversations about the temporality of agency. First, there is now a considerable literature on the idea that we are *selves*—that is, we have a personal identity and are unified across time into a single ongoing person—in virtue of the fact that we construct (though not always consciously) stories about our lives that unify ourselves across time. We are narrative selves. This ability to narratively unify the different parts of our temporal existence into a single self has seemed to many to be a precondition for being an agent—someone who can govern and be responsible for the course of her life across time.

Second, there is the idea that in taking something to be a reason for action, as, for example, we might take the fact that a carton of eggs comes from cage-free chickens as a reason for buying it rather than a different carton, we are doing something that reaches into the future. In taking something to be a reason, we adopt, in however modest a fashion, a principle of choice and we commit not just our present self but our future self as well; our future self must either continue to act on that principle or else come up with an intelligible account of why that principle should be discarded or modified.

Third, there is the idea that what makes our lives meaningful and gives us an interest in going on into the future is our caring deeply about some one or more things in a way that gives what we care about normative priority in our lives. That is, the things we care deeply about are also what we aim to make our lives about, are resistant to sacrificing, take care to preserve, and the like.

Last is the idea that planning, in the most general sense of framing intentions that settle the question of what we will do in the future, is central to the human exercise of agency. Such plans might be quite simple, as in deciding what to prepare for breakfast, while others involve plans in the more everyday sense of laying out a complex course of action for achieving a more temporally remote aim, such as the complex plans involved in relocating to a new home.

What these quite different philosophical views share in common is a basic methodological strategy. The strategy is one of attending to the temporality of agents, particularly their future orientation, in order to correctly describe important features of agents: their unity, their giving themselves reasons, their being motivated to lead their lives, and their engaging in intentional action.

In what follows, I adopt the strategy of attending to the temporality of persons for purposes of exploring some central ways in which evaluators connect themselves to their present and their future, and of trying to understand why they sometimes find themselves disconnected from their present and their future.

Chapters 2 and 3 consider two different things we typically have in mind when we describe our lives as meaningful or meaningless. On the one hand, we *evaluate* the quality of our lives as a whole or the quality of more limited time expenditures. As beings with a life's time to dispose of, one of our central concerns is that of doing so meaningfully. "Meaningful" is a term of qualitative evaluation. Chapter 2 is devoted to determining what meaningful living consists in. I resist the dominant approaches to meaningful living that require meaningful lives be devoted to agent-independently valuable pursuits. Instead, I suggest that we get a more useful and plausible account of meaningfulness by tying meaningful living to the agent's pursuit of ends that she takes herself (perhaps mistakenly) to have reason to value.

In addition to using "meaningful" as a term of evaluation, we sometimes use "I find my life meaningful (or meaningless)" to indicate our *motivation* (or lack thereof) to continue on toward the future. That is, in addition to evaluating the meaningfulness of what we are doing with our time, one of the basic ways we as agents connect ourselves to our future is simply by taking an interest in it. Taking a motivating interest in the future, however, can be lost, as those who have suffered depression well know. In losing interest in their future, agents lose the motivation to deliberate, choose, and act, and thus to continue leading the life of an agent. Chapter 3 focuses on what enables and what undermines our taking a motivating interest in our own future and leading the life of an agent. This involves explaining how valuing the particular pursuits and relationships that occupy our time could produce a *general* interest in living into the future. It also involves examining the background assumptions about what the future will be like, on which depend our interest in leading the life of an agent who actively takes herself into the future through her choices and plans.

Being motivated to deliberate and to act on their deliberations is one way agents *take* themselves into their future, actively striving to determine its shape rather than passively awaiting the temporal unfolding of events. Hope is another way, and this is the subject of chapter 4. Minimally, in hoping, we take ourselves into the future by adopting a preference among several possible temporal unfoldings of events and imaginatively inhabiting that preferred future. But we often talk as though hope plays a more significant role in our taking ourselves into that future: hope *motivates*. This motivational role is especially important in the kind of hope that I will call *practical hope*—a hope for the success of our own activities, such as the hope that our efforts to make new friends will succeed. This practical hope differs from hope merely for the occurrence of some desirable thing, like sunny weather, in that it is connected to the exercise of agency. Practical hope for the realization of our aims plays an important role in motivating us to take, and continue taking, ourselves into the future, even when obstacles and setbacks disrupt our plans. Chapter 4 examines this motivational role of practical hope in sustaining our practical pursuits. Although hope is often taken to be a motivationally important emotional attitude, it is not at all obvious what hope's motivational "oomph" consists of or even why hope should be necessary. After all, in embarking on our pursuits, we have motivating reasons to do so. So, what work is left for hope to do, and how could it do that work if not by supplying an additional motivating reason?

Practical hope, of course, presupposes that agents have already made one kind of connection with their future by settling on some goal for the future. The most obvious way that agents connect themselves to their futures is by managing the trajectory of their lives—what they aim for—within shorter and longer temporal segments of a lifetime. In framing simple intentions, in forming more complex but provisional plans that might be revised or abandoned depending on how things work out, and in making commitments that we are resistant to revising, we lock in future actions to a lesser or greater degree and attach ourselves more or less tightly to a particular vision of the future.

Chapter 5 examines these differing degrees to which we settle on future actions and attach ourselves to a particular envisioned future, clarifying what is involved in making a commitment, rather than merely intending or provisionally planning. My main interest, however, is in assessing the reasons that favor settling the future more or less firmly. It might seem important, and certainly has seemed so to many philosophers, to lock in the future in the particularly strong way that commitments effect: it is important to the narrative unity of a life and important for leading a meaningful life. Chapter 5 explores those thoughts by critically raising the question "What good is commitment?" and then sorting out better from worse reasons for forging a strong link between one's present and future by making commitments.

While a lack of interest in one's own future and hopeless despair are significant, and common sources of a disconnection from the future, boredom is perhaps the most common source of disconnection from both the present and the future that evaluators experience. Indeed, one of the unintended consequences of committing oneself to spending one's time in a particular way is boredom. But why do evaluators so often find themselves bored? Taking issue with a view, prevalent in psychology, that boredom is a problem, I argue in chapter 6 that it is virtually an inevitable feature of being an evaluator who lives through time and makes decisions about how to spend her time. We end up bored for a variety of quite different reasons—our daily life is filled with "have-to-dos"; we find ourselves with more time on our hands than we know what to do with; we suffer the monotony of spending extended time with the same value quality; and sometimes our chosen life course ends up going nowhere. Indeed, boredom attends some of the most typical things that evaluators do.

In boredom, we disconnect from our present by losing interest in it. In discontentment, we disconnect from our present by refusing to accept the present we have gotten, as opposed to the better present that could have been. In contentment, by contrast, the present we have appears preferable to alternative temporal unfoldings of events that would have been worse. In chapter 7, I argue that contentment and discontentment—unlike being happy, unhappy, pleased, or displeased—are distinctively connected to our temporality, and in particular to our ability to imagine alternative, counterfactual temporal unfoldings of events. Contentment and discontentment are also distinctively connected with our nature as evaluators. In particular, they are connected with our use of standards—*expectation frames*—for what will count for us as a "good enough" turn of present events. Whether we focus on the better or the worse counterfactual present, and whether we find our present situation good enough, depends on what goods we think we ought to have been able to expect to find in the present. Those expectation frames are, however, open to choice. Although throughout the book I largely avoid giving explicit advice on how to do valuable time, in this last chapter I do offer advice: a disposition to employ expectation frames that enable contentment is a virtue.

One of my aims in writing this book was to consider topics related to the psychology of agency and evaluation that have been surprisingly underdeveloped in philosophy, given how central they are to our lived experience. A second aim was to look at those topics in ways that unsettle what seem to me to be both initially plausible and common assumptions. Those assumptions include the ideas that being interested in one's own future depends on deeply caring about some project or relationship; that taking oneself to have a reason to do something by itself motivates (or fails to motivate) quite independently of how agents imagine their future; that hope supplies a motivating "oomph" that, by itself, explains how the hopeful are able to withstand setbacks and surmount obstacles to their practical pursuits; that boredom is a problem and something people can (and should) try to avoid by making different and better choices about how to spend their time or by becoming a different sort of person; and finally, that discontentment with the imperfect present is always a reasonable and motivationally important attitude for agents to have.

In addition to the central theme of an evaluator's connection to and disconnection from her own present and future, there are two subthemes running through these chapters. The first is the *difficulty* of leading the life of an evaluator across time. For any sentient being who has desires, whether a human being, a horse, or a hamster, simply *having* a life is bound to be difficult at times. Pain, fatigue, hunger, illness, frustration, and fear are ordinary features of sentient life. But beings like us, who not only have but also *lead* a life and evaluate the way our time gets spent, face additional difficulties. Agents are vulnerable to becoming demoralized when their efforts to control their futures are ineffective and when they cannot secure themselves adequately against disastrous misfortune. They are vulnerable to losing a sense of the meaningfulness of their lives and thus of the point in trying to shape their futures. Agents routinely confront obstacles and setbacks in attempting to achieve their aims and thus find themselves needing to adopt some policy about whether those difficulties are reason to change course or reason to employ coping strategies. In the face of such obstacles and setbacks, agents must also find supplementary motivational resources beyond the good reasons they originally had for pursuing particular goals. For human agents, the sheer quantity of time that they must determine how to spend may itself pose difficulties, most obviously during periods of enforced waiting, excess leisure, and limited or unattractive options. That both the trajectory of a whole life and specific portions of the future are subjects of evaluation and planning may also pose difficulties. The long-range view of the future makes it natural to plan long-term activities, relationships, identities, and so on, but pursuing valuable and interesting lifetime aims may not fit well with spending temporal parts of one's life in valuable and interesting ways. Many of the things we do in the course of leading a life—submitting to norms for what has to be done with one's time, spending extended time with what one values, and determining what one is and is not willing to take an interest in—are a setup for boredom with the very life one has chosen to lead. Finally, the very fact that we are evaluators who can always imagine what would be better, and the fact that we are doers who need to attend to the obstacles in the way of achieving our plans but who can safely disattend what is going right, biases us toward discontentment with our present circumstances. That bias is exacerbated by cultural influences that encourage discontentment and discourage grateful appreciation of the goods in our imperfect present.

A second subtheme in this book is the *importance of small things*—features of evaluators' lives that, at first glance, don't seem particularly important to doing valuable time. One sort of small thing is the set of activities and experiences that, in our rank-ordering of what's valuable, have only minor value and we don't care about in a deep, identity-defining way—for example, petting one's cat or living where the sunlight has a particular quality. Some of these small things, I will suggest, may nevertheless play an important role in our being attracted to our own future and in our feeling that our lives are being spent in meaningful or attractive ways.

A second sort of "small thing" concerns what we actually expend our life's time on in the course of a day or a week. In thinking about meaningful living, it's tempting to think just about the big things—big in evaluative importance and big in temporal extent—that one's life is about, such as one's career or long-term relationship. We tend to overlook how these big things involve lots of small time expenditures on instrumental and constitutive activities. In overlooking these smaller activities, we may fail to see and reckon with the costs of what our lives have come to be about.

Yet another "small thing" is what fails to capture our interest or what bores us. The experience of boredom—an attitude often connected with the trivial or unimportant things in our lives—may itself seem a small thing in comparison to evaluative attitudes like resentment at injustice or pride in one's accomplishments. However, vulnerability to boredom, I will suggest, is inescapably connected to our capacities for evaluation and agency.

Finally, there are the "small things" that constitute modest goods in imperfect circumstances. As evaluators capable of imagining what would have been better, and even better yet, than what we presently have or are experiencing, it is tempting to ignore the actual goods in our imperfect situation. But as I will suggest in the final chapter, there is reason to think that being disposed to appreciate and be grateful for those small goods is a virtue.

In the rest of this introductory chapter, I take up two preliminary topics. The first is what it means for evaluators to be future oriented. Chapters 3 and 4 focus specifically on the ways evaluators connect and disconnect themselves from their future, given what they anticipate that future to be. So, it will be helpful to have a specific account of how the content of the future is given in present experience and in present decision-making contexts. The second preliminary topic is what "leading a life" means. We might have two quite different things in mind when we say that evaluators "lead" their lives. On the one hand, we might mean choosing what we want to *characterize* our lives—this might be thought of as the ingredients of a life plan or a narrative identity. On the other hand, we might mean simply having a *normative outlook* and making choices on that basis about how to shape the course of the future, rather than either letting ourselves be drawn along by our strongest impulses or passively suffering the temporal unfolding of events. Appreciating at least some of the reasons evaluators find *leading* their lives difficult requires keeping in mind both of these senses of "leading a life." If we focus just on the first sense, we lose sight of all the ways evaluators spend their time that they might regard as peripheral to the overall characterization of their lives but that nevertheless are the subject of decision-making and choice. We also lose sight of the ways evaluators choose to spend time that feels more like using up rather than leading a life. Moreover, as I will argue in chapters 2 and 5, there can be real tensions between the choices that give meaningful and interesting shape to a whole life and the choices that make local segments of time meaningful and interesting.

HAVING A FUTURE

We are temporal beings. We do not just persist through chronological time the way stars and marigolds do. We have a future in the sense that we understand that the course of present events unfolds toward a future. We make present decisions precisely in order to determine our future actions and, we hope, to affect the specific way events will unfold over time. We also have a future, rather than merely persist toward it, in that we understand ourselves as possessors of a life that has to be led—which is to say, a lifetime that has to be filled up by us in one way or another. Future life time stretches out ahead as both a resource, as we have time available in which to do things, and a burden, as we will have to decide what to do with the immediate, mediate, and long-range parts of that lifetime. Finally, we have a future in the sense that we have, sometimes consciously and sometimes nonconsciously, a sense of what our own future will or might look like, such that we can anticipate and previsage in imagination both specific and global features of that future—as, for instance, one might anticipate being hungry by evening or imagine one's living environment next year. Our future thus has a *content*, although, of course, the anticipated content of the future may not match events as they actually unfold. It is that contentful sense of what the future will look like that makes the future largely unsurprising when it arrives and that also forms the background for our present choices.

I will say more about the first two points—that we understand the present as unfolding toward the future, and that we understand ourselves as having a lifetime to be spent—in later sections of this chapter. Here, I want to focus on the idea that the future toward which we are directed has a *content*. By "content," I do not mean the way the future will actually turn out. I mean the future as we imagine, anticipate, predict, assume, or sense it will be.

Phenomenologically, the content of the future appears in our present experience in a variety of ways. Most obviously, we make the content of the future present through conscious reflection on it. Reflective recall is often about the future. For example, you recall the intentions and plans you adopted earlier for what is still in the future at this point, or you recall the work schedule you've been assigned for next week. Similarly, present deliberation and planning bring into view what you may or will do in the future, as well as your expectations about what the future context of action will be. You consider, for example, who to invite to a future party on the basis of your expectations about who will be in town on that future date and which people are likely to enjoy that future party. Making predictions—for example, that August will be hotter than May—and taking stock of the possible ways the future might unfold obviously involve direct reflection on the future. Conscious reflection on the future also includes *previsaging* it, to use Richard Wollheim's helpful term.[1] Similar to the way that experiential memory

---

[1] Richard Wollheim, "Ourselves and Our Future," in *How Many Questions? Essays in Honor of Sidney Morganbesser*, ed. Leigh Cauman, Roberet Schwartz, and Charles Parson (Indianapolis, IN: Hackett, 1983), 366–383, 382–383.

allows us to make the past present by recalling what the past was like, imaginative pre-visaging enables us to inhabit, in advance, the possible, likely, or definite future.

The future also *saturates* the present at a nonreflective, nonconscious level. We do not typically find the immediate future surprising nor do we need to rely on conscious reflection about the future in order to navigate toward it. That is in part because we experience the inanimate objects and animate beings in our world as temporally persisting into the future, so we aren't surprised to find they are still there later on. Moreover, we develop, over time, a substantial understanding of the continuities and discontinuities of experience. We learn, for example, what the weather is typically like in various seasons, how congested traffic is at certain times of the day, which people tend to be cheerful or grumpy, and which pet likes to sleep on the bed. Much of this background understanding, which enables us to anticipate the future without consciously reflecting on it, is also intermittently the subject of conscious noticing and reflecting. But some of our background understanding of what the future will be like is simply a result of habituation to the future. Think, for example, about how you might expect, without consciously thinking about it, that your car will start, that the electricity in your house will be working when you wake up, or that your arthritic hip will ache when you walk. You come to expect these simply because they have routinely been the case. When we have been habituated to the future, we typically discover what future we were expecting only when those expectations are not fulfilled.

One important expectation about the future is that of one's own future action. Routines and habits that are established by reflective choice (for example, deciding to be an early riser), or by not considering the option of handling a repetitive situation differently from before (for example, gravitating to the same seat in the classroom one consciously chose the last time), settle the question of future action. So, too, do intentions, provisional plans, and commitments. Social conventions for organizing one's activities in terms of work weeks, weekends, bedtime, dinnertime, and the like, as well as social understandings of age-appropriate activities in the human life cycle, also contribute to our having a background sense of what we will be doing at different future times.

In short, the time we inhabit is, unlike chronological time, not a string of separable instants but, rather, a time in which the past is retained and the future is anticipated in the present. And unlike chronological time, lived temporal dimensions have a content. My future is not a blank. It is instead richly filled in with the content of my predictions, speculations, imagination, intentions, plans, routines, habits, and acquired expectations. And the ways that the future is not filled in, too, can be a kind of content. The indeterminate future may, for example, appear ripe with opportunities, a field of open possibilities, a place of uncertainty and risk, or full of unfamiliar things.

The future toward which one is oriented in the present has not only a content but also a *qualitative character*. This is in part because particular features of the future—events, actions, locations, and so on—have a qualitative character we can appreciate in advance by calling them to mind in the present. You recall, for example, an upcoming chore that you regard as onerous or a planned trip to a peaceful countryside. But one's sense of the future generally—apart from reflection on some anticipated bit of it—also typically has a qualitative feel. Often this is in virtue of some contents of the future dominating one's general sense of (some stretch of) the future. For instance, that onerous chore on your schedule colors the entire upcoming day by being what everything else is leading up to. Or, a loss over which you continue to grieve weighs down the future. The future may also acquire its qualitative character from general characteristics of the future's contents: the future may be a place of continuing loneliness or bad luck or physical debilitation. And, of course, the future is often simply more of the same, so that whatever qualitative character colors the present also extends into the future.

The qualitative character of the future figures in the lives of agents as both a datum for decision making and a motivating influence on present and future action. Among the considerations we factor into our decision making is the qualitative character of the future. Sometimes that qualitative character provides a reason to act to change that qualitative character of the future. Your present invariant and unexciting routine, for example, stretches into future months—a reason to alter that future by planning now for some future novelty. Sometimes the qualitative character of the future provides a reason for or against an action already under consideration. In timing a special outing, you consider the qualitative character of different future dates—ruling out, for example, dates anticipated to be dominated by stress. That you will be too stressed at some future date to enjoy the outing is an instrumental reason for not choosing that date, since the aim of enjoyment will not be served if you do. Put differently, the decisions we make about future actions often turn, in part, on how we expect to feel in that future context, including what mood we expect to be in. Will we, in that future context, be in a frame of mind conducive to what we now consider doing then?

This is to say that there are two different kinds of reasons for action that play a role in decision making. On the one hand, there are normative considerations of the value of the activities and aims themselves, and instrumental considerations of the best means for bringing them about. You consider, for example, whether a water aerobics class is choiceworthy, whether it is more choiceworthy than a Zumba class, and what you need to do to get signed up for and pay for the class. On the other hand, there are considerations concerning whether a choiceworthy activity is worth doing, given the qualitative character of the future context and the frame of mind you will be in then. The qualitative character of the future context may impede realization of the aim of the activity—as in the example of being too stressed to get the aimed-for enjoyment from an outing. But it may also impede appreciating the value of the activity. So, for example, although you may be able to play a good game of chess while distracted with worry about looming deadlines, when such a qualitatively bad future saturates the present, you are unlikely to appreciate playing the game. As evaluators, we aim not just to fill our lives with choiceworthy activities but also to appreciate the value of those activities when they are under way. Thus, inability to appreciate what you judge to be valuable may make the activity ultimately not worthwhile.

In addition to being a datum for decision making, the qualitative character of the future is motivationally significant insofar as it makes getting to the future more or less attractive. Our motivating interest in our future lives is the subject of chapters 3 and 4.

LEADING A LIFE

Evaluators lead their lives in both a narrow and a broad sense of the phrase. In the narrow sense of the phrase, "leading a life" refers to making and acting on choices about the *characterizing* features of a *whole* life in accord with normative preferences that are not substantially constrained by contextual factors such as a lack of resources. In this narrow sense, you determine how to lead your life by answering the question "What do I want to do with my life?" In considering how to answer that question, you are thinking of your life as the expanse of time you have to be alive in and that is up to you to give a shape to—or if you like, a narrative storyline. You are thinking about it as *a* life, rather than merely a sequence of hours, days, and years. That the question of how to lead a life is raised about a life you think of as *a* life—and one that will be characterizable, at the end of the day, in virtue of your choices—does not mean that leading a life requires determining what to devote the entirety of your life to and then committing yourself to those activities, projects, relationships, identities, and so on. It does, however, mean thinking in fairly broad terms about the principal things you want your life to contain. Among the things you want your life as a whole to contain might be some time-limited activities, such as getting a college degree or serving a stint in the military. In addition, the answer to "What do I want to do with my life?" may be partial or provisional. Very few people, I suspect, are well-positioned to say with any clarity, confidence, or completeness what they want to do with temporally remote parts of their lives. Most, however, can say what they want to do with a portion of their lives, understanding that portion as part of a whole life, and understanding their choices as contributing to the narrative characterization of their whole life. Those life-characterizing choices may also be provisional. You may provisionally decide you want to lead your life as a teacher but remain open to changing course depending on how things turn out, including what new opportunities emerge.

Life-characterizing choices are, of course, always made in real-life contexts that impose constraints on what can be chosen. There will be limited resources, opportunities, talent, time, physical abilities, and so on that restrict the options. However, beyond a certain level—which I plan to leave unspecified—one's options can be so constrained as to make the description "leading one's life" inappropriate, or at least to require adding a qualification like "as best one can under the circumstances."

Concerned with the principal things you want your life to contain, leading a life in this narrow sense will typically involve settling on a way of life, a set of roles (such as teacher or parent), long-term relationships, social identities, the development of skills and character traits that you consider important, and the like. While these characterizing features of a life entail some specific activities—for example, if you decide to be a parent, you will be changing diapers—what is being chosen are not context- and time-specific activities but, rather, a characterizing feature of a life that will entail some set of, often as yet indeterminate, context- and time-specific activities. (For example, it is only as your life as a parent unfolds that you discover what context- and time-specific choices you face.) Moreover, in deciding how to lead your life, you are not paying attention to all the subordinate preferences you have—for example, seeing movies starring Philip Seymour Hoffman rather than Pierce Brosnan; nor are you paying attention to the fact that a considerable amount of your lifetime will be spent in ways that have very little to do with the characterizing features of your life (consider, for example, the amount of time you spend commuting, grocery shopping, and channel surfing).

This takes us to the broader sense of "leading a life." In the narrow sense, the emphasis is on leading *a life*. In the broad sense, the emphasis is on *leading* a life. Here, the relevant contrast is between actively leading a life by making choices on the basis of a normative outlook—what you might think of as a complete listing and rank-ordering of what you value and disvalue, however minor some of the things on that list might be—and merely having events happen to you or simply following your strongest impulse. Only agents lead a life, because only agents determine for themselves what they value, what they will do, and what they will aim for. In this broader sense, you are as much leading a life when you choose which movie actor you prefer to watch as when you select which career path to follow. And you are leading a life just as much when you choose under substantial constraint as when your preferences have free play. (Even if it's cereal that tastes like twigs or nothing at all for breakfast, there's still an evaluative choice to be made.) If we think about what it means to lead a temporal life in this broader sense, we might think the primary question agents must answer is "How do I want to spend my time?" Here, the time to be spent includes both a lifetime and temporally specific segments of that lifetime, such as one's afternoon or the time in the doctor's waiting room (*Field & Stream* or *People* magazine?). One's aim, in this case, is to spend time in ways that best reflect one's normative outlook, no matter the context or subject of choice.

Why might it be important to keep in mind that leading a life can be construed either narrowly or broadly? One main reason is to forestall the temptation to think of the meaningfulness of the lives people lead primarily in terms of whole-life characterizations—what a life is *about*. If we focus on whole-life characterizations, we will be tempted to think that the most meaningful lives are ones about important things—say, service to humanity or producing great art. Since most of us lead less impressive lives yet still find them meaningful, we might then succumb to a different temptation—namely, to locate the meaningfulness of what characterizes our lives in something entirely subjective, such as finding our life satisfying. But had we started with a broader conception of what leading a life amounts to—spending our time in ways that reflect our normative outlook—we might have seen that leading a meaningful life is neither a matter of doing impressive things nor a matter of doing subjectively satisfying things (though it might include both) but, rather, about how we spend our time, including the time of ordinary, everyday life. Developing a normative outlook conception of meaningful living will be the focus of chapter 2.

A second important reason for keeping the narrow versus broad construals of "leading a life" in mind is that we stand a better chance of noticing how people sometimes trade off the meaning a life gets by being about something for the kind of meaning that simpler and less time-extended projects and experiences provide (and vice versa). Moreover, the kind of careerist approach to leading a meaningful life involved in making one's life *about* something fits only certain kinds of lives. Making one's whole life about something meaningful may be largely out of reach if one lacks ample resources, substantial control over how one's life proceeds, and suitable options for making that life about something meaningful. And that approach ill-fits childhood, or when facing a terminal illness, or suffering the beginning stages of dementia. Yet leading a meaningful life under these variously constrained circumstances still seems possible.

SPENDING TIME

Focusing on the broader sense of "leading a life" draws our attention to the different ways we do spend time. The English language is full of idioms for spending time. Many of these suggest analogies between spending time and spending money or some other resource. In addition to spending time, we squander time, budget time, use up time, and manage, commit, and dispose of time. Like money, time can be misspent or invested wisely. Time is something one can have too much of. We find ourselves with time on our hands, more time than we know what to do with, and time to burn, so that we have to pass or while away the time. Like other resources, one can also be short on time.

Not all spending of time involves doings aimed at achieving something. There are plenty of passive expenditures of time, as when you spend time lolling on the beach, not doing much of anything. Some expenditures mainly amount to spending time with a particular value quality rather than in pursuit of something valuable. Spending time at an art museum or with friends is like this. And not everything that people choose involves spending time. Most obviously, very short-term actions, like saying "hello," while taking place in time, count as spending time the way paying out a penny counts as spending money. Such very short-term actions do not compete with other options for the available time; nor do they solve the problem of how to fill up time; nor do they satisfy evaluators' interest in doing something meaningful with their time.

In thinking about how evaluators spend their time, it is useful to distinguish four different categories of time expenditures: primary, filler, entailed, and norm-required. In *primary spending*, you use your time on things you think are worth pursuing for their own sake. More precisely, primary spending is the *expenditure of time on activities that are your ends*, and thus are connected to your normative outlook.[2] In chapter 2, I suggest that meaningful living occurs during primary time expenditures, and I have more to say about what a normative outlook is. Candidates for primary spending are all those things that, should there be time, resources, and opportunity, you would opt to spend time doing for their own sake.

Although the most obvious instances of primary spending are life-characterizing activities and relationships—what I have called *leading a life in the narrow sense*— primary spending is not limited to what takes priority in one's normative outlook. You are just as much engaged in primary spending when you choose to spend your evening watching your favorite television show or you volunteer to pass out political flyers for a few hours as when you spend time working in your chosen career. What distinguishes primary spending is that it answers to your assessment of what is worthwhile to include in your life for its own sake, and thus worth making time for, if possible. Because you are using up your life's time on the very things you want to constitute your life, you are as it were using up your time on being you.

---

[2] I do not mean by "end" *whatever* we aim at, such that some ends may be chosen for purely instrumental reasons. I am restricting "ends" to those aims that we do not adopt purely for instrumental reasons but, rather, find worth doing for their own sake. Of course, some of these ends might be chosen for instrumental reasons in addition to noninstrumental reasons. So, for example, someone who enjoys cooking might set as an end the creation of a fantastic dinner to serve her guests; she values the process of creating a fantastic dinner for its own sake, and she also values doing so as an instrumental means toward hosting a successful dinner party.

You can't always be doing things that answer to your conception of what is worth including in your life for its own sake. The time that can't be used in primary spending still has to be spent some way, if only by taking a nap. *Filler spending* is what we do while waiting, or when we're too tired or ill or unmotivated to do much of anything else, or when we lack the opportunities or resources for primary spending, or when there's simply too much time on our hands. The line between primary and filler spending is, roughly, that between what we hope there will be time for or deliberately make time for and what we wouldn't waste time on were it not for the excess time on our hands. Thus, filler spending might naturally be described as a way of wasting time while waiting to meaningfully spend time.

Filler spending has an ambiguous status in the lives led by evaluators. On the one hand, even if filler time is spent in normatively unimportant ways, evaluators still need to decide what to do with those extra bits of time. Thus, when you are engaged in filler spending you are leading your life in the broad sense of that phrase—you are choosing how to spend your time in light of what you value. On the other hand, filler spending involves spending time in ways you wouldn't have chosen, except for the fact that you have time on your hands that can't be devoted to primary spending. Thus, it seems equally natural to describe filler spending as an agent's way of waiting to lead a life, rather actually leading it.

What you choose to primary-spend your time on often entails both expected and unexpected ways of using that time. This is *entailed spending*. Most obviously, primary spending choices call for taking the instrumental means necessary to spend time doing the things you value doing. Spending time commuting, for example, is a necessary means toward spending time working at the job you prefer to have. For some, work itself is an entailed expenditure of time—one works solely to receive the paycheck that funds one's primary expenditures of time during nonwork hours. One important subcategory of entailed spending on instrumental means is spending time to overcome problems and recoup from setbacks that have arisen in the course of pursuing activities you choose to primary-spend time on. For example, your computer crashes, other essential equipment malfunctions, you misplace the key to your office, paperwork gets lost, co-workers haven't done what you depended on them to do, and so on. The discussions of hope and commitment in chapters 4 and 5 draw attention to the fact that evaluators must adopt policies that, in effect, determine how much time they are willing to spend dealing with obstacles and setbacks.

When your primary time expenditure is on a complex activity comprising a set of subordinate tasks, you may not regard spending time on all the constitutive tasks as primary spending—that is, as worthwhile or meaningful ways of spending your time, especially given that temporal resources are limited. Consider the primary expenditure of time in a career. At least some of the tasks that the career includes may well be regarded as neither particularly worthwhile nor meaningful but, rather, simply unavoidable aspects of the career. The time spent on those tasks qualifies as entailed spending rather than primary spending. It is possible for most of one's time to be taken up in such entailed spending. This is particularly likely when one chooses to primary-spend time in a way of life because of the value of that way of life rather than because of the cumulative value of the constituent activities in that way of life. For example, consider what one of Betty Friedan's interviewees for her book, *The Feminine Mystique*, said about her time spent as a wife and mother:

> Ye Gods, what do I do with my time? Well, I get up at six. I get my son dressed and then give him breakfast. After that I wash dishes and bathe and feed the baby. Then I get lunch and while the other children nap, I sew or mend or iron and do all the other things I can't get done before noon. Then I cook supper for the family and my husband watches TV while I do the dishes. After I get the children to bed, I set my hair and then I go to bed.[3]

Insofar as these are constituents of being a wife and a mother, there is a sense in which she is primary-spending when she does the dishes. But to appreciate this she must describe what she does with her time quite abstractly—not as "doing the dishes" but as "being a wife and mother." That abstract description, however, renders invisible the concrete reality of what she is doing and the fact that doing the dishes is not something she chooses because it is itself worthwhile but is instead entailed spending. When we, like Friedan's housewife, can see ourselves as primary-spending only by abstractly describing what we are doing, that time spent will have a mixed character. We are both spending our time on what is worthwhile and using ourselves up on specific activities that are not and thus do not, in themselves, make for meaningful living.[4] What this suggests is that assessing the meaningfulness of one's life is not simply a matter of one's dominant, career-like pursuits being primary time expenditures. Assessing the constituent activities of those primary time expenditures is relevant as well—a point I return

[3] Betty Friedan, *The Feminine Mystique* (New York: Dell, 1964), 23.
[4] Harry Frankfurt's illuminating discussion of the complex relationship between the value of final ends and the value of instrumental means in "On the Usefulness of Final Ends" (in his *Necessity, Volition, and Love* [Cambridge: Cambridge University Press, 1999], 82–94, especially 90–91) draws attention to the importance of taking into account, when selecting final ends, the kinds of activities that a particular selection will involve one in. Tal Brewer observes that while we may find no intrinsic value in a constituent activity viewed as a time-slice, we may find a constituent activity intrinsically valuable when contextualized in a larger narrative of what we are doing ("Savoring Time: Desire, Pleasure, and Wholehearted Activity," *Ethical Theory and Moral Practice* 6 [2003]: 143–160, 152–153).

to both in the next chapter on meaningful living and in the fifth chapter on the value of commitment.

Some entailed expenditures are neither instrumentally necessary to nor constituent components of one's primary time expenditures. Instead, they may simply be contingently connected but unavoidable under the circumstances. A primary expenditure of time in a particular job, for example, can with bad luck entail spending time with crabby co-workers or a domineering boss. One then ends up, as a contingent matter of fact, spending time dealing with interpersonal shrapnel.

Finally, there is *norm-required spending*. Norms of morality, etiquette, law, workplaces, and so on place various requirements on how individuals spend their time. The law, for example, requires that citizens spend time filing income tax reports and that felons spend time in prison. Norms of etiquette require (or at least used to require) that one spend time writing thank-you notes for gifts. Workplaces may pressure employees to "volunteer" to spend time outside working hours doing such things as attending a retreat or networking over golf. While living in accord with a kind of norm might seem worth your while, the particular time expenditures required by those norms may or may not qualify as primary time expenditures. So here, too, our time expenditures may have a mixed character.

Entailed and norm-required spending, like filler spending, have an ambiguous relation to leading a life. Because entailed expenditures are entailed by the very activities and relationships that one regards as choiceworthy and as meaningful ways of spending a life, there is a sense in which these entailed expenditures of time just are how one has chosen to lead one's life. But because agents would often be happy to dispense with the entailed expenditures of time—as Friedan's housewife might be pleased if the time expenditures in her chosen life as wife and mother resembled her husband's a bit more—agents can have reason to regard entailed expenditures as taking up or wasting time rather than contributing to the leading of a life. A similar point applies to norm-entailed spending. While it may be a matter of importance that one's life be lived in accord with a kind of norm—say, norms of etiquette—the particular time expenditures required by those norms may or may not qualify as primary time expenditures. For my neighbor, for example, writing thank-you notes is a point of pride and a source of connection to her childhood. She might reasonably regard writing thank-you notes as something she wants to make time for in her life, and thus as a primary time expenditure. By contrast, I begrudge each minute spent writing thank-you notes, even while acknowledging the legitimacy of the norm and of norms of etiquette generally. One focus of chapter 6 is the connection between norm-required expenditures of time and boredom.

Why do these distinctions between types of time expenditures matter? They matter, first, because they suggest what I think is the most plausible way of thinking about what it means to lead a meaningful life. The meaningfulness of a life is a function of one's primary time expenditures. Primary time expenditures, I have suggested, cut across both big things—one's value priorities in choosing what will characterize one's life—and small things—personally valued activities, experiences, and relationships that one hopes there will be time for even if they do not enter into the characterization of one's life.

Second, these distinctions between different ways of spending time suggest that the measure of a meaningful life is not simply *how valuable* the subjects of one's primary time expenditures are but also *how much* of one's life's time is not being spent on filler, entailed, and norm-required expenditures of time. Both the nature and the difficulty of leading a life are obscured when we talk about leading a life in comparatively atemporal terms as a matter of making choices about what activities, aims, ideals, relationships, or standards of conduct best reflect our values. Organizing one's life around what one values most, especially if this involves organizing one's life around long-term ways of life, may come with very high levels of filler, entailed, and norm-required expenditures of time. Recall Friedan's housewife. Alternative organizations around either lesser values or shorter-term projects and relationships may significantly reduce the filler, entailed, and norm-required expenditures of time. This fact should lead us to think more carefully about how valuable organizing one's life around long-term commitments really is.

Third, attention to kinds of time expenditures brings into much sharper focus how difficult it is to lead a life. We may prize the fact that human persons have a future and lead a life while nonhuman animals do not (or at least not in anything like the robust way humans do). But one cost of having a future is consciousness of the ways our lifetime gets used up in filler, entailed, and norm-required spendings. And one cost of leading a life is that the choices we make in order to lead our lives as agents involve us in entailed time expenditures—in instrumental activities, in coping with obstacles and setbacks, in constituent activities of complex pursuits—and sometimes in filler time expenditures while waiting or spinning our wheels that seem more like wasting or using up a life than leading it. Moreover, when the future is dominated by filler, entailed, and norm-required spendings, or in other ways precludes primary spendings, it may be unattractive and boring enough to generate disinterest in the very business of leading one's life, or at least of leading portions of one's life. Leading a life is difficult. And it is difficult in ways that exceed the difficulty of making up one's mind about what one values.

2

Geographies of Meaningful Living

The philosophical literature on meaningful living is substantial not simply because this topic is of fundamental human importance but also because it is significantly unclear what "meaningful" does or should identify when applied to a life. The concept is significantly unclear in large part because we have a plurality of intuitions about which lives are meaningful and what makes them meaningful; these intuitions sometimes pull in conflicting directions or simply are not shared. So, no account of meaningfulness in life simply clarifies a concept whose meaning is already fairly clear. Inevitably, one must argue that one among many reasonable candidate analyses *should be adopted* as a privileged account of the meaning of "meaningful life."

One way to go about this constructive, rather than merely clarifying, project is to ask "Where in our conceptual geography is 'meaningful' best located?" Or put differently, "What conceptual work do we want the concept to do?" Here, there are two broad options. One is the geography of *agent-independent value,* whereby we think that an agent's pursuits have value independent of what the agent herself thinks of them.[1] "Meaningful" is in the neighborhood of "admirable," "humanly good or excellent," and "significant." It is to be connected with accounts of distinctively valuable human capacities and their exercise, of human achievement and contribution to human progress, and of the duty of beneficence, particularly supererogatory discharges of that duty. Central to the geography of agent-independent value is, of course, the formulation of correct standards of assessment, as well as comparative evaluations of how different lives rate according to that standard. In this geography, the primary work of "meaningful" is evaluative and commendatory.

---

[1] "Agent-independent value" should be read quite broadly. "Independent" need not mean "independent of *any and all* evaluating activity." Indeed, you might think that nothing could be valuable were there no beings capable of evaluation, and thus that there are no agent-independent values in *that* sense. But you still might think that values are independent of what any *particular* agent thinks, perhaps because values are socially constructed, or are what ideal knowers would collectively agree upon. I include all these possibilities as "agent-independent values" and exclude only the dependence of value on the judgments of particular individuals. The latter I call "agent-dependent value." I say a bit more about agent-independent value in footnote 5.

Alternatively, one might locate "meaningful" in the geography of *agency* and *agent-dependent* assessments of value, where we think that an agent's pursuits have value specifically for her given her reasons for valuing them. Within this geography, "meaningful" is to be connected with accounts of humans as end-setters and as bearers of a normative and/or narrative identity, of the relation between the agent's valuational and motivational systems,[2] of the kinds of reasons that can enter into deliberation, and accounts of various reason-responsive attitudes (pleasure, desire, satisfaction, caring, love[3]). This is also the geography of integrity, understood as what the agent stands for,[4] personal autonomy, and accounts of the importance of adopting others' ends as one's own. Within this geography, the primary work of "meaningful" is not commendatory. Instead, it is something more on the order of picking out lives that can survive the agent's own evaluative reflection and whose election is intelligible to the agent.

These two geographies prioritize different viewpoints from which meaningfulness is to be assessed. The first prioritizes the third-person perspective, particularly the idealized one of the correct evaluator. The second prioritizes the first-person perspective, in particular how one's life appears to oneself given one's own normative outlook. They also diverge on the kind of account of meaningfulness to be offered. The first proposes a *substantive* account of meaningfulness. If we are to correctly assess the degree of meaningfulness in different lives, we need a substantive account of what the standard is and what kinds of life activities satisfy the standard. The second can at most propose a *procedural* account of meaningfulness in terms of the general shape that deliberation about and the temporal organization of life activities must take in order to yield a meaningful life, but without specifying a single substantive, agent-independent standard.

One might think these are not competing geographies: the geography of agent-independent value is the geography of *real* meaningfulness; that of agency and agent-dependent value is the geography of *seeming* meaningfulness. And one might think this because any account of meaningfulness that doesn't tether the concept to an agent-independent standard of value will have the unfortunate implication that lives devoted to trivial or immoral pursuits could turn out to be meaningful. Thus, any first-person, subjectivist conception of meaningfulness will be overly permissive.

My aim here is threefold: First, I raise concerns about the adequacy of an agent-independent conception of meaningfulness. This will not be a decisive argument against that conception; I'm dubious such an argument could be constructed. The goal is simply to motivate a more careful and less dismissive consideration of the alternative

[2] For example, Gary Watson, "Free Agency," *Journal of Philosophy* 72 (1975): 205–220.
[3] For example, Tal Brewer, "Savoring Time: Desire, Pleasure, and Wholehearted Activity," *Ethical Theory and Moral Practice* 6 (2003): 143–160, 152–153; Harry Frankfurt, *The Reasons of Love* (Princeton, NJ: Princeton University Press, 2004).
[4] Cheshire Calhoun, "Standing for Something," *Journal of Philosophy* 92 (1995): 235–260.

agent-dependent option. Second, I aim to lay out an agent-dependent conception of meaningfulness that I hope will look like a viable candidate for real meaningfulness—certainly more so than caricatures of subjectivist views suggest. Specifically, I aim to defend the view that what you expend your life's time on contributes meaning to your life when it is an end that you, in your own best judgment, have reasons to value and thus reason to use yourself up on. This is not the whole of the view, but it is the heart of it. And third, I take up the overly permissive objection.

AGENT-INDEPENDENT CONCEPTIONS
OF MEANINGFULNESS

An agent-independent conception of meaningfulness attempts to isolate those characterizing features of a life that have agent-independent value and, in virtue of this, are suitable to confer meaning. The task, then, is to consider a variety of possible characterizing features and try to determine which ones best capture our ordinary assessments of more or less meaningful lives.[5] Among characterizing features contributing to the meaningfulness of a life might be that the life makes a positive difference to the lives of human and nonhuman others; that it involves developing various moral and nonmoral excellences; that it includes friendships, love relationships, or other significant human connections; that it achieves something of relatively enduring importance; that it involves the development and exercise of distinctively human capacities, such as the capacity for aesthetic appreciation; that it be the kind of life that we might describe as a flourishing human life or one that is consistent with individual well-being. And the list might be extended.[6]

---

[5] Susan Wolf uses the term "objective value" to capture what I mean by "agent-independent value"—namely, to refer to the fact that there is *some* sense in which the evaluative standard is independent of the individual whose life is alleged to be meaningful or meaningless such that we might reasonably argue with others about that standard, hope to reach agreement, hold others and not just ourselves to that standard, and be mistaken about what that standard is (Wolf, *Meaning in Life and Why It Matters* [Princeton, NJ: Princeton University Press, 2010]). Both Wolf and Thaddeus Metz (*Meaning in Life: An Analytic Study* [New York: Oxford University Press, 2013]) classify accounts of meaningfulness via an "objectivist" versus "subjectivist" framework, but mean different things by this. Metz classifies a view that appeals to what "all human agents would prefer upon the dispassionate consideration of their properties while abstracting from the way in which they would bear on their own lives" as subjectivist (Metz, *Meaning in Life*, 178). Wolf would, I assume, regard this as an objectivist account. My own division between agent-independent and agent-dependent measures more closely tracks Wolf's way of dividing the field.
[6] For a comprehensive survey of extant substantive accounts and a critical evaluation of them, see Metz's *Meaning in Life*. The substantive account offered may be at different levels of abstraction, some looking more list-like (e.g., Robert Audi, "Intrinsic Value and Meaningful Life," *Philosophical Papers* 34 [November 2005]: 331–355; David Schmidtz, "The Meanings of Life,"

There is no doubt that we actually *do* appeal to considerations like these in reflecting on whether we are doing something meaningful with our life's time. We sometimes do set out to get more of these valuable things into our life story or view our lives with regret that our circumstances or personal failures have cut us off from one or more of these avenues of meaning. The question, though, is not whether reflecting on the agent-independent value of what we are doing with our lives is *relevant* to assessing how meaningfully we are disposing of our lives but, rather, whether an agent-independent conception correctly captures the *way* that such reflections function in determinations of meaningfulness.[7]

Let me suggest some reasons for being dubious. Recall, first, my observation that the principal work done by an agent-independent conception of meaningfulness is commendatory. We have a rich evaluative language in the conceptual territory of meaningfulness already on hand for commending lives: significant, impactful, admirable, humanly excellent, distinctively human, flourishing, and the like. One possibility is that the commendatory term "meaningful" just is equivalent to one of these other commendatory terms, and this would be revealed once we fully work out the substantive conception of both "meaningful" and some other evaluative concept, such as "significant." This need not be a wholly unwelcome or uninteresting result. Rawls, for example, gives us an account of oppression which turns out to be equivalent to political injustice; and this gives us a useful way of understanding what oppression is. But it is also not a wholly welcome result, either. In the case of oppression, one might have thought that the value of having this concept is that it picks out something that is not identical with political injustice. That is, its value lies in its doing distinctive conceptual work not performed by other closely allied evaluative notions, such as those of political injustice, wrongful harms, social group inequalities, and the like.[8]

Similarly, it is not a wholly welcome result if "meaningful" could be fully cashed out via some alternative evaluative concept—say, "significant"—such that we could drop reference to meaningfulness altogether and say all that we want to say by writing essays

in *Life, Death, and Meaning: Key Philosophical Readings on the Big Questions*, 2nd ed., ed. David Benatar [Lanham, MD: Rowman & Littlefield, 2010]). Others offer a general, abstractly described feature of meaningful lives (e.g., Metz's own fundamentality account of meaningfulness).

[7] The agent-independent theorist claims (a) that assessments of agent-independent value are all that matter, and (b) that the assessment is to be determined by appeal to the correct agent-independent standard. By contrast, one might think, as I do, that (a) assessments of agent-independent value matter but are not all that matter, and (b) the evaluative assessment is to be determined by the agent's own best judgment.

[8] Sally Haslanger makes this sort of point and highlights the importance of deciding what work we want a concept to do in "Gender and Race: (What) Are They? (What) Do We Want Them to Be?" *Nous* 34 (March 2000): 31–55; and "Oppressions: Racial and Other," in her *Resisting Reality: Social Construction and Social Critique* (New York: Oxford University Press, 2012).

and books about significant lives instead.[9] Here again, one might have thought that the value of having a concept of meaningfulness is that it picks out something not identical with significant (or whatever other evaluative conception is driving the analysis of meaningfulness). That is, its value lies in its doing *distinctive* conceptual work not performed by other, closely allied evaluative notions.

In view of this, agent-independent conceptions of meaningfulness must do one of two things. On the one hand, they could bite the bullet and affirm that "meaningful" does no distinctive conceptual work. Consider, for example, one of the agent-independent conceptions of meaningfulness that appear in Thaddeus Metz's survey of meaning in life accounts:

> A human person's life is more meaningful, the more that she lives in the ways all human agents would prefer upon the dispassionate consideration of their properties while abstracting from the way in which they would bear on their own lives.[10]

"More meaningful" here collapses quite clearly into "intersubjectively preferable," or simply "better."

Alternatively, the agent-independent theorist could try to secure distinctive work for the concept of meaningfulness by excluding some agent-independently valuable ways of living. "Meaningful" would then do distinctive work because it picks out a limited range of agent-independently valuable activities, relationships, and the like. Consider these two accounts, also drawn from Metz's survey:

> A human person's life is more meaningful, the more that she makes others in the world better off than they would have been without her influence.[11]

> A human person's life is more meaningful, the more that she actively makes progress towards highly worthwhile states of affairs that cannot conceivably be realized because our knowledge of them changes as we strive to meet them.[12]

The difficulty here is that, since our background conception of what makes bettering others' lives or making progress toward highly worthwhile states of affairs

[9] Thaddeus Metz argues explicitly for the equation of "meaningful" and "significant" in "The Meaningful and the Worthwhile: Clarifying the Relationships," *Philosophical Forum* 43 (2012): 435–448.

[10] Metz, *Meaning in Life*, 178. He bases this measure on Stephen Darwall's rather different account of meaning in *Impartial Reason* (Ithaca, NY: Cornell University Press, 1983), 163–166.

[11] Metz, *Meaning in Life*, 189.

[12] Ibid., 205.

agent-independently valuable is doing the work of enabling us to pick out these sorts of things as meaningful, narrower conceptions of meaningfulness like these naturally invite the objection that they wrongly exclude. The first of these two accounts excludes making oneself better off even by such apparently meaningful activities as studying an academic discipline, while the latter appears to exclude quite a lot including friendships and other intimate relationships. If being agent-independently valuable is what enables the items in the conception to be recognized as meaningful, then what rationale could there be for excluding other valuable ways of living?[13] One might try to avoid this objection by proposing that "meaningful" picks out agent-independently valuable life contents that are *sufficiently* valuable or valuable in the *right way* to make the life significant or a humanly good or excellent life; but then we are back to thinking that "meaningful" could be replaced by one of these other evaluative concepts.

Let me turn now to a second worry about agent-independent conceptions. Given that we often raise questions about the meaningfulness of our own lives, one bit of work one might think a concept of meaningfulness should do is answer the question, "Which activities, relationships, projects, experiences would be most meaningful for *me* to choose?" Insofar as agent-independent measures provide us with a measurement standard for assessing more versus less meaningful lives, they provide a method of answering the question. But on these measures there may well be a plurality of options that rank equally. With respect to these, the advocate of an agent-independent standard must say it is a matter of indifference which you choose, at least so far as the meaningfulness of your life goes (though, of course, not a matter of indifference so far as the feasibility of the option goes, given your talents, opportunities, and resources). For example, if on a particular conception, being a philosophy professor and being a biology professor rank as equally good, then in your search for meaning it makes no difference which you choose. To continue to wonder "But which would be more meaningful *for me*?" is to fail to understand meaningfulness.

As with the previous worry about the concept not doing distinctive work, this is not a wholly unwelcome conclusion. It's exactly what one would expect if an agent-independent conception were the right one. But we are now trying to determine whether this is the right sort of conception. To that end, it's relevant to note that the

---

[13] Metz's own quite capacious measure of meaning manages to cover animal rescue work as a meaningful activity only insofar as it involves the use of our rational capacities, but not insofar as it involves reducing animal suffering. See Metz's own comments on this feature of his view in *Meaning in Life*, 239.

conclusion that, among equally agent-independently valuable pursuits, none could be more meaningful specifically for you is also not a wholly welcome conclusion.

Consider, for example, a different domain where talk about meaningfulness arises—that of meaningful gifts. It seems not only unremarkable but also correct to think that someone selecting a meaningful gift should give some consideration to its agent-independent value, but also to what the receiver would appreciate receiving. We pick meaningful gifts by taking stock of what the recipient values, not just what we think she should value. In short, in the gift-giving domain, it is not a misunderstanding of meaningfulness to ask, for example, "But which among these equally good books would make the most meaningful gift *for her*?"

Turning back to the domain of meaningful lives, consider the fact that Mother Teresa surely had a plurality of options for serving the poor—in terms of both location and what she aimed to do for the poor. On an agent-independent conception, it was a matter of indifference which she chose as far as making her life meaningful went. The real Mother Teresa, however, was adamant that the service be specifically in India and that her primary service be to bring the souls of the poor to Christ. It was only *this* option that she heard Christ's voice asking her to choose. The agent-independent theorist must say that being barred by her Church superiors from pursuing this option and required to pursue a different venue for serving the poor would not have been a cost in meaningfulness.

There is, obviously, no way of forwarding this as a criticism without sounding question-begging. Anyone committed to an agent-independent conception will think there would have been no cost in meaningfulness for Mother Teresa, though there might have been costs in something else, such as satisfaction. My point here is not that this latter view is clearly *wrong*; the aim is to pump intuitions that would lead a person who is undecided about which conception of meaningfulness is better to think that this implication of the agent-independent conception is not wholly welcome. And it might seem especially unwelcome in light of the availability of alternative conceptions that permit both the agent-independent value of one's pursuit and the agent's own take on that pursuit to play a role. These are what I will call *agent-independent-plus* conceptions.

But first, one final worry. Agent-independent conceptions seem to entail a maximizing approach to living meaningfully. If living more meaningfully is better than living less meaningfully, and living more meaningfully just means that you are spending more of your time on more agent-independently valuable activities, then the most meaningful life is one in which you devote quantitatively more time to qualitatively more objectively valuable activities. Not only ought one not to lead a life *devoted* to reading science fiction, collecting Beanie Babies or baseball cards, and reading *Field & Stream*, but one ought not to *include* these activities so long as there are more valuable options.

Consider, for example, one of our earlier examples: a human person's life is more meaningful the more she makes others in the world better off than they would have been without her influence. A version of the over-demandingness problem that confronts maximizing act-utilitarianism when put into play in a world full of suffering and need appears to confront anyone who aims to live increasingly more meaningfully, according to this conception.

The maximizing concern here is not that the agent-independent theorist lacks resources to avoid recommending a life narrowly focused on one thing. Thomas Hurka, for example, argues that a perfectionist conception of the good life (one possible agent-independent standard for measuring meaningfulness) should also be concerned with *balancing* physical, theoretical, and practical perfection.[14] The concern is that striving for a more meaningful life by always choosing the agent-independently best (and Hurka's balancing account is an account of the objectively best life) will inevitably crowd out spending time on less valuable projects that one might intelligibly think contribute more rather than less meaning to one's life. I once spent considerable time designing and making dozens of stuffed mice to give to shelter cats at Christmas. It was not the agent-independently best use of my time. But given my foster-care work, concern for cat welfare, commitment to this particular shelter, and enjoyment of creating and making, I had reasons to think it a more meaningful use of my time. As with the two other worries, my aim here is not to present a decisive objection to agent-independent conceptions (since it is not), but to draw into view a familiar way of thinking about meaning that they fail to capture and that invites the thought that crowding out a plurality of less valuable activities in order to devote all of your time to the most agent-independently valuable activities may not be the most meaningful way of living.

AGENT-INDEPENDENT-PLUS CONCEPTIONS

There are philosophical conceptions of meaningful living available that simultaneously tether meaningfulness to an agent-independent standard of value, while at the same time enabling "meaningful" to do distinctive work and avoiding the indifference among the equally good objection. (I do not think they avoid the maximizing objection, but I will not argue that here.) I call these *agent-independent-plus* accounts,

---

[14] Thomas Hurka, "The Well-Rounded Life," *Journal of Philosophy* 84 (1987): 727–746. There are also resources for the objectivist about meaning to justify spending time in less or nonmeaningful ways. Enjoying simple pleasures might provide an essential psychological respite that prepares one for reengaging with more meaningful activities. And the pursuit of meaningfulness can be trumped by other considerations, such as the need to earn a living or the duty to fulfill minor moral obligations.

since they require that meaningful living be occupied with the agent-independently valuable, but add the agent's personal attitudes as either a second necessary condition for meaningfulness or simply allow personal attitudes to contribute to meaning while being neither necessary nor sufficient for it.

Both Susan Wolf and Thaddeus Metz have recently defended quite different versions of agent-independent-plus accounts.[15] On Wolf's view, a meaningful life is bound up with activities, projects, experiences, relationships, and the like that are genuinely valuable by some agent-independent standard and are not simply thought to be so by the agent. However, a meaningful life must also have a particular *subjective quality*, one that might be characterized as being actively engaged with, or drawn to, or in love with the objectively valuable parts of one's life that supply its meaning. She summarizes her conception of a meaningful life in a slogan: "meaning arises in a person's life when subjective attraction meets objective attractiveness."[16] On Metz's fundamentality theory of meaning, meaningful living depends on the agent-independent value of activities that are oriented toward matters of fundamental human concern. That a life is so oriented is sufficient for meaning, but an array of judgment-sensitive attitudes may also contribute to the meaningfulness of a life.

While avoiding some of the not wholly welcome implications of agent-independent accounts, agent-independent-plus accounts face a different difficulty, which is potentially avoidable but not without cost. The difficulty is that the fact that an activity is agent-independently valuable and the fact that it is the target of personal attitudes look like two very different kinds of reasons and thus two different measurement scales for meaning, rather than a single unified one.

Although agent-independent-plus accounts may stipulate that meaningfulness requires or is enhanced by the right kinds of subjective attitudes, this looks ad hoc. The explanation of why meaningful lives require, as on Wolf's view, two such very different components cannot be that we just would not count anything as a meaningful life

---

[15] Wolf, *Meaning in Life*. Another, earlier example is John Kekes's "The Informed Will and the Meaning of Life," *Philosophy and Phenomenological Research* 47 (September 1986): 75–90. Readers may be more familiar with the terminology "hybrid account" for a view like Wolf's. I introduce the new term "agent-independent-plus" because Metz denies that his is a hybrid view, regarding it instead as an objective measure of meaning. Nevertheless, his complex account of meaningfulness acknowledges a subjective, agent-centered component (namely, orientation of the person's rational self, including her judgment-sensitive attitudes) in addition to the main agent-independent component of the life's in fact being oriented toward things of fundamental human importance. In order to focus on the similarities between the two views (they both include a subjective component) while acknowledging significant difference (they construe that component differently), I've avoided the term "hybrid" in favor of something entirely new.

[16] Susan Wolf, "Meaning and Morality," *Proceedings of the Aristotelian Society*, New Series, 97 (1997): 299–315, 305; Susan Wolf, "Happiness and Meaning: Two Aspects of the Good Life," *Social Philosophy and Policy* 14, no. 1 (1997): 207–225, 211; Susan Wolf, *Meaning in Life*, 9.

that is either devoid of agent-independently valuable activities or devoid of subjective engagement. Similarly an appeal to intuition cannot be the sole reason for allowing, as on Metz's view, subjective attitudes to contribute to meaning. Given how different the two components are, it is not enough for a theory to fit our intuitions. It must also make sense of those intuitions. At first glance, it looks as though whatever reasons we have to accept the claim that meaning is a function of agent-independent value are also reasons to think that one's subjective attitude doesn't really matter.[17] Whatever reasons we have to accept the claim that meaning is (at least partly) a function of subjective engagement are reasons to think that the degree of agent-independent value doesn't matter, or doesn't matter as much as the arguments for including an agent-independent component led us to believe.

The ad hoc-ness problem is more or less severe depending on how one understands the subjective component. One initially plausible option is that it involves caring about, engagement with, and loving what one spends time on for personal reasons. Mother Teresa, a devout Catholic, was passionate about her work in India because she believed that Jesus had called her to that work and she loved him. If subjective engagement with what makes one's life meaningful depends on personal reasons, this would solve the indifference problem that agent-independent accounts face: among equally agent-independently valuable options, some are more meaningful for me to choose than others because I have personal reasons for choosing them. Unfortunately, this option also exacerbates the appearance that two quite different measures are being combined in an ad hoc way: a first-person measure that appeals to the agent's personal reasons and a third-person measure that appeals to actual agent-independent value.

Because such an account measures meaningfulness by appeal to quite different reasons—personal reasons and agent-independent value—one wonders why the subjective and agent-independent standards for meaningfulness couldn't be applied entirely separately. Consider, for example, an avid gardener who recognizes that volunteering in the local soup kitchen, however tedious and boring, is nevertheless a more agent-independently valuable activity than tending her garden, however fulfilling she finds the latter. She might manage the conflict by allowing some time for both—less than the soup kitchen deserves and less than her passion for gardening prompts. How

---

[17] Both Wolf and Metz, along with many others, reject attitudinal subjectivist conceptions of meaning on the grounds that *mere* subjective attitude—whether that be feelings of fulfillment, caring, or commitment—cannot by itself make a life meaningful. We cannot make a life devoted to the trivial meaningful simply by caring a lot about those trivial things. This is part of the overly permissive objection to subjectivist accounts. If one accepts this reasoning, then it is hard to see why subjective attitudes would be necessary for or contributors to meaning, even when oriented toward what has agent-independent value. As I will shortly suggest, this problem is not insurmountable, but it comes at a cost.

much has the avid gardener thereby enhanced the meaningfulness of her life? Having understood the arguments for each component, the avid gardener might think she's done a pretty good job of adding meaning to her life by applying the two standards independently of each other. But if subjective attraction must meet objective attractiveness in order to contribute meaning, the avid gardener has contributed little to the meaningfulness of her life by adopting this strategy. Her subjective attraction only meets something of minor worth—tending the garden. Her soup kitchen work doesn't appear to count, unless we suppose that her choosing it entails some degree of engagement, however modest.

There is the additional problem that the disconnect between the subjective and agent-independent components deprives us of a principled way of deciding between rivaling options. Suppose, for example, you recognize that one option is more agent-independently valuable, but you care less about it or appreciate it less (say, helping two homeless people from whom you feel alienated); and you recognize that a second option is less agent-independently valuable, but you care more about it or appreciate it more (say, helping one homeless person you care a lot about). What then? Which makes your life more meaningful?[18]

I said that the severity of the ad hoc-ness problem depends on how one construes the subjective component in agent-independent-plus accounts. An alternative would be to understand meaningful living on analogy with knowing and the subjective attitudes that contribute to meaningfulness on analogy with the beliefs that count toward knowing. Just as it isn't sufficient, in order to know, that one's epistemic attitude of belief accidentally latches onto true propositions—one must also have access to justifying reasons—so it isn't sufficient, in order to live meaningfully, that one's subjective attitude accidentally latches onto what is agent-independently valuable. Those attitudes must be appropriately responsive to, and involve appreciations of, agent-independent value. This is, I take it, Metz's view or close to it.[19]

With this seemingly improved version of the subjective component in mind, let us turn to Mother Teresa's account of her passionate commitment to her work with

---

[18] The example is from Thaddeus Metz's "Utilitarianism and the Meaning of Life," *Utilitas* 15, no. 1 (2003): 50–70, 68. His own answer is that we may get more meaning in our lives by *not* pursuing what has more agent-independent value and instead by pursuing something of lesser agent-independent value whose value we can better appreciate, desire, and engage with in a positive emotional way. But one wonders why this is the right answer and why, given the importance of agent-independent value on agent-independent-plus views, the subjective should here have such clout.

[19] It may also be Wolf's view. She observes, "Insofar as meaningfulness in life is a subjective matter . . . it is important to stress her *perception* of activities or objects of the activities with which she is involved as having objective worth" (Wolf, "Meaning and Morality," 304–305).

the poorest of the poor in India, since her life is routinely cited as an exemplar of a meaningful life.

Mother Teresa worked for years to gain Church approval to establish the Missionaries of Charity in India so as to educate the poorest children and care for the sick and dying, because she heard the voice of Christ asking her to do this and had a series of visions reinforcing that request. The Voice, as she called it, said to her

> I want Indian Nuns victims of my love, who would be Mary and Martha, who would be so very united to me as to radiate My love on souls. I want free Nuns covered with my poverty of the Cross—I want obedient Nuns covered with my obedience on the Cross. I want full of love Nuns covered with My Charity of the Cross—Wilt thou refuse to do this for Me?[20]

and

> I want Indian Nuns, Missionaries of Charity who would be my fire of love amongst the poor, the sick, the dying and the little children. The poor I want you to bring to me and the Sisters that would offer their lives as victims of My love—will bring these souls to Me. You are I know the most incapable person—weak and sinful but just because you are that—I want to use you for My glory. Wilt thou refuse?
>
> Little one, give Me souls—Give me the souls of the poor little street children.—How it hurts, if you only knew, to see these poor children soiled with sin.—I long for the purity of their love.—If you would only answer and bring me these souls—draw them away from the hands of the evil one. If you only knew how many little ones fall into sin every day. There are plenty of Nuns to look after the rich and well to do people—but for My very poor, there are absolutely none. For them I long—them I will love. Wilt thou refuse me?[21]

Whatever reasons philosophers have for holding up Mother Teresa's life as an exemplar of an agent-independently valuable and meaningful life, they are surely not Mother Teresa's reasons. From her point of view, her work was made valuable and meaningful by its being asked of her by Christ, by its prospect of uniting the souls of the dying with God and saving children from sin, and by her status as an obedient, loving spouse of Christ. Some of her reasons were reasons for thinking her work was specifically

---

[20] Brian Kolodiejchuk, ed. and comm., *Mother Teresa, Come Be My Light: The Private Writings of the "Saint of Calcutta"* (New York: Doubleday, 2007), 96.
[21] Ibid., 98.

meaningful for her to be doing: her communication with, love of, and marriage to Christ. Some of her reasons were, in her best judgment, reasons for anyone to regard this work as agent-independently valuable and thus meaningful: saving the souls of the neglected poor. From a more secular-minded philosophical point of view, her reasons-responsive subjective attitudes, governed by a mistaken metaphysical view and conception of the good, failed to latch on to what made her work agent-independently valuable. If correctly reasons-responsive subjective attitudes are either a necessary condition or a contributing source of meaning, we must conclude, respectively, that Mother Teresa's life either wasn't meaningful or that her life would have been more meaningful had she had different metaphysical views and a different conception of the good.

This, I think, is the wrong conclusion. Given the plurality of metaphysical views and conceptions of the good that people might hold, we end up with an *overly restrictive* conception of meaningfulness if we rule out all but the correctly (however we would determine this) reasons-responsive subjective attitudes from playing a role in the meaningfulness of a life.

The point here is not that a good conception of meaningfulness should be compatible with liberal tolerance for diversity of views (though this would not be a wholly unwelcome feature in my book). The point is that the story I have told so far prompts the thought that this would be an overly restrictive conception of meaningfulness.

Were "meaningful" simply equivalent to "significant" or "humanly excellent," Mother Teresa's life would (presumably) qualify as a meaningful life because the assessment could be made fully third-person by appeal to whatever the correct standard of agent-independent value is. But the not wholly welcome implications that "meaningful" does no distinctive work, and that agents have no meaning-related reasons for choosing among equally valuable options, together perhaps with an ordinary intuition that the agent's take on her life matters to meaningfulness, led us to think an agent-independent-plus view might be better. But while appeal to a subjective component would address all three reasons for moving beyond a straight agent-independent view, there was a risk that such a view would be ad hoc and that the subjective and agent-independent components might recommend different things. This led us to think about meaningfulness on analogy with knowing: the agent's subjective attitudes must be appropriately responsive to the agent-independent value of what she spends her time on. It's hard to see, however, how those attitudes could be appropriately responsive to agent-independent value if the agent has completely mistaken reasons for thinking her project has agent-independent value—as I am assuming that Mother Teresa did. Given how varied people's metaphysical and evaluative views are, it seems likely that many of us have similarly mistaken reasons. This "corrected" agent-independent-plus view thus rules out as living meaningfully (or fully meaningfully) not only those whose mistaken views lead them to expend their lives on trivial or immoral pursuits but also those whose mistaken views lead them to spend their time on what are in fact agent-independently valuable projects. And that seems overly restrictive. Perhaps we can do better by locating "meaningful" in a different geography.

A NORMATIVE OUTLOOK CONCEPTION
OF MEANINGFULNESS

Agent-independent and agent-independent-plus conceptions of meaningfulness assume that "meaningful" belongs on the conceptual geography of agent-independent evaluation and that the principal work of "meaningful" is commendatory. Their primarily third-person view of lives, from which lives like Mother Teresa's and Albert Einstein's appear exemplary, also invites us to locate "meaningfulness" on the temporal geography of a career. One asks, "What is, or was, the life centrally about?" and, "How do the projects and relationships that define the life's career rate on an agent-independent standard of value?" The items in that life career are naturally described fairly abstractly—for example, helping the destitute in India or creating fundamental theories in physics.[22]

This is not, I want to suggest, the first-person temporal geography of meaningfulness. Relocating "meaningful" on a different, noncommendatory *conceptual* geography looks more appealing once we remind ourselves of what the first-person *temporal* geography looks like. From the first-person perspective, you are intimately familiar with where your time is going on a daily, weekly, monthly basis. Thus, for anything that you are doing or plan to be doing in the short term or long term, it is natural to ask, "Is this a meaningful use of my life's time?" The question has bite, because anything you do takes time, and you are mortal. So there will be a cost for anything you do. The cost will be your life's time. Given that you are temporally extended, the cost is not just *to* you, but *of* you. In short, whatever you spend your time on uses up a bit of you. So, it matters a great deal how you spend our time.

I suggested in the introductory chapter that we spend our time not only in pursuing things we value for their own sake—primary spending—but also with merely filler, entailed, and norm-required time expenditures. Focusing on these categories of actual time expenditures suggests a different way of thinking about what it means to lead a meaningful life. *Meaningful living involves expending your life's time on ends*

---

[22] Neither an agent-independent nor agent-independent-plus conception of meaningfulness *necessitates* our taking a careerist approach to a meaningful life. But for most people's lives, we know very little about what their daily lives look like. So, taking stock of what the life was centrally about, abstractly described, is typically the best we can do from the third-person perspective.

that in your best judgment you have reason to value and thus reason to use yourself up on. Given that for many ends, their pursuit comes with temporal costs in the form of entailed spending, it will be important, as I suggested in chapter 1, to reflect on concrete descriptions of those pursuits and on whether the value of your ends justifies paying their temporal costs. I call this a *normative outlook* conception of meaningfulness. It occupies not the conceptual geography of agent-independent evaluation but the geography of agency and agent-centered value judgments. This is a subjectivist conception of meaningfulness.[23]

In setting ends, agents appeal to a plurality of reasons. Without trying to be exhaustive, let me suggest that the reasons for valuing an end to which agents appeal fall into at least three general categories. First, there are the kinds of reasons that look a lot like what agent-independent and agent-independent-plus theorists are concerned with: *reasons-for-anyone* to regard a particular activity as worthwhile, and worthwhile to a particular degree. They support our views about what activities are impersonally valuable.

To illustrate, suppose I adopt dressage riding as one of my ends. Among my reasons for thinking this is a worthwhile activity are the facts that riding dressage is excellent exercise, involves teamwork, offers opportunities for socializing with others, and requires dedication, skill, focused attention, and self-control. You don't have to like the sport or have reasons to choose it as an end for yourself to recognize that the sorts of reasons I offer support the claim that this is a choiceworthy sport.

Reasons-for-anyone typically are public reasons in the sense that they are part of a common pool of reasons that can be drawn on to justify the demand that others agree with us in our judgments of value. Reasons-for-anyone are a particularly important class of reasons because they figure prominently in interpersonal evaluative practices that involve reason-giving and reason-receiving: giving advice, making recommendations, exhorting, criticizing, correcting, condemning, justifying, and defending.

Having reasons-for-anyone enables us to justify to others our particular choices of ends to spend time on. Having reasons-for-anyone is also typically important to our being able to justify our choice of ends to ourselves. If, as someone who understands

---

[23] Wai-hung Wong also works out a subjectivist, reasons-based account of meaningfulness in "Meaningfulness and Identities," *Ethical Theory and Moral Practice* 11 (2008): 123–148. His view, like the one I propose here, also permits reasons other than "objectively good reasons" to be reasons for valuing. Stephen Darwall's very brief account of meaningfulness in *Impartial Reason* (165–166), though not identical, is also similar to the account I offer. He suggests that among the agent's (necessary) reasons is the agent's belief that the worth of what she occupies her life with is intersubjectively available—that others can recognize and affirm it—or, as I would say, there are *reasons-for-anyone* to value it. The importance that a particular intersubjectively valuable activity has to oneself will also be, in his view, a function of one's situation, commitments, and preferences, or what I am calling *reasons-for-me.*

that there are reasons-for-anyone and who engages in public reason-exchanging practices, such as giving and receiving advice, you attempt to adopt as an end something for which you can provide no or only weak reasons-for-anyone, you will be poorly positioned to make sense to yourself of why you adopt this end. Why should this be a candidate at all for an end of yours if there is little or nothing you could say to others on behalf of it either from the pool of public reasons that you actually share with others or the not-yet-public reasons that you think others should share with you?

In speaking of a public pool of reasons that are actually shared, or reasons that you think should be in that pool, it should be clear that by "reasons-for-anyone" I do not mean what ought to count for us as reasons from some ideally rational perspective that is not shaped by the cultural histories of our collective thinking about what should count as good reasons or by our own deliberative perspectives. I don't know how we could be certain we had finally and infallibly latched on to that kind of reason. The reasons-for-anyone that figure into our actual deliberation about what is choiceworthy are reasons that are accessible to us either because we—or some limited group of we— share those reasons or because those reasons are *reachable* from where we conceptually are now. Of course, since you are working from within your own deliberative perspective, you may appeal to reasons-for-anyone that others do not accept because they draw on a different shared pool of reasons. Mother Teresa might have said in defense of the choiceworthiness of her work in India that God commands us to care for and save the souls of the sick and destitute. She draws on a pool of reasons common to a large set of religious believers, but not to everyone.

In addition to reasons-for-anyone, there will be *reasons-for-the-initiated*. Some of the reasons we have for valuing what we adopt as ends are reasons that only a person who is familiar with the activity could have. To continue with the dressage example, outsiders to horse sports see that there are reasons-for-anyone that tell against adopting any horse sport as an end: the facts that one will eventually get stepped on, knocked down, and thrown; that one will be exercising in blistering heat and freezing cold; that it's expensive; and the like. Despite these negative reasons-for-anyone, insiders to horse sports can appreciate reasons that make it all worth it. Such reasons-for-the-initiated are, in part, something like what Alastair MacIntyre had in mind for internal goods that are accessible only to participants in a particular practice.[24] In dressage, achieving and experiencing lightness and impulsion in the horse and harmony between horse and rider are reasons for valuing dressage that only the initiated would appreciate.

[24] Alastair MacIntyre, *After Virtue: A Study in Moral Theory*, 2nd ed. (Notre Dame, IN: University of Notre Dame Press, 1984).

Finally, there are *reasons-for-me*. Reasons-for-me are the reasons you have as the particular person you are—rather than as an "anyone" or as "one of the initiated"—for choosing this end, sticking with it, and spending as much time on it in the face of temporal and other costs as you do. Reasons-for-me include such things as what the activity symbolizes for you, its connection with your past, the fact that you made a commitment, its suiting your personality and natural talents, that others would be disappointed in you if you didn't adopt this end, that you enjoy or love it, and so on.[25] During childhood, for example, trucks pulling horse trailers down the highway came to symbolize for me an unattainable level of wealth and privilege (though surely many of those horse owners were neither wealthy nor privileged). Horse ownership's symbolizing a special kind of fortunate life is among the reasons-for-me for valuing dressage as an end the way I do.

Although reasons-for-me cannot be offered to others to justify the worthiness of one's end, they can be offered to others to make interpretive sense of one's selecting just this activity as one's end. Many activities are equally worthwhile, and there will be whole sets of activities for which the same reasons-for-anyone can be given. The reasons-for-anyone that I gave for dressage could be given for virtually any sport. Reasons-for-me will, then, play a particularly important role in deciding between equally worthy activities.

In framing a normative outlook—a set of hierarchically ordered ends—one of the things we reflectively consider is the general choiceworthiness for anyone of various pursuits that a life's time might be spent on. We reflect on the hierarchy of choiceworthy pursuits supported by what, in our best judgment, are reasons-for-anyone. Since the hierarchy is supported solely by reasons-for-anyone, we may also call it an intersubjective or impersonal hierarchy of value. The rank-ordering of choiceworthy pursuits is, of course, determined from within our own deliberative view, a viewpoint we expect to be shared or at least aim to be shareable. Represented schematically, where V1 to V3 represent degrees of choiceworthiness for anyone from highest to lowest, and where a's, b's, and c's represent different practical activities, that hierarchy of value looks something like this:

$$V1: a_1, a_2, a_3 \ldots . a_n$$
$$V2: b_1, b_c, b_3 \ldots . b_n$$
$$V3: c_1, c_2, c_3 \ldots . c_n.$$

[25] It is tempting to describe these as reasons why an end has *personal* or *agent-centered* value. I avoid using those terms here, since I want to preserve a distinction between the purely personal reasons we have for selecting ends (reasons-for-me), and the "personal" or "agent-centered" value that ends have when they are adopted *for reasons* (that may include reasons-for-anyone and reasons-for-the-initiated, and not just reasons-for-me).

So, for example, various humanitarian activities might, in our best judgment, appear among *a* activities, various choiceworthy professions among *b* activities, various sports among *c* activities, and various pastimes like reading mystery novels or watching movies on some lower tier. Such a hierarchy of generally choiceworthy pursuits provides us with an intersubjective guide to adopting our own ends and constructing our own normative outlook. It is this intersubjective guide to selecting ends that I take agent-independent and agent-independent-plus accounts to be concerned to help us with.

Framing a conception of the hierarchy of choiceworthy pursuits is not yet a normative outlook. In adopting ends and rank-ordering them, we take into account not only the reasons-for-anyone that there are but also the reasons-for-me that one has and the reasons-for-the initiated that one has acquired. The point of your framing a normative outlook is to guide your practical activity by clarifying what, for you, in light of these different kinds of reasons, is worth spending time on for its own sake and how much time is worth spending. Your normative outlook specifies what, for you, counts as primary time expenditures. Schematically represented, a normative outlook might look something like this:

- V1: a_{12}, c_{14}
- V2: a_2, a_{62}, b_9, c_5
- V3: a_1, b_6, b_7, c_{28}, c_{96}, c_2

Notice that because the value-ordering of ends is based on more than reasons-for-anyone, it may well not track the hierarchy of (in our own best judgment) agent-independently valuable pursuits. Some of the highly choiceworthy *a* activities may figure in your normative outlook in a lower value tier than some *c* activities that you judge less agent-independently choiceworthy. Many choiceworthy activities won't figure in your normative outlook at all. You might recognize that golf is a choiceworthy sport, but the fact that there are reasons-for-anyone to choose this sport may not give you enough reason to choose it. Working in a soup kitchen might be, for you, simply entailed spending connected to some abstractly describable end like "helping others," rather than itself being one of your ends. It is because meaningfulness tracks normative outlook rather than agent-independent value that spending quantitatively more time on agent-independently more worthwhile activities doesn't necessarily make for more meaningful living.

MANAGING THE TEMPORAL PURSUIT OF VALUE

As I suggested in chapter 1, what you do can have a variety of time-related costs. You might be spending very little of your time on your ends at all. Instead, you might just be wasting time—being lazy, procrastinating, failing to even set ends. Or your circumstances might be so constrained that there is nothing you are able to do that you want for an end; you might be physically or mentally debilitated, or lacking the necessary material resources, or imprisoned, or put in a position where all your energies must go to just making a living. In short, "Am I doing something meaningful with my life?" might arise in response to the apparent dearth of time spent pursuing your own ends. Given circumstantial constraints, there may be nothing you can do about a negative answer. Alternatively, reflecting on the question of meaning may lead you to see that amid what seemed a relentless wasting of time, you are in fact managing to pursue some of your ends. Or you may come to see that you need to set some ends or be more diligent about pursuing the ones you have.

What you do can also have time-related costs, not because you're wasting time but because your ends aren't worth the time expense. "Am I doing something meaningful with my life?" might arise in response to the apparent mismatch between your reasons for adopting particular ends and the amount of time you spend pursuing them. You might have reasons for adopting the end of working Sudoku puzzles or hunting for bargains, but your reasons may not justify spending as much time on those ends as you do. That you are spending more time pursuing an end than it is worth may not be something you can do anything about. Perhaps you are recovering from a severe illness and haven't the energy to pursue any but the least taxing ends. Alternatively, reflecting on whether your ends are worth as much time as you're spending on them may lead to your seeing that you aren't using your time wisely and need to do some time management in order to invest more of your time in what really matters to you.

A related temporal cost arises because there may simply not be enough time in a lifetime to pursue all of one's ends. Pursuing one end (or one set of ends) tends to eliminate time for the pursuit of other ends. This is particularly true of ends whose pursuit involves time-consuming constituent activities, many of which may not themselves be forms of primary spending but are instead entailed or norm-required spending. Consider once again Betty Friedan's housewife, from chapter 1, whose description of her day is entirely in terms of entailed and norm-required time expenditures. While she is primary-spending on her chosen way of life, the amount of norm-required and entailed spending that comes with that life eliminates time for other primary expenditures. "Am I doing something meaningful with my life?" sometimes invites reflection on whether or not one is really willing to have an end (or set of ends) that so consumes one's time, especially in entailed and norm-required (and sometimes also filler) spending, crowding out other options for primary time expenditure.

I am not suggesting that there is a correct answer to the question of how much crowding out can occur without diminishing the meaningfulness of one's life. I am, however, suggesting that individuals must be able to make sense to themselves of shouldering the temporal costs of their ends. And reflecting on the meaningfulness of one's life may be occasioned precisely because other ends are being crowded out by entailed and norm-required time expenditures.

The finitude of human lives raises additional time-management concerns. I have been using "end" to refer to what you value pursuing for its own sake, and thus what for you would count as primary spending. I have not been using "end" to refer specifically to those pursuits you actually engage in. Some of your ends will, you hope, be realizable in your lifetime; others will not. When people make bucket lists, they are thinking about their ends, even if those ends likely won't be realized.

Within any particular temporal horizon—this week, this year, your lifetime— you will be able to pursue only a subset of your ends. But which subset? One thought might be that you should start at the top of your normative outlook. What do you value most? Devote your time to that, even if doing so eliminates time for lower-ranked ends. In short, maximize within your normative outlook. Perhaps loving obedience to Christ through serving India's poor topped Mother Teresa's normative outlook, so she maximized by investing all her time in that. Without judging that such persons make a mistake, one might nevertheless think there is another reasonable approach to managing the temporal pursuit of ends: spend less time on what tops one's normative outlook so that one has more time for equal- or lower-ranked ends.[26] Or, one might revise one's normative outlook, removing some really time-consuming end from one's normative outlook so as to pursue other ends—as politicians sometimes give up running for another term or for higher office in order to spend more time with their family.

While the answer to the practical question of how to manage the pursuit of ends under temporal constraints might be *guided* by thoughts about relative rankings within a normative outlook, it doesn't strike me as decisively *settled* by one's normative outlook. Which time-management style one adopts—"spend more time on each of fewer ends" or "less time on each of more ends"; "keep the high-ranked but time-consuming end" or "drop the high-ranked, time-consuming end"—seems more reasonably thought of as just that: a *style* of temporal management. As with other styles, some just seem to suit a person better than others. Thus, two people who share the same normative outlook might end up, within the same temporal horizon, pursuing different sets of ends. (I return to the topic of different styles for managing

---

[26] Valerie Tiberius argues that the ability to divide one's attention and energy between goals that complement each other, rather than "becoming the kind of person who obsessively pursues one project to the exclusion of any other," is a virtue. See her "Value Commitments and the Balanced Life," *Utilitas* 17, no. 1 (March 2005): 24–45, 27.

the pursuit of value within a finite life in chapter 5, when we come to the topic of commitment.)

For now, I simply want to observe that one of the ways agent-independent accounts of meaning go wrong is that they treat the question of meaning as entirely a question of how valuable one's projects are. They ignore the fact that some highly valuable projects use up considerable amounts of time in norm-required and entailed spending that may not be very valuable at all. Agent-independent accounts also ignore the fact that people pursue value within a finite life. The finitude of life means that people will have to adopt some policy for managing their pursuit of value that addresses the question of whether they will or will not allow valued but less worthy activities to be crowded out by more worthy activities.

THE SUBJECTIVITY OF THE AGENT'S BEST JUDGMENT AND THE OVERLY PERMISSIVE OBJECTION REVISITED

In assessing the agent-independent conception of meaningfulness, I said that the question is not whether reflecting on the agent-independent value of what we are doing with our lives is relevant to assessing how meaningfully we are disposing of our lives but, rather, whether an agent-independent conception correctly captures the *way* those reflections function in determinations of meaningfulness. Agent-independent and agent-independent-plus conceptions think that meaning is supplied by agent-independent value facts that the agent tries to latch on to. I agree that this is what agents are trying to latch on to. But I don't think meaning (as opposed to value) is supplied by those facts. Meaning is supplied by the agent's best judgment about what those facts are, along with her reasons-for-the initiated and reasons-for-me.

That different sorts of reasons enter into the selection of ends explains, I think, our being pulled toward two different conceptions of what makes a life meaningful. On the one hand, reasons-for-anyone are likely to play a prominent role in our adoption of ends. So, it is not surprising that we are pulled toward thinking that meaningful lives are ones devoted to activities that are valuable or excellent according to an agent-independent standard, or as I would prefer to say, are supported by reasons-for-anyone. On the other hand, reasons-for-anyone are not the only reasons, and sometimes we have particularly strong or numerous reasons-for-me or reasons-for-the-initiated for selecting particular ends even if they are not the most worthy activities. Among those reasons we may find our attraction, love, feelings of fulfillment, desire for and appreciation of an activity—feelings that may be particularly strongly connected with one's reasons-for-me and reasons-for-the-initiated. So, it is not surprising that we are pulled toward thinking that meaningful lives are ones that feel satisfying or attractive.

As should be clear now, I think it is a mistake to describe this pull in terms of being pulled toward both an agent-independent account of meaning and toward a subjective attitude account of meaning, and thus as resolvable by adopting an agent independent plus account. All assessments of meaning are fundamentally subjective: they appeal to the individual's own reasons for spending her life's time the way she does. Because individuals adopt ends for their own reasons, subjectivity is built into the evaluation of ends from the get-go—not added on to an evaluation of the agent-independent worth of a life's activities.

If it seems as though we could rank the meaningfulness of lives, like those of Albert Einstein or Mother Teresa, without knowing anything about how they feel about their lives, it is because we simply assume, quite reasonably, that in pursuing physics or service to the poor, respectively, Einstein and Mother Teresa were pursuing their own ends. That we would not retract the assessment of Mother Teresa's life as meaningful upon discovering her loneliness and feelings of being abandoned by God is because we assume she continued to have service to India's poor as her end despite her alienation—not because her service continued to be a kind of excellent activity. Indeed, in her letters she is adamant about her unwavering commitment to God and obedience to what he willed for her life.

Meaningfulness may in some cases be subjective in an additional sense: what makes your disposing of time meaningful is that you have strong or numerous reasons-for-me for pursuing some of your ends, such that the value you place on your ends cannot be made sense of solely by appeal to reasons-for-anyone that justify an assessment of the worthiness of your ends. The resistance we may feel to the way agent-independent accounts of meaning demote the meaningfulness of our more ordinary lives when compared to a Mother Teresa's extraordinary life is, I think, a resistance to discounting reasons-for-me (and reasons-for-the initiated) as good reasons for selecting the ends whose pursuit makes our lives meaningful.

We have now arrived at the overly permissive objection. Suppose the agent gets it wrong. Her best judgment isn't right. She thinks, for example, that what the destitute need most is to have their souls saved rather than to be relieved of destitution. Or worse, she thinks the richest of the world should be bombed. A normative outlook conception of meaning counts these as meaningful lives. Isn't this overly permissive?

In assessing this objection, it's important to be clear on the difference between the kind of subjectivist view I've been proposing and an attitudinal subjectivist view, since the charge of over-permissiveness appears in the literature in response to the latter view. Attitudinal subjectivists think that what makes an activity meaningful are mere positive personal attitudes, quite apart from the agent's evaluative reasons for having those attitudes. You simply enjoy, feel satisfied by, care about, or love what you're doing.[27]

The principal reason repeatedly offered for rejecting an attitudinal subjectivist conception of meaning is that it yields sharply counterintuitive judgments of what lives are meaningful. Here is but one of a multitude of fantastical examples from critics of subjectivist conceptions: were it one's passion, assembling the largest ball of string would be a meaningful way of spending one's life.[28]

Beyond being intuitively compelling, what specific flaw in attitudinal subjectivist conceptions of meaning are such counterexamples designed to reveal? Most obviously, they are designed to draw attention to the uncommendable nature of such a life. Assembling the largest ball of string is not a valuable activity by any plausible agent-independent standard. If we assume that "meaningful" does the work of commending, then it will be a fatal flaw of any conception of meaningfulness if it commends clearly uncommendable lives. I have, however, been arguing that it is not a foregone conclusion that "meaningful" must be located in the conceptual geography of commendation. It is thus open to any subjectivist to resist the overly permissive objection by simply denying that "meaningful" is commendatory in the way agent-independent theorists think it is.

Still, even granting that "meaningful" does not commend because it is not equivalent to "significant" or "humanly excellent," there seems something intuitively wrong with counting mere passion—for string collecting, no less!—as sufficient for meaning. What is the source of that intuition? I suggest it is this: were *mere* passion meaning-conferring, this would place the string collector's activities beyond criticism, *even by the string collector himself.* There would be no space for the string collector to even raise the question of whether his passions are tracking what is valuable.[29] The counterexample has force because it draws attention to the way an attitudinal subjectivist conception of meaning places beyond criticism ways of living that naturally invite criticism, including by the string collector himself. But notice that this interpretation

---

[27] Although I have a great deal of sympathy for Frankfurt's approach to meaningfulness, it does appear to be an attitudinal subjectivist one on which caring itself, and no reason-giving features of what is cared for, makes a life meaningful. For a thorough critique of Frankfurt on this point, see Susan Wolf, "The True, the Good, and the Loveable: Frankfurt's Avoidance of Objectivity," in *Contours of Agency: Essays on Themes from Harry Frankfurt*, ed. Sarah Buss and Lee Overton (Boston: MIT Press, 2002), 227–244.

[28] Thadeus Metz offers a helpful compendium of counterexamples appearing in the literature (*Meaning in Life*, 175). John Koethe suggests the string collecting example in his "Comment" in Wolf, *Meaning in Life*, 67.

[29] Susan Wolf uses this to argue against equating meaningfulness with feelings of fulfillment. On such a view, one could not make sense of the possibility of thinking one is living a meaningful life and being wrong.

of the force of the counterexample is neutral between agent-independent and agent-dependent construals of the basis for criticism. One might criticize a passion for being directed toward something that lacks agent-independent value as assessed from some ideal third-person point of view. Alternatively, both we and the string collector might criticize his passion for failing to be properly responsive to his own reasons, including his own assessments of agent-independent value.[30]

Precisely because subjective attitudinal conceptions do not require that meaning-conferring attitudes be responsive to any particular sorts of reasons, or even to any reasons at all (hence the objector's emphasis on *mere* feelings of fulfillment, caring, etc.), they render unintelligible the choice of what to expend a life on. We the spectator cannot get a grip on what the string collector tells himself about the meaningfulness of what he does. An attitudinal subjectivist eliminates from the conception of meaningfulness the very things that would enable the person who claims to have a meaningful life to explain the intelligibility, and thus the meaningfulness, of his choices—his reasons. Attitudinal subjectivist measures thus fail to cite a suitable kind of subjective basis for meaningfulness. In short, the overly permissive objection, insofar as it relies on the force of fantastical examples, fails to cut against subjectivist measures of meaning generally. It cuts against those on which the having of reasons for one's attitudes is irrelevant.

It is important to be clear here about why "I like it!" is, on the view I am proposing, unlikely to be sufficient to ground claims about the meaningfulness of what one is doing. Psychologically normal, adult human beings are familiar with interpersonal practices of reason-giving, such as giving advice, criticizing, and justifying. As I suggested earlier, central to those reason-giving practices is an appeal to the public fund of reasons-for-anyone. "I like it!" will be a decisive reason for selecting an end and devoting a life's time to it only if that reason survives reflective consideration of all the sorts of reasons one has—including the reasons-for-anyone that favor or disfavor that selection. It is virtually unimaginable that a psychologically normal adult would, using his best judgment, set string collecting as a primary end worth using up his life's time on.

The situation is different for those with disordered, limited, or undeveloped cognitive abilities. One might, for example, imagine children setting major, time-consuming ends by appeal solely to "I really like it!" These are not lives that *we* would find

---

[30] To believe that devotion to string collecting is exactly what her reasons support is (to lift Nomy Arpaly's words) to see "her as so immensely removed from our experience of healthy adult humans that we might need a global revision of what we believe about our species" ("Comment," in Wolf, *Meaning in Life*, 88). Or, as I suggested earlier, those who are familiar with reasons-for-anyone and the evaluative practices of criticism, advice, and defense that those reasons enable will be hard pressed to explain even to themselves why collecting string is choiceworthy.

meaningful to live. And it is an unfortunate thing when psychological disorders or cognitive deficits prevent an individual from leading the kind of meaningful life that normal, psychological healthy adults can, since they are cut off from activities that we have reason to think are valuable or excellent in one way or another. However, questions about meaningfulness are not, I have been arguing, simply questions about the excellence of one's activities, and they are not reducible to the question of whether one is living a humanly flourishing life, or making contributions to the good, exercising distinctively human rational capacities, developing one's virtue, or the like. They are instead questions about whether one is spending one's life's time pursuing one's ends—that is, primary-spending one's time.

Conceivably, psychologically abnormal or cognitively limited individuals are doing just that when they consume their time with something we regard as trivial.[31] It is a strength of the normative outlook account that it can acknowledge that children, the mentally ill, and the cognitively limited can lead meaningful lives. Acknowledging that they are leading meaningful lives does not prevent us from counterfactually thinking that were they not limited in the ways they are, the life they are presently living is not as meaningful as it could be. But this is just to say that if they were different they would have chosen different ends, and we think it would be a good thing if they were different. Where psychological deficiencies are remediable, such counterfactual claims have a good deal of force.

The more serious challenge for the normative outlook view comes from less fantastical counterexamples than string collecting. What does the normative outlook conception permit us to say about and to people—who might be ourselves—who appear to be frittering away their lives in more ordinary trivial pursuits or, worse yet, in immoral ones?[32] Well, quite a lot.

First, if one wants to commend the life of Mother Teresa or Albert Einstein, by all means one can do so. We have plenty of evaluative language on hand for making that commendation. By the same token, we have plenty of evaluative language on hand for criticizing the life-fritterer. The couch potato is not leading a humanly excellent, flourishing, good, or significant life. That Hitler's normative outlook made his life meaningful does not bar us from condemning him for choosing morally monstrous ends;

---

[31] I am indebted to Nomy Arpaly's discussion of the differences between what might make a psychologically healthy adult's life meaningful and what might make a cognitively limited child's life meaningful ("Comment," in Wolf, *Meaning in Life*, 86–89).

[32] Valerie Tiberius also poses and responds to a similar objection to her subjectivist account of living well in *The Reflective Life: Living Wisely With Our Limits* (New York: Oxford University Press), 99–101, 193.

nor does a Kantian duty of beneficence to adopt others' ends as our own extend to promoting others' immoral ends.

On the normative outlook conception, "meaningful" and "meaningless" cannot be used, respectively, to commend a life for being devoted to the valuable or condemn a life for being devoted to the valueless. It is not a substantive, evaluative conception. However, the normative outlook conception of meaningfulness can be used to commend procedurally successful and to criticize procedurally unsuccessful end-setting. On the normative outlook conception, it would not be amiss to hold Mother Teresa up as an exemplary instance of a meaningful life. Her letters reveal her to have been an exemplar of someone who deliberated in depth and over a long period of time about what ends to set, the reasons for setting those ends, and the reliability of her own reasons (for example, the warrant for believing that the Voice she heard was in fact the voice of Christ). If we assume that the string collector is a normally developed human being, familiar with and a participant in practices of reason-giving, then absent an extraordinary story on his part, we must assume he has simply not bothered to set ends and thus has not engaged in the very processes necessary for meaning-making. He is an example to us all of a meaningless life.

The subjectivist view I have been recommending does not disable us, as the subjective attitude conception does, from critically engaging with others over the meaningfulness of their lives. Meaningfulness requires that a life's time expenditures be guided by the person's normative outlook. We may, as in the string collector case, have reason to think the person hasn't given sufficient (or perhaps any) attention to framing a normative outlook in the first place. In other cases, we might think the reasons-for-anyone a person offers for choosing ends aren't very good ones, and we may try to persuade him that he's wrong. For example, parents sometimes disagree with their children about the choiceworthiness of pursuing a philosophy major. To the extent that reasons-for-anyone figure into the child's defense of the meaningfulness of a philosophy major, those reasons are fair game for parental disagreement. In yet other cases, we might think that the normative outlook a person thinks she has is not the one we're inclined to say she really has, since her own reasons-for-anyone, reasons-for-the-initiated, and reasons-for-me support something different. In particular, one might worry that people who are narrowly focused on the agent-independent value of what they are doing have neglected to take stock of their reasons-for-me that favor a different option. In yet other cases, we might think a person's normative outlook is likely to change with new experiences, greater knowledge, and changed circumstances, and so a long-term commitment that is meaningful now is unlikely to remain meaningful into the future (tattooing one's chest with the present girlfriend's name being a simple and obvious example). In yet other cases, we might suspect that a person is using a time-management policy that isn't the one he would have chosen had he reflected on what he wanted the temporal management of his pursuit of value to look like. If a pluralist strategy is what really suits him, but he is using a maximizing strategy, devoting all his time to top-ranked ends and allowing lower-ranked ends to get crowded out, he is not living as meaningfully as he could. Finally, there is all that entailed, norm-required, and filler time expenditure that gets in the way of meaningful living. In at least some cases, it will be the person's own fault for not doing as much primary-spending as she could. All of these considerations can make it appropriate to point out that the person is not leading a meaningful life at all or not as meaningful a life as she could be.

3

Taking an Interest in One's Future

The aim of the previous chapter was to determine what counts as an answer to the question, "Is what I am doing with my life meaningful?" The quality of meaningfulness at issue here is one that attaches to particular activities or life-courses, where it is assumed that some have more meaning than others. I argued in chapter 2 that if "meaningful" is to do distinctive conceptual work, we should not equate "meaningful" with "agent-independently valuable." I also argued that if we are to have a single criterion of meaningfulness, we should reject agent-independent-plus accounts as well. Your doing something meaningful with your life is not a matter of your engaging in pursuits that are both agent-independently valuable *and* toward which you have positive subjective attitudes. It is instead, I suggested, a matter of expending your life's time on ends that, in your best judgment, you take yourself to have reason to value for their own sake and thus to expend your life's time on. In this chapter, I turn from a focus on the *evaluative* conception of "meaningful living" to the *motivating interest* we take—or sometimes lose—in our own future. Taking such an interest is one of the basic ways we connect ourselves to our future.

Having at least some interest in one's own future appears to be critical to actively leading one's life. In chapter 1, I distinguished between "leading a life" in the narrow sense of deciding what characterizing features we want our life as a whole to have, and "leading a life" in the broader sense of deciding how to expend time, including making lowly decisions about how to fill time when we have no choice but to waste it. That we are motivated to lead a life in either of these senses would seem to depend on our taking an interest in our own future and thus having an interest in shaping our future lives. Absent a motivating interest in our own future—as, for example, happens in depression—we still might find reasons to forge ahead; one might continue on out of a sense of duty to others or to God, or because there is no alternative short of suicide to doing so, or on the basis of hope that a motivating interest might later be recovered. However, losing an interest in our future undercuts a central motivation for taking ourselves into the future via our agential activities.

I begin by examining the connection between meaningfulness and interest in the future and by explaining how finding particular pursuits meaningful could give us a *general* interest in our future. That our future appears open to meaningful living, however, is only part of the explanation of why we take an interest in our future. The bulk of this chapter is devoted to exploring other parts of our idea of the future that condition our interest in actively taking ourselves into the future through our own agency.

CREATURELY INTEREST

Taking an interest in one's own future and finding one's life meaningful might naturally be thought to be connected. Indeed, one reason for including some subjective component in a conception of meaningfulness—whether by adopting an attitudinal subjectivist, or an agent-independent-plus, or a normative outlook conception of meaningfulness—is to capture that intuitive connection. As Wolf suggested, people who find their lives meaningful care about, feel engaged by, and are satisfied by their present and prospective lives, and thus they take an interest in the future. But exactly how are meaningfulness and interest in the future connected?

One possibility, suggested by Richard Taylor, is that there is a basic creaturely interest in continued activity that itself makes life meaningful, independent of our evaluation of life pursuits, precisely because it give us an interest in our future.

In the course of thinking about what sort of meaningfulness might survive the fact that, within a geological time frame, human activities produce only ephemeral goods and thus appear ultimately pointless, Taylor proposes that the pointlessness of human endeavors is nevertheless compatible with taking an interest in them. A motivating sense of meaningfulness comes from "within us," and is a function of one's taking an interest in, and deeply involving one's will in, the activities with which one occupies one's time.[1] In his view, our involvement in those activities does not depend on either the value of those activities or their having an ultimate point, but simply on a basic creaturely interest in being active. Taylor takes both humans and animals to have this basic interest in activity (and aversion to the boredom of having, finally, completed everything there is to do). This, in his view, suffices to make life subjectively meaningful independent of how we evaluate our activities. As he says of beings with this creaturely interest, "their endless activity, which gets nowhere, is just what it is their will to pursue";[2] and "it is the doing that counts for them, and not what they hope to win by it."[3]

---

[1] Richard Taylor, *Good and Evil* (Amherst, NY: Prometheus Books, 2000), 333–334.
[2] Ibid., 333.
[3] Ibid.

I agree with Taylor that the interest we take in our lives is independent of theoretical reflections on the point or pointlessness of our activities within a geological time frame. His view nevertheless seems incomplete. Human interest in leading a life is surely more complex and conditional than Taylor suggests. Brute animal drive to be active doesn't exhaust for us (and probably not for some animals) the nature of taking an interest in living. That interest is likely to be conditional on all sorts of things, including thoughts about whether what one is doing with one's life is valuable and thus meaningful in an evaluative sense. (In chapter 6's examination of boredom, we will take a closer look at what conditions interest in present activities.) Moreover, while Taylor's short answer to the question of what interests us in our future explains our interest in our immediate future, it does not explain our interest in the future that falls beyond, and sometimes well beyond, present activities. Nor does it explain variations in the degree to which we take a motivating interest in our future. Depressed people may, for example, have some kind of creaturely interest in continued living, but beyond that have very little motivating interest in proceeding into the future. And those who are not depressed may take a greater or lesser motivating interest in their future. "What conditions our motivating interest in the future and thereby enables us to be interested in the business of leading the life of an agent?" thus needs a more complex answer than just "a brute interest in activity."

INTEREST IN AN EVALUATIVELY
MEANINGFUL FUTURE

Both agent-independent-plus and my normative outlook conceptions of meaningfulness suggest one way we might connect the evaluation of how well we are disposing of our lives with our motivating interest in our own future. Finding your life's pursuits meaningful is intrinsically connected to your having positive subjective attitudes toward those pursuits. On Wolf's agent-independent-plus account, the meaningfulness of your life depends on your being subjectively attracted to the agent-independently valuable things you spend your life's time on—you care about them, feel engaged by them, and are satisfied by their pursuit. On the normative outlook conception, the meaningfulness of your life depends on your having your own reasons for valuing the ends you pursue. You have not only reasons-for-anyone to acknowledge that they are worthwhile ends for anyone to choose, but also additional reasons to adopt them as ends for yourself and thus to adopt an engaged valuing attitude toward them. Thus, either an appeal to subjective attraction or a valuing attitude toward what you are doing with your life's time might explain why you take an interest in your future.

While it may seem obvious that we will take an interest in our future so long as their contents are valued by us, we might nevertheless wonder how that is possible.

A personal valuing attitude toward some activity—say, ballroom dancing—is, after all, simply a pro-attitude. It is not a temporally oriented attitude. So, a bit more needs to be said about the connection between such pro-attitudes and temporally oriented interest in the future. How is the valuing attitude taken toward an end connected to taking an interest in one's future where that end is realized, given that valuing attitudes are not essentially future oriented?

In addition, if your valuing attitudes toward your ends is to interest you in going on in general—that is, to give you a motivationally global interest in your future—your valuing particular pursuits would have to have psychologically global motivational effects. In presenting her agent-independent-plus theory, Wolf assumes that subjective attraction will have these larger motivational effects, thus attaching us in a particularly robust way to our future. In her terms, subjective attraction "roots us motivationally"[4] and gives us a reason to take an interest in the world and in ourselves in general, including a reason to live.[5] But how could valuing attitudes toward particular ends give us a motivationally global interest in our future? Let us take up these two questions in order.

Valuing Attitudes and Interest in Particular Bits of the Future

Our first question was: "How is the valuing attitude taken toward an end connected to taking an interest in the future where that end is realized given that valuing attitudes are not essentially future oriented?" Valuing attitudes toward ends can make the future attractive only to the extent that they are connected with an anticipation of, expectation of, or imaginative projection of oneself into a future in which the objects of those valuing attitudes have a place. We project ourselves into the future through future-oriented desires, hopes, aims, future-oriented practical reasoning (planning), and temporally extended activity. To value ballroom dancing as an end, for example, is to be disposed to having a variety of future-oriented desires (for example, to sign up for the Rhumba class), hopes (for example, that there will be opportunities for ballroom dancing), and aims (say, of entering and winning the next competition), and with those aims, plans for how to realize them and the execution, over time, of those plans.

Desires, hopes, aims, and plans are intrinsically future oriented. Desires and hopes are for the materialization of some states of affairs in the future. Settling upon aims involves framing intentions to realize them in the future. Making good on the intention to realize an aim in the future requires planning how to do so—plans that may be

---

[4] Susan Wolf, "Meaning and Morality," *Proceedings of the Aristotelian Society*, New Series, 97 (1997): 299–315, 306.

[5] Ibid., 303.

more or less complex and whose execution may extend over longer or shorter periods of time.[6] In desiring, hoping, aiming, and planning, we thus anticipate, have expectations about, and imaginatively project ourselves into a future in which desires or hopes have been satisfied, aims realized, and plans carried out. When valued ends are the object of desires, hopes, aims, plans, and temporally extended activity, valuing attitudes get connected to a conception of the future as one that is hospitable to our lives being bound up with what we take ourselves to have reason to value for its own sake and thus what would make future living meaningful. Valuing attitudes toward ends thus render the future attractive precisely because, and to the extent that, they are connected with a variety of psychological states in which one imaginatively projects oneself into—or, in Wollheim's terms, previsages—a future in which involvement with the valued end has a place.

That valuing attitudes toward ends get connected with an imaginative projection of ourselves into a future bound up with those ends explains why losing or being cut off from things we value, or their being damaged beyond repair, undercuts our interest in the future. To have such valuing attitudes, under conditions of loss, is to continue imaginatively projecting oneself into the future via now unsatisfiable desires and an acute sense of the loss of what one had hoped for, aimed at, and planned for as one's future. The future that one now anticipates appears unattractive because of its lamentable difference from the future that one continues to imagine as what-would-have-been or what-one-had-hoped-for.

A Motivationally Global Interest in the Future

Let's turn now to the second question: "How could valuing attitudes toward particular ends give us a motivationally global interest in our future?" In having ends, we adopt valuing attitudes toward particular relationships, activities, and experiences. You have as an end, say, reading mystery novels. The most obvious motivational effect of your valuing the reading of mystery novels is that you would take an interest in reading mystery novels in the future. The fact that you value reading mystery novels would explain why you take a motivating interest in that bit of your future that involves reading mystery novels—say, the evenings that you've set aside for doing so. But the fact that you value reading mystery novels does not, by itself, explain why you would take a general interest in your future—an interest that has psychologically global motivational effects. Why do we take a motivating interest in our future in general, including all those bits

---

[6] Michael E. Bratman, *Intention, Plans, and Practical Reason* (Cambridge MA: Harvard University Press, 1987).

of the future that are not the focus of desires, hopes, aims, and planning, such as getting dressed in the morning, answering the phone, and chatting with the Starbucks barista?

In chapter 1, I suggested one possibility. The future saturates the present both in virtue of our consciously previsaging what we hope or expect it to contain and in virtue of our nonreflective sense of the future. The future that saturates the present, I suggested, has not only a content but also a qualitative character as a result of some of the contents of the future dominating one's general sense of the future. This idea of the future is also *unitary*—a conception of The Future rather than a part of the future. Taken together, this would explain how the value attached to bits of the anticipated future could interest one not just in that part of one's future but also in one's future generally. We get up in the morning, get dressed, and get the day's activities under way against a background conception of a future in which there will be space, among everything else that the future holds, for involvement with what makes life meaningful. So, one explanation of our interest in our future—our being "motivationally rooted," as Wolf says—is that we live in the present *under the idea of a unitary future whose qualitative character is dominated by those bits of the future that constitute meaningful living.*

A second, related explanation of our motivationally global interest in our own future is suggested by deep normative identity views of the self. Normative identity is deep, it might be thought, when there are some valued attachments, projects, or self-conceptions that are so fundamental to one's sense of normative identity that one couldn't envision being oneself without them.[7] In Frankfurt's terms, fundamental carings impose "volitional necessities" on us.[8] Acting against what we care most deeply about is unthinkable—something we could not bring ourselves to do. In establishing the boundaries of the will, such deep attachments determine one's core normative identity as an agent. Korsgaard proposes that a similarly deep, normative identity

---

[7] Just how one should understand these identity-defining normative commitments is a matter of controversy. Harry Frankfurt understands them to not be reason-based (but reason-generating) carings that might conflict with what one evaluatively "endorses" as being *worth* caring about (Frankfurt, "On the Necessity of Ideals," in his *Necessity, Volition, and Love* [Cambridge: Cambridge University Press, 1999], 108–116). Gary Watson, by contrast, identifies identity-defining commitments with what one reflectively *endorses*. If one cares too much, one may act in ways that one does not reflectively authorize. Thus, agency can be defeated by deep carings—what Frankfurt calls volitional necessities—if they have not been reflectively endorsed (Gary Watson, "Volitional Necessities," in *Agency and Answerability: Selected Essays* [Oxford: Oxford University Press, 2004]). Nomy Arpaly agrees: "Harry Frankfurt's agents who surrender to 'volitional necessity,' may be very true to themselves but they do not *control themselves*; it may be said that on the contrary, *their selves control them*, as it were" (Nomy Arpaly, *Unprincipled Virtue: An Enquiry into Moral Agency* [New York: Oxford University Press, 2003], 122).

[8] Harry Frankfurt, "The Importance of What We Care About," in his *The Importance of What we Care About: Philosophical Essays* (Cambridge: Cambridge University Press, 1988) , 86ff; and "On the Necessity of Ideals," in *Necessity, Volition, and Love.*

consists in the "description under which you value yourself, a description under which you find your life to be worth living and your actions to be worth undertaking."[9] That self-conception gives rise to unconditional obligations the violation of which would mean being "for all practical purposes dead or worse than dead."[10] And in Bernard Williams's terms, deep identity consists in having some ground projects or commitments that are the condition for one's having an interest in going on at all, and thus that are objects of categorical desires.[11]

If this idea is recast in terms of normative outlook, not everything in our normative outlook is equally central to our self-conception. Some ends will be especially important to our sense of who we are, what we stand for, and what makes our lives meaningful. Our taking a motivating interest in the future—being "motivationally rooted" in our lives—often depends heavily on our being able to project ourselves forward in time via the network of desires, hopes, aims, and plans that flow specifically from what is most central to one's normative outlook and deep self-conception. Our having a motivating interest in the future—and thus an interest in leading a life—may therefore depend on our ability to live in the present *under the idea of a future in which our deepest self has a place.*

INTEREST IN USING ONE'S AGENCY TO TAKE ONESELF INTO THE FUTURE

So far, I have suggested that our taking a globally motivating interest in our own future, and thus in leading our lives, depends on our living in the present under an idea of the future whose content and qualitative character are connected to our conception of meaningful living and, in particular, where our deepest self has a place. In short, the idea of the future under which we live in the present must be sufficiently attractive for us to be motivated to take ourselves there. In the next chapter, I will describe this motivating interest in the future generally as *basal hopefulness.* Basal hopefulness is not hope for this or that particular future occurrence, but a more basic, globally motivating interest in the future.

Are there other things that condition our global interest in the future—our basal hopefulness—besides the meaningfulness of our future life? Yes. For beings like us who lead lives—who actively take ourselves into a future—the idea of the future must be one in which exercising our agential capacities makes sense. We need a background idea of our future selves and circumstances within which, and on the basis of which, the activities

---

[9] Christine Korsgaard, *The Sources of Normativity* (Cambridge: Cambridge University Press, 1996), 102.

[10] Ibid.

[11] Bernard Williams, "Persons, Character and Morality," in his *Moral Luck: Philosophical Papers 1973–1980* (Cambridge: Cambridge University Press, 1981).

of agency make sense. I call these agency-related conditions on our interest in the future *background frames of agency*. One important background frame of agency is our sense of the future as open to meaningful living. But this is only one of a set of crucial background frames of agency. In the rest of this chapter, I explore three additional background frames of agency: lack of estrangement from one's own normative outlook, a belief in the effectiveness of instrumental reasoning, and confidence in one's relative security from disastrous misfortune and indecent harm. The absence of these background frames is *volitionally disabling*. When a person is volitionally disabled she is unmoved to take herself into the future. So, let us begin with the notion of volitional disability.

Agency and Volitional Disability

Getting a fix on the background frames of agency that condition our interest in actively leading our lives is important to a full account of what makes agency possible. There is by now an extensive philosophical literature, much of it inspired by the pioneering work of Harry Frankfurt, on what it would mean to constitute oneself as an agent in the first place (and thus to become something more than, as he puts it, a mere wanton) and on how agency might be *internally defeated*.[12] Becoming an agent means determining which bits of one's psychology one wants to be moved by and thus which will count as reasons to act. The fact that I have particular desires may not be up to me, but it is up to me whether I count them as providing considerations to be weighed in deliberating about what to do. We fail to act as agents when inclinations that we do not authorize move us rather than our own reasons. A central threat to agency is, thus, failure to exercise control over our own inner states. Because they typically cause agents to act against their better judgment, obsessions, compulsions, irresistible urges, overwhelming aversions, addictions, and weakness of will are paradigm instances of states that impair agency by defeating the agent's motivating reasons.

There is also an extensive philosophical literature on the *circumstantial conditions* necessary for the development and exercise of agency. Determining the causal conditions

---

[12] Frankfurt, *Importance of What We Care About*; Gary Watson, "Free Agency," *Journal of Philosophy* 72 (1975): 205–220; Watson, "Volitional Necessities," 129–159; Christine M. Korsgaard, "Self-Constitution in the Ethics of Plato and Kant," *Journal of Ethics* 3 (1999): 1–29; Korsgaard, *Sources of Normativity*; Michael E. Bratman, *Faces of Intention: Selected Essays on Intention and Agency* (Cambridge: Cambridge University Press, 1999); Michael E. Bratman, "Reflection, Planning and Temporally Extended Agency," *Philosophical Review* 109 (2000): 35–61; Arpaly, *Unprincipled Virtue*, 91–123; J. David Velleman, "Identification and Identity," in *Contours of Agency: Essays on Themes by Harry Frankfurt*, ed. Sarah Buss and Lee Overton (Cambridge, MA: MIT Press, 2002), 91–123; J. David Velleman, "The Possibility of Practical Reason," *Ethics* 106 (1996): 694–726; Richard Moran, "Frankfurt on Identification: Ambiguities of Activity in Mental Life," in Buss and Overton, *Contours of Agency*, 189–217.

necessary for developing and exercising agency enables the formulation of normative principles about how individuals or political institutions ought to treat those who are capable of constituting themselves as agents. Those normative principles include ones barring coercion, strong paternalism, and deception, because these ways of treating people impede their ability to deliberate and choose. They also include principles enjoining the social availability of an adequate array of options for choice and sufficient material means for the exercise of meaningful agency.

The possibility of agency thus depends on constituting oneself as an agent, on one's will not being internally defeated by one's impulses, and on living under agency-supporting circumstantial conditions. In addition, the possibility of agency depends on the absence of volitional disability—the *disengagement* of the will from actively leading a life as a result of lost interest in one's own future.

Depression and kindred volitional disabilities, such as demoralization, centrally involve disengagement from the agential activities of reflecting, deliberating, choosing, and acting.[13] What is most striking about depression is that depressed individuals are unable to get themselves to act on their own deliberative conclusions about what to do, and sometimes unable to initiate deliberation, even in the absence of countervailing motivations.

Volitional disabilities differ fundamentally from phobias, addictions, irresistible urges, weakness of will, and similar losses of self-control. Irresistible urges and overwhelming aversions defeat agency by supplying powerful motivational forces that compete with what we want to determine our will—namely, our own conception of what we want our lives to look like. That defeat of the will presupposes that we are already engaged in the project of leading a life. By contrast, in depression, we do not run up against overpowering motivational forces; instead, we find our reasons for action simply depleted of their normal motivational force. That depletion is not best viewed as the result of depression functioning as a kind of ghostly internal dam that blocks the hydraulic force of motivating reasons, thus defeating agency. Rather than causing the internal defeat of an engaged will, volitionally disabling depression involves disengagement of the will, and consequently disengagement from the project of being an agent and leading a life. As a result, quite simple everyday tasks, such as getting out of bed or deciding which pair of pants to wear, come to seem impossibly difficult.[14] Worse, being oneself may come to seem impossibly difficult as one finds oneself unable to carry out

---

[13] I take the term "volitional disabilities" from Gary Watson (Watson, "Volitional Necessities"). He uses the term more broadly than I do here to include irresistible impulses and overwhelming aversions—that is, desires that conflict with and defeat the agent's will. I am using "volitional disability" to refer more narrowly to disengagement, not also defeat, of the will.

[14] Those who suffer from depression continue to have views about what they ought to do, both pragmatically and morally, and about the identity-defining features of their lives that they

one's projects and plans, engage with the persons and things one values most, or strive to meet one's own moral and nonmoral standards.

"Major depression is one of the most common forms of psychopathology world-wide."[15] It commonly attends poverty, victimization by violent assault, low-status occupations, and caretaker roles, with women experiencing depression at twice the rate that men do.[16] While depression is often caused by significant losses—the loss of loved ones, a central relationship, a job—and thus loss of meaningful living, it also has other causes, including the experience of undergoing bypass surgery or suffering a heart attack, financial or other stress, loss of control over gratification and relief from suffering, unexpected disability, being faced with an insolvable problem, growing old, a negative self-conception, and loss of social status or reputation.[17] Furthermore, leading a meaningful life is no guarantee against volitionally disabling depression. Recall from the previous chapter Mother Teresa's ongoing depression and despair in the midst of a life devoted to what she took to be most important.

Or, consider the case of Larry McMurtry. McMurtry had a passion for books. He owned some 200,000 books and read voraciously at a fast clip, and he typically had several books at the same time that he was in the process of reading. After he underwent quadruple bypass surgery, he fell into a deep depression—a fairly common event for men who go through bypass surgery. Describing his life after surgery, he says:

> The content of my life, which had been rich, began to drain rapidly away. . . .
> [M]ore or less overnight staying informed ceased to matter to me. . . . From
> being a living person with a distinct personality, I began to feel more or less like

continue to believe they ought to take an interest in, such as their family relationships, hobbies, or career, even if they cannot take such an interest. Thus depression is typically attended with both guilt about one's inability to conduct one's life as one believes one ought (for example, to get out of bed) and longing for one's lost, motivationally engaged self.

[15] Elizabeth Sparks, "Depression and Schizophrenia in Women: The Intersection of Gender, Race/Ethnicity, and Class," in *Rethinking Mental Health and Disorder: Feminist Perspectives*, ed. Mary Ballou and Laura S. Brown (New York: Guilford Press, 2002), 279.

[16] "The common interpretation in the literature is that women are at higher risk for experiencing depression due to differences in socialization between women and men in our society, different learned styles of coping with emotional distress, and innate biological differences" (Sparks, "Depression and Schizophrenia in Women," 283). In addition, women are more likely to find themselves exposed to the stress factors that contribute to depression: poverty, violent assault, being a caretaker, occupying a low-status job (Susan L. Simonds, *Depression and Women: An Integrative Treatment Approach* [New York: Springer, 2001], 32).

[17] Christopher Peterson, Steven F. Maier, and Martin E.P. Seligman, *Learned Helplessness: A Theory for the Age of Personal Control* (New York: Oxford University Press, 1993); Aaron T. Beck, "A Cognitivist Analysis of Depression," in *The Nature of Melancholy: From Aristotle to Kristeva*, ed. Jennifer Radden (Oxford: Oxford University Press, 2002), 317–323.

an outline of a person. . . . I became, to myself, more and more like a ghost, or a shadow. What I more and more felt, as the trauma deepened, was that while my body survived, the self that I had once been had lost its life.[18]

For two and a half years, McMurtry was completely unable to read. And, "the sense of grief for the lost self," he says, "was profound. I didn't feel like my old self at all, and had no idea where the old self had gone. But I did know that it, he, me was gone, and that I missed him."[19]

What is significant here is that McMurtry's life before depression is bound up with something that makes his life meaningful and which he continues to value during depression. Even after he has become motivationally uprooted so that he no longer takes an interest in staying informed, he continues to define himself in terms of this former project. What's missing is the motivational force of his continued, but ghostly, attachment to books. And this suggests that we need a more complicated psychological story than so far developed about what conditions interest in our own future and thus provides a background frame of agency.

One background frame of agency, I have suggested, is our living with the idea of a future whose content and qualitative character is connected with meaningful living. Let us turn now to three additional background frames, whose disruption is commonly registered in depression: (1) lack of estrangement from one's own normative outlook, (2) a belief in the effectiveness of instrumental reasoning, and (3) confidence in one's relative security from disastrous misfortune and indecent harm. Those who are estranged from their normative outlook lack the desire to pursue what they value, including what they most deeply value, even when their lives afford them opportunities to do so. Those who lose confidence in the effectiveness of instrumental reasoning or in their security from disastrous misfortune have reason to give up on planning generally, not just planning connected to their most important concerns.

Estrangement

In Michael Cunningham's *The Hours*, we meet the character Laura Brown at a point in time when she is struggling with her estrangement from her own normative outlook.[20] Laura is married, has one young child, and is pregnant with a second. What is most central to her normative outlook as she conceives it is being a good mother, a good

---

[18] Larry McMurtry, "From *Walter Benjamin at the Dairy Queen*," in *Unholy Ghost: Writers on Depression*, ed. Nell Casey (New York: Perennial, 2002), 69.
[19] Ibid., 70.
[20] Michael Cunningham, *The Hours* (New York: Farrar, Straus and Giroux, 1998).

wife, and a competent caretaker of her family's home; and she in fact has a husband who adores her, a son who is almost painfully attached to her, and a pleasant suburban home. Even so, unwelcome bits of her psychology disrupt her story about who she is and will be, estranging her from her own normative outlook. She sometimes resents her child, finds her husband mystifyingly alien, feels incompetent at mothering and homemaking, and longs for her lost possibilities. Shortly before planning suicide, she experiences a brief moment when it seems as though she has overcome her estrangement from her normative outlook and her own reasons for action.

> It seems suddenly easy to bake a cake, to raise a child. She loves her son purely, as mothers do—she does not resent him, does not wish to leave. She loves her husband, and is glad to be married. It seems possible (it does not seem impossible) that she's slipped across an invisible line, the line that has always separated her from *what she would prefer to feel, who she would prefer to be*. It does not seem impossible that she has undergone a subtle but profound transformation, here in this kitchen, at this most ordinary of moments: She has caught up with herself. She has worked so long, so hard, in such good faith, and now she's gotten the knack of living happily, as herself, the way a child learns at a particular moment to balance on a two-wheeled bicycle. It seems she will be fine, she will not lose hope. She will not mourn her lost possibilities, her unexplored talents (what if she has no talents after all?). She will remain devoted to her son, her husband, her home and duties, all her gifts. She will want this second child.[21]

Unfortunately, her estrangement from her normative outlook returns, resulting in an attempted suicide.

The fictional character of Laura Brown echoes the narratives of depressed women interviewed by Dana Crowley Jack in her book, *Silencing the Self: Women and Depression*.[22] Jack's interviewees articulate conceptions of what they want most that involve being good wives and caretakers. They want to be supportive, compliant, unselfish, quiet, cheerful, cooperative—in short, they want to live up to their own and their culture's conception of a good woman. But like Laura, unwelcome bits of their psychology disrupt, without immediately motivating a revision in, their normative outlooks. As a result, they find themselves estranged from the very normative outlooks that they take to define their identities as agents.

[21] Ibid., 79 (emphasis mine).
[22] Dana Crowley Jack, *Silencing the Self: Women and Depression* (Cambridge, MA: Harvard University Press, 1991).

This estrangement is not simply a matter of no longer being able to sustain a particular self-conception—in Laura's case, as someone who loves her son purely and is glad to be married—in the face of thoughts, feelings, and desires that tell against that self-conception.[23] Discovering "I thought I was this kind of person, but now I realize I'm not," and thus giving up a particular picture of one's psychology, isn't the same as coming to feel estranged from one's values. Not uncommonly, giving up smug illusions about how well one's actual desires, beliefs, and feelings track what one aspires to desire, believe, and feel goes hand in hand with renewed identification with one's normative outlook and to better embodying it.

Nor is estrangement from one's normative outlook simply a matter of finding that one doesn't want to act on the deliberative conclusions one reaches about what to do, given one's ends. People often find some (or even much) of what they value—say, being polite to telemarketers—unappealing at the level of desire and emotion, without their feeling estranged from what they value. This is to say that estrangement isn't equivalent to large chunks of one's psychology being at odds with one's normative outlook (although estrangement often involves this).

Rather, to be estranged from one's own normative outlook is, on one hand, to continue to think that if one is going to have a normative outlook at all, one's present normative outlook is the one that one wants to have. This is what makes the normative outlook *one's own*. On the other hand, one comes to feel that one is not capable of being the person who values these things, who deliberates on their basis, and who is moved to act in keeping with them.

By "not capable of being the person who values these things," I do not mean just that it has come to seem too difficult to embody in one's actions the normative outlook one has called one's own. The incapacity has to do with there being something missing from *the way in which one holds* the normative outlook. It is held, as it were, in a bloodless, intellectual way that is detached from one's perceptual, desiderative, and emotional experience.[24] Frankfurt's distinction between caring and desiring is useful in explaining what it might mean to hold one's own normative outlook in this defective way.

Frankfurt argues that caring—finding things, persons, and ideals to be important to oneself—is not a matter of feeling or of desire, but of commitment to having specific motivationally effective desires in one's psychological economy. Such commitment is "a disposition to be active in seeing to it that the desire is not abandoned or neglected"

[23] On not being able to sustain a particular self-conception, see Velleman, "Identification and Identity," 227–244.
[24] See Michael Stocker's discussion of the way in which those suffering spiritual maladies, including depression, lack full-blooded desire, in "Affectivity and Self-Concern: The Assumed Psychology in Aristotle's Ethics," *Pacific Philosophical Quarterly* 64 (1983): 211–229.

and to refresh the desire should it begin to fade, reinforcing "whatever degree of influence he wishes it to exert upon his decisions and upon his behavior."[25]

> Insofar, then, as a person considers something important to him and hence something that he needs, he will also normally consider it important to him to desire it. Furthermore, he will be similarly motivated to prevent himself from losing his desire for it. It is good for us to be motivated to satisfy our needs. So it is a good idea for us to sustain that motivation and to support it whenever it might otherwise tend to fade.[26]

There is no incompatibility, on this view, between caring about something and having insufficiently motivating desires to take care of it. By extension, there would seem to be no incompatibility between a person's regarding something as an end of hers but finding that her desires relating to it have faded. So, one might care about, or value as an end, the doing of philosophy, but find that, during a particular period of time, one's desires related to philosophical activity have faded. Frankfurt does not mention the possibility that one might lose the appropriate motivating desires altogether, having failed to be able to rekindle them, but that would seem a reasonable psychological possibility. And this is what I have in mind by estrangement from one's own normative outlook. Laura Brown, for example, has to tell herself that her son is lovable and that her marriage is a good thing; she has ceased to be able to feel that it is or to have the appropriate mothering and wifely desires.[27]

When a normative outlook is held in this defective way, acting on the basis of it produces a feeling of unreality, as though the person who animates that normative outlook is a fiction of herself, even though there is no other self (no other normative outlook

[25] Harry G. Frankfurt, "On Caring," in his *Necessity, Volition, and Love*, 162.

[26] Ibid., 164.

[27] In "Valuing and the Will" (*Nous* 34, Supplement 14 (2000): 249–265, 260–261), Michael Bratman suggests a similar point about the possibility of failing to have first order desires connected to the higher order self-governing policies:

> Could one have a policy of treating, say, helping others as a justifying end in motivationally effective deliberation, and yet still not have a first-order desire in favor of helping others? I think the answer is yes. However, actually to treat helping others in this way in motivationally effective deliberation will, I think, involve some such first-order desire (in the broadly generic sense of "desire"). In the absence of such a desire, then, the cited policy will involve a commitment to coming to have the desire. Should we say that such a higher order policy, in the absence of the first-order desire, suffices for valuing? Well, it is not by itself a kind of valuing characteristic of self-determined activity, for that requires valuing that really does control action. But we might still say that this is a kind of (somewhat attenuated) valuing, related in indicated ways to the motivationally more robust valuing I have highlighted.

with which she identifies) that is the real self. In narrating his experience of depression, Larry McMurtry captures precisely this experience of estrangement: "During this period, I began to feel that I, too, was one of my imposters, doomed to impersonate a person I now no longer was. I became, to myself, more and more like a ghost, or a shadow. What I more and more felt, as the trauma deepened, was that while my body survived, the self that I had once been had lost its life."[28] Cunningham's Laura has a similar experience of impersonating her own self: "she is again possessed (it seems to be getting worse) by a dreamlike feeling, as if she is standing in the wings, about to go on stage and perform in a play for which she is not appropriately dressed, and for which she has not adequately rehearsed."[29]

That one could be estranged from what one values may still seem oxymoronic. How could one's own values not feel like one's own? After all, making up one's mind about one's normative outlook isn't just the impersonal, intellectual exercise of asking "What things are agent-independently good or worthwhile?"—an exercise that might supply answers with which one fails to resonate. Making up one's mind is the more personal exercise of asking "What do *I* have reasons (for-anyone, for-the-initiated, for-me) to adopt as ends?"

One may thus be tempted to adopt an alternative interpretation of Laura Brown and of Jack's interviewees. One might, for example, think that these women are not in fact estranged from their own normative outlooks, but have simply misidentified their actual normative outlooks. Jack herself takes that view. She argues that at the heart of women's depression is a split between two voices—one the voice of "immediate experience" that expresses what these women really value, and one the internalized voice of cultural norms of womanhood. Because their "authentic" self is at odds with the culturally sanctioned view of what is normatively valuable,[30] these women censor their authentic selves and misdescribe their *real* normative outlooks even though doing so "requires tremendous cognitive and emotional activity to curb the self."[31] Thus, Jack takes these women's depression to be occasioned by their insistence on leading a life in which their own normative outlooks cannot find expression, a life from which, quite naturally, they come to feel alienated. In other words, they are depressed because they are leading lives in which their deep self-conceptions have no, or insufficient, place.[32]

---

[28] McMurty, "From *Walter Benjamin at the Dairy Queen*," 69.

[29] Cunningham, *The Hours*, 43.

[30] According to Jack, "The Over-Eye persistently pronounces harsh judgment on most aspects of a woman's authentic strivings, including her wish to express herself freely in relationship, her creativity, and her spirituality. Because the judgments of the Over-Eye include a cultural consensus about feminine goodness, truth, and value, they have the power to override the authentic self's viewpoint" (*Silencing the Self*, 94).

[31] Jack, *Silencing the Self*, 49.

[32] Along these lines, Marya Schechtman develops (without entirely agreeing with) the popular idea that a person's "true self" is to be identified not by asking what the agent self-consciously

Nomy Arpaly suggests a variant of this view—one on which the women would not be, as on Jack's view, merely parroting cultural norms when they claim to be expressing their own normative judgments about the importance of being good wives, but that nevertheless avoids the conclusion that I've suggested that these women are estranged from what is (really) their own normative outlook.[33] Arpaly points out that in deliberating about what to do, including what life-courses to pursue, individuals may fail to take into account all their relevant beliefs and values and, consequently, misjudge what the right course for themselves really is. They end up feeling dissatisfied, restless, and ill-motivated. If Jack's depressed women are like this, then the problem is not that they act on the basis of an inauthentic, internalized cultural voice. They have not misidentified their normative outlooks in that sense; they may truly value their marital relationships and living up to the ideal of a good wife. But in their deliberation they discount other reasons that they have, reasons that would lead them to a different conclusion about the value, all things considered, of marital self-sacrifice. As a result, they deliberate irrationally and reach mistaken deliberative conclusions. It is no wonder, then, that they find themselves unmotivated to act on their own deliberative conclusions, since their deliberation does not adequately reflect the reasons that they have.

On both of these interpretations, the depressed women still have motivating reasons for action from which they are not estranged. It's just that they have, in one way or another, lost sight of those reasons. Had they only deliberated on the basis of their *own* or their *complete* reasons for action, they would have recognized that their true ends are not ones from which they are estranged, and they would have come to different conclusions about what they should be doing.

It is surely true that some people silence their normative outlooks in order to conform, while others take inadequate account of their normative outlooks when they deliberate. When individuals are obviously repressing strong and persistent desires, there is prima facie reason to suspect that the repressed desires may be more indicative of the person's true normative outlook than are the person's avowals. The situation is otherwise, however, in cases where a person loses interest in her normative outlook

---

endorses but by attending to her robust inclinations. Robust inclinations, in Schechtman's view, are relatively stable, coherent, and powerful desires that constitute desiring to lead a particular kind of life. In order to conform to their own or others' ideas of who they should be, individuals may try to repress their robust inclinations, with the consequence that they experience frustration, anxiety, emptiness, and depression. Marya Schechtman, "Self-Expression and Self-Control," in *The Self?*, ed. Galen Strawson (Malden, MA: Blackwell, 2005).

[33] Arpaly, *Unprincipled Virtue*, see especially 33–51. For example, Arpaly considers the case of Emily, the chemistry Ph.D. student who, in deliberating about her chosen vocation, discounts facts about her lack of talent in chemistry and the way this profession prevents her from exercising other talents. She thus reaches conclusions about staying in the Ph.D. program that do not accurately reflect the range of her reasons.

but in the absence of any evidence that some strong, persistent, and more identity-defining desires are being repressed. Laura Brown, for example, isn't obviously repressing anything. We know that later she will abandon her husband and child, become a lesbian, and pursue a career as a librarian. But at the time of her depression, there is virtually no indication that there is something else she wants more than the life she has. The absence of some alternative, truer normative outlook with which she identifies (if only she would admit it) is part of what makes this particular way of losing interest in one's future so devastating. One is estranged from the only present and future self one wishes to have.

Estrangement from one's own normative outlook is an ordinary hazard of agency. We constitute ourselves as agents both by rejecting some kinds of inclinations as acceptable reasons for action and by selecting among desirable aims, attachments, projects, and life trajectories that cannot all be accomplished in a single lifetime.[34] Rejected inclinations are not necessarily eliminated from one's psychology. And unchosen but desirable paths of living often do not cease to be attractive. As a result, the very process of self-constitution occurs against a backdrop of inclinations and normative attractions that can disrupt agency.[35] Most obviously, rejected inclinations and normative attractions provide the occasion for weakness of will. They may entice us to act contrary to what our own normative outlook requires, thus defeating agency. But rejected inclinations and normative attractions provide the stuff not just for weakness of will but also for becoming estranged from one's own normative outlook. What one is most deeply psychologically attracted to, as well as what one finds oneself persistently repulsed, frustrated, uninterested, or bored by, may conflict with what one values. Laura Brown persistently found herself uninterested in mothering despite the priority of motherhood in her normative outlook.[36] One may refuse to have one's agency defeated by

---

[34] See Connie S. Rosati's discussion of the way that agency is inherently tied to the possibility of regret in "Mortality, Agency, and Regret," in New Trends in Philosophy: Moral Psychology, ed. Sergio Tennenbaum (Amsterdam: Rodopi, 2007), 231–260. Consider also Marya Schechtman's observation that "the romantic picture of a well-formed self just waiting to be set free is a nice one, but unlikely to be true. Our natures will more plausibly involve contradictory inclinations, and self-destructive ones. Unless we repress at least some of our natures we are likely, as Frankfurt says, to act in ways that are incoherent or self-undermining" (Schechtman, "Self-Expression and Self-Control," 60).

[35] By "normative attraction" I mean those things that we continue to regard as good, desirable, and a potential part of some individual's personal good, but that we have not chosen as part of our own personal good—at least not for this lifetime. The point here is that constructing a self is not just (or even largely) a matter of outlawing fully unacceptable desires, but of naysaying, or "silencing," desires that would, were one to have many lifetimes, be acceptable. Connie Rosati develops this point at length in "Morality, Agency, and Regret."

[36] For a real-life example, one might think of Mother Teresa, much of whose posthumously published correspondence concerns the deep depression she experienced throughout most of her work in India and her psychological inability to engage with the work she continued to prioritize

giving in to those inclinations, attitudes, and normative attractions that conflict with what one values.[37] But securing one's agency against defeat by rejected bits of one's psychology does not secure one's agency against estrangement. As Gary Watson says of a case of managing to act on one's endorsements rather than on one's nonendorsed carings: "Whether this achievement is enough to help her to carry on is another question entirely";[38] and "she is likely to feel empty, just 'going through the motions.'"[39] That is, she is likely to feel estranged from the very normative outlook she endorses and from what she wills on the basis of that outlook. Hence, there is the depersonalizing experience of feeling that one is just going through the motions, impersonating someone who has one's normative outlook.

My point here is that it is a mistake to think that because a person has ceased to identify psychologically with her normative outlook, there must be something else—some other hidden or silenced or ignored normative outlook with which she really does identify. Perfectly ordinary experiences of having lost one's religious convictions, or one's love for one's spouse, or one's interest in one's career—and wanting it back—tell against that idea. There are equally ordinary experiences of simply coming to be bored with the ends—the ideals, type of intimate relationship, career, political or religious commitments, family life, intellectual pursuits, and the like—that constitute one's normative outlook. To understand what we might call "existential" boredom, we need not suppose there is something else that interests the agent that she just isn't pursuing. That is, one need not suppose that there must always be something that one really values that explains one's estrangement from, including boredom with, what one says one values. (I will have more to say about boredom with one's own ends in chapter 6.)

In sum, most of us, most of the time, simply take for granted the way our normative outlook feels meaningful and interesting and nonfictional. Most of us, most of the time, take for granted that the evaluative structure of the world presented in our perceptions, desires, and emotions will generally coincide with the normative outlook we intellectually affirm, and thus that we are capable of being the kind of person who holds the normative outlook we do. This is a background frame of ordinary agency. But it is a frame that can be disrupted. The result is an estrangement from one's normative outlook that drains one's own reasons of motivational force; and to the extent that

---

in her normative outlook. See Brian Kolodiejchuk, ed. and comm., *Mother Teresa, Come Be My Light: The Private Writings of the "Saint of Calcutta"* (New York: Doubleday, 2007).

[37] Gary Watson argues, rightly I think, that when caring and endorsement part company, acting on what one cares about would defeat one's agency, since only in acting on our endorsements do we *authorize* the outcome (Watson, "Volitional Necessities," 121).

[38] Ibid.

[39] Ibid., 120.

deliberation and action are still possible, deliberating and acting feel like impersonating an agent rather than being one.

Demoralization

So far, I have focused only on conditions under which agents may find themselves unmoved by their own deliberation about what constitutes meaningful living for them. The possibility of agency, however, depends not only on being moved by one's deliberation but also on being moved to deliberate in the first place. The point of deliberation is to affect the world through one's actions (or inactions). Under normal conditions, we take for granted that deliberation has a point: our actions do affect, or stand a good chance of affecting, the world in the ways we intend. Most of us, most of the time, simply take for granted the practical efficacy of our deliberating and acting. But that background frame can be disrupted, resulting in a demoralizing loss of confidence in one's ability to function as an agent.

Demoralizing loss of confidence in the practical efficacy of agency is not all of a piece. For some, demoralization results from a loss of confidence in the *efficacy of instrumental reasoning.* For others, demoralization results from a loss of confidence in one's *security from tragic misfortune or from indecent harm.*

Poverty, social marginality, cultural dislocation, domestic abuse, unpredictable trauma, and chronic illness, as well as lesser harms, may produce the demoralizing experience of one's instrumental reasoning being ineffective. Agents may find themselves without the necessary material resources for action, or the cultural and linguistic tools for understanding and navigating their world, or the physical abilities to do what they expect themselves to be able to do, or the talents and abilities to carry off their plans, or safe and predictable social relationships on which to rely. Some of these factors, such as material resources or predictable social relationships, are part of the circumstantial conditions of agency: what we can effectively do is limited by the instruments available to us. But all these factors can also condition one's interest in reasoning instrumentally, because too much of one's life, or the most important parts of one's life, are not under one's own control but, rather, are controlled by good and bad luck or by other people. Poverty, for example, means that even the simplest plans, such as taking a bus to work or supplying one's children with required school pencils, are chronically vulnerable to derailment. For a refugee, lack of cultural literacy makes plans chronically vulnerable to going awry because one doesn't understand how things are done, and one may lack sufficient cultural literacy to discern when one doesn't know enough to engage in effective instrumental reasoning. Women who live with abusive men may find that even the simplest plans, like having access to the car keys or visiting a friend, are vulnerable to being undermined by the abuser's choices. When exercising one's agency has ceased to be reliably connected to producing intended effects, deliberation may well seem pointless and the future hopeless.

In his well-known work on depression, Martin Seligman proposed using learned helplessness as a model for depression.[40] Experimental subjects—both dogs and college students—who were subjected to uncontrollable negative outcomes (Seligman used electric shocks) learned that the outcome of their behavior was independent of their behavioral response. They learned they were helpless. The distinctive features of learned helplessness are diminished motivation to try to control outcomes, a belief in the inefficacy of responding, and difficulty learning that responding is efficacious. College students, for example, after being subjected to inescapable shock, simply sat and took shocks that were escapable. Dogs subjected to uncontrollable shocking, when given the opportunity to escape being shocked by jumping a barrier, didn't do so. The experimenter had to repeatedly carry the dogs over the barrier away from the shock, and the dogs only very slowly learned that they could escape shock by themselves.

Because a similar "paralysis of the will"[41] distinguishes depression, Seligman proposed using learned helpless as an explanatory model for depression. Just as learned helplessness is caused by learning that responding is independent of reinforcement, so depression, on his model, is caused by "the belief that action is futile."[42] Seligman rejects the idea that depression involves a generalized pessimism, and argues that it derives from a "pessimism specific to the effects of one's own skilled action."[43] What paralyzes the will is the uncontrollability of one's circumstances and thus the ineffectiveness of one's instrumental reasoning. Demoralized depression registers the practical inefficacy of agency and thus the pointlessness of engaging in deliberation.[44]

Closely related to the demoralizing loss of control that makes deliberation seem pointless is demoralizing confrontation with the insecurity of human life against tragic

---

[40] Martin E. P Seligman, *Helplessness: On Depression, Development, and Death* (San Francisco: W.H. Freeman, 1975).

[41] Ibid., 83.

[42] Ibid., 93.

[43] Ibid., 86.

[44] Seligman observes that both learned helpless and depression can be a response to our lacking control over *positive* events in our lives. He suggests, for example, that the common phenomenon of "success depression"—the depression people sometimes feel after achieving major goals—is because the rewards following success are disconnected from present instrumental action: "I suggest that what produces self-esteem and a sense of competence, and protects against depression, is not only the absolute quality of experience, but the perception that one's own actions controlled the experience. To the degree that uncontrollable events occur, either traumatic or positive, depression will be predisposed and ego strength undermined. To the degree that controllable events occur, a sense of mastery and resistance to depression will result" (ibid., 99).

misfortune, indecent harm, and death. Here, however, what one comes face to face with is not the ineffectiveness of instrumental reasoning but, rather, the general inhospitableness of the world to humans' pursuit of value. Trauma victims can suffer both forms of demoralization. Being victimized by unpredictable human violence may undermine confidence in one's ability to discern when one is safe and thus to protect oneself through instrumental reasoning.[45] Being victimized by unpredictable human violence may also fundamentally alter one's perceptual awareness of the world. The risk of suffering human violence, once merely a bit of intellectual knowledge, now becomes part of one's daily lived experience.[46] The world that, pre-trauma, seemed reliable, predictable, and safe, and thus a world hospitable to human planning and action, takes on a different aspect. What becomes acutely apparent is the way our lives as agents are hedged with risk.

For most of us, most of the time, the insecurity of life against disastrous misfortune is a fact to which we do not consciously attend and that we do not affectively register. But when the background frame of confidence in the hospitableness of the world to ongoing human agency is disrupted, one may lose the sense that deliberation has a point.

In sum, we lead our lives under an idea of our future—of who we will be and what life circumstance we will find ourselves in. Taking a motivating interest in our own future depends on our being able to sustain an idea of our future under which future-oriented desiring, hoping, aiming, and planning make sense.

As the discussion of meaningful living earlier in this chapter suggests, an interest-generating idea of the future includes the background assumption that the future will be hospitable to our lives continuing to be bound up with what we value. But reflection on the nature and causes of depression and demoralization suggest that the idea of the future under which we presently live is more complex. Our taking an interest in our future depends only in part on anticipation of a future bound up with what we value. I have argued that our taking an interest in our future—and consequently, in leading a life—depends on additional background frames of agency being in place. These latter frames are attitudes toward and beliefs about our own continuing agency that, under normal conditions, are simply taken for granted as we lead our lives and that thus do not enter into our normative reflection, deliberation, planning, and intending. Rather,

---

[45] Susan Brison observes that one effect of unpredictable trauma is loss of faith in induction. See Susan Brison, *Aftermath: Violence and the Remaking of a Self* (Princeton, NJ: Princeton University Press, 2002), 66.

[46] I am relying here on Karen Jones's distinction between "intellective risk assessment" and "basal security." See Karen Jones, "Trust and Terror," in *Moral Psychology: Feminist Ethics and Social Theory*, ed. Peggy DesAutels and Margaret Urban Walker (Lanham, MD: Rowman & Littlefield, 2004).

they provide a kind of background idea of our future selves and circumstances against which, and on the basis of which, the activities of agency make sense. Those frames include lack of estrangement from one's own normative outlook, a belief in the effectiveness of instrumental reasoning, and confidence in our relative security from disastrous misfortune. Those background frames can be disrupted. And when they are, we may find our agency not defeated, but emptied of significance.

4

Motivating Hope

In Chinua Achebe's classic novel *Things Fall Apart*, the main character, Okonkwo, is "ruled by a great passion—to become one of the lords of the clan. That had been his lifespring" and what he is totally invested in hoping for.[1] This dominant passion springs from an even deeper and consuming fear of being an unmanly failure like his father, who was lazy, improvident, weak, a coward, unable to take care of his family, laughed at by fellow clansman, deeply and inescapably in debt to many, and in short, an unmanly failure. That fear is, ultimately, "the fear of himself, lest he should be found to resemble his father."[2] As a result, Okonkwo totally invests himself in becoming the best among men; and indeed, over time, in virtue of his hard work and inflexible will, he becomes a wealthy farmer, marries three wives, becomes a great and respected warrior, and earns two honorific titles.

But after achieving the life he had hoped for, Okonkwo inadvertently kills a clansman's son. As punishment, he is required to live in exile for seven years, where he must entirely rebuild his life, including overcoming the disappointment of his eldest son's conversion to Christianity. During these seven years of exile, which he regrets as wasted among men who were not bold and warlike, Okonkwo remains hopeful, imagining a future in which he not only regains his place but achieves even greater honor:

> He knew that he had lost his place among the nine masked spirits who administered justice in the clan. He had lost the chance to lead his warlike clan against the new religion. . . . He had lost the years in which he might have taken the highest titles in the clan. But some of these losses were not irreparable. He was determined that his return should be marked by his people. He would return with a flourish, and regain the seven wasted years. . . . [T]he first thing he would do would be to rebuild his compound on a more magnificent scale. He would build a bigger barn than he had had before and he would build huts for two new wives. Then he would show his wealth by initiating his sons into the *ozo* society.

[1] Chinua Achebe, *Things Fall Apart* (New York: Anchor Books, 1959), 131.
[2] Ibid., 13.

Only the really great men in the clan were able to do this. Okonkwo saw clearly the high esteem in which he would be held, and he saw himself taking the highest title in the land.[3]

These hopes are almost immediately disappointed upon his return. During his exile, the clan itself has undergone major change in response to the presence of missionaries and the missionary church, school, trading stores, and government. His clansmen pay little attention to his return; his sons must wait two years to be initiated; and the once warlike men have "become soft like women."[4] Things go from bad to worse. Officials of the white government interrogate Okonkwo and five other leaders about the burning of the missionary church. The six are briefly imprisoned, taunted, and hit with a stick. The town meeting held upon their release, which Okonkwo hopes will produce a declaration of war, is interrupted by a government messenger demanding that the meeting end. Still hoping to live as a manly warrior and leader, Okonkwo kills the white messenger. Only then does Okonkwo finally realize that his clansmen will not do the manly thing and go to war, that his world has changed beyond repair, and that the future self he imagined becoming will not materialize in this new world. He hangs himself.

Okonkwo's story ends with his losing a motivating interest in his future, because his deepest self no longer has a place in that future. His period of exile, however, is dominated by hope; and this appears to be what sustains him in his plans to rebuild his life during those seven years.

People hope both for states-of-affairs over which they have no control and for the realization of their ends through their own efforts. As agents, the hope that matters most is what I call *practical hope*—hope for success in the pursuit of ends we value. Practical hope is often thought to play a motivationally critical role when our pursuit of ends is unlikely to meet with success or we need to be able to pick ourselves up from setbacks and continue striving to succeed, as Okonkwo did.

The standard belief-desire model of hope, however, is not well equipped to explain the special motivational role practical hope plays in buoying us against setbacks or low odds of success. On the belief-desire model, hope consists in part in a *belief* that a state-of-affairs is possible but not assured.[5] Hope thus differs from mere wishing for the impossible and from counting on the assured.[6] Hope also consists in a *desire* that,

---

[3] Ibid., 171–172.

[4] Ibid., 183.

[5] See, for example, R. S. Downie, "Hope," *Philosophy and Phenomenological Research* 24 (1963): 248–251; J. P. Day, "Hope," *American Philosophical Quarterly* 6 (1969): 89–102.

[6] The conventional rules for determining when the believed probability is too low or too high for one to be able to claim to be hoping for, as opposed to wishing for or planning on, are complex. We tolerate and, indeed, encourage children to actively hope for things we would regard as mere

among possible ways that the temporal unfolding of events might proceed, the pre-ferred option actually materializes or is brought about.[7] Many instances of hope fit the belief-desire model. Often all we mean when we talk about hope is that we think that a prospect is possible and that we prefer it to other options. We use "I'm not very hopeful that . . . " and "I'm not going to pin my hopes on that occurring" to indicate our prob-ability assessment. We use "I'm *really* hoping that . . . " or "That's my fondest hope" to indicate strength of preference. On this belief-desire model, all the motivational work of hope is done by the constituent desire.

In difficult circumstances, however, we talk about hope as though it supplied some special motivational oomph: "Keep your hopes up!" "Don't lose hope!" These uses of hope language suggest that the motivational dimension of hope is not limited to the fact that hope is a species of desire—namely, desire under conditions of uncertainty that the desired end will emerge in the temporal unfolding of events. There seems to be some feature, other than the constituent desire, in virtue of which hoping in diffi-cult circumstances is motivationally valuable. Accordingly, Philip Pettit distinguishes between "superficial" belief-desire hope and the "substantial," especially motivating hope that sustains practical pursuits under difficult circumstances.[8] The distinctive feature of substantial practical hope is what Margaret Walker calls its " 'efficacy,' a spe-cial or extra motivational power."[9] It is tempting to describe such substantial hope in terms of the distinctive phenomenology of hopeful motivation. Walker mentions the feeling of "energy, elevation, buoyancy,"[10] of "being oriented alertly and longingly" toward the realization of one's hopes.[11] Victoria McGeer describes hope as "a way of

wishful thinking in adults—for example, the hope to become an astronaut or the president of a country. As a general rule, people can hope for things they believe are highly unlikely when having one's hopes realized depends entirely on luck or is very important; one can hope one has bought the winning lottery ticket, or that one will survive pancreatic cancer. But when realizing one's hopes depends in part on one's agency, we generally insist on greater realism: a C student who knows that getting an A, while theoretically possible, would require skills he doesn't pres-ently possess and is unlikely to develop in time, can wish for an A, but not hope for one.

[7] Hope is one of a category of emotional attitudes that might be described as *reactions to the plurality of temporal possibilities*. In anxiety and fretfulness, we take seriously the possibility that events will unfold badly. In regret, we imaginatively entertain possibilities for how events might have unfolded in the past and how things would stand now had they so unfolded. Remorse and guilt respond to alternate possibilities for one's own past actions—"Had I only not done that!"

[8] Philip Pettit, "Hope and Its Place in Mind," *Annals of the American Academy of Political and Social Sciences* 592 (2004): 152–165.

[9] Margaret Urban Walker, "Hope(s) After Genocide," in *Emotions and Mass Atrocities: Philosophical and Theoretical Perspectives*, ed. Thomas Brudholm and Johannes Lang (New York: Cambridge University Press, forthcoming).

[10] Ibid., 11.

[11] Ibid., 10.

positively and expansively inhabiting one's agency" in which our energies are oriented toward the future.[12]

Suppose there is a motivationally important form of practical hope that amounts to something more than just a belief in the possibility of and a desire for a preferred outcome. *What does that "substantial" hope consist in, and how does it do its motivational work?* A satisfactory answer will need to do two main things. First, the account will need to identify the exact *source* of the motivational problem that arises under difficult circumstances. As we'll see, identifying that source is much more difficult than it appears at first glance. It might seem that the pursuit's being difficult—for example, it is beset by setbacks in the way Okonkwo's pursuit of manly success was—is inherently demotivating. I argue, however, that this is not the case. Second, a satisfactory account of practical hope will need to identify the feature of hope *in virtue of which* hope is a motivating attitude. If it is not a desire that provides the motivation (as on the belief-desire model), then how does practical hope motivate? Giving a substantive answer to that question requires going beyond the sometimes tempting "Energizer bunny" view of hope, whereby we think of hope as a kind of fuel, like super-charged batteries, that provides a motivational push.[13] These two tasks are connected; identifying the source of the motivational problem that hope is supposed to solve will guide us to the correct account of the feature in virtue of which hope is able to solve that motivational problem.

BASAL HOPEFULNESS

In thinking about the kind of hope that is motivationally important in sustaining practical pursuits under difficult circumstances, we need to distinguish two quite different, although related, states that we call hope: *basal hopefulness* (which I mentioned in chapter 3) and *substantial practical hope*. My primary interest is in understanding the latter, substantial practical hope. But since loss of basal hopefulness, not just loss of practical hope, can threaten our interest in continuing in practical pursuits, getting clear on the difference will prevent confusion later on. And what I have to say about the phenomenological idea of the future involved in basal hopefulness is relevant to the analysis of practical hope I provide later.

---

[12] Victoria McGeer, "The Art of Good Hope," *Annals of the American Academy of Political and Social Sciences* 592 (2004): 100–127, 104.

[13] Robert Solomon criticizes what he calls the "hydraulic model" of emotions, a view of emotions that has at least partial roots in Freud, where emotions are thought to be impulses that push us along and where there is no further explanation of how emotions are able to do this that connects the motivating aspect of emotions with how we think about our circumstances. Robert C. Solomon, *The Passions: Emotions and the Meaning of Life* (Indianapolis: Hackett, 1993), 77–88.

Basal hopefulness is what I described in chapter 3 as an interest in the future generally, or globally, rather than in particular future outcomes.[14] Basal hopefulness consists in taking this interest and doing so on the basis of one's phenomenological idea of the future. So, I begin by calling back into view the idea of the future that I described in chapter 1.

The Phenomenological Idea of the Future

As I suggested in chapter 1, the phenomenological idea of the future plays a central role in our being future-oriented creatures. As evaluators and agents, we have desires, aims, intentions, and plans *for* the future. We are future-oriented creatures partly in virtue of this capacity to have future-oriented states in which we take seriously the fact that what we do now will bring about our own future. But this is not all that makes us future-oriented beings. We also live and act under a phenomenological idea *of* the future.

As the emphasis on "phenomenological" might suggest, "idea" here is meant to capture primarily our sense of the future, rather than our beliefs about or a conceptualization of the future. Emphasizing that this is a *phenomenological* idea of the future is also meant to draw attention to features that distinguish this idea of the future from what I call the *planning* idea of the future. In making plans—for example, about which restaurant to book for dinner or which college to attend—we rely on consciously held beliefs about the future, such as how crowded a restaurant will be at 6:00 P.M. or the likelihood of being accepted by a particular college. The phenomenological idea of the future differs from such a planning idea in several ways. Most centrally, having a phenomenological idea of the future is a matter of inhabiting the future. We inhabit the future in part by being drawn to previsage a particular future in our imagination; the student who knows that being accepted by Princeton is unlikely, may nevertheless be drawn to previsaging her college life there. Okonkwo inhabits, by being drawn to previsage, a future where he has built a more magnificent compound. In part, we inhabit the future by living now under an unreflective sense of what the future will be like. As this last point suggests, the content of the phenomenological idea of the future may be neither part of conscious awareness nor readily accessible to conscious awareness. Larry McMurtry, mentioned in chapter 3, may, like many men depressed after heart surgery, have been unreflectively living under the idea of a future of reliably robust

---

[14] For other work on basal emotions, see Karen Jones on basal security ("Trust and Terror," in *Moral Psychology: Feminist Ethics and Social Theory*, ed. Peggy DesAutels and Margaret Urban Walker [Lanham, MD: Rowman & Littlefield, 2004], 7–16); Robin Dillon on basal self-respect ("Self-Respect: Moral, Emotional, Political," *Ethics* 107, no. 2 [1997]: 226–249); and Matthew Ratcliffe on pre-intentional hope ("What Is It to Lose Hope?" *Phenomenology and the Cognitive Sciences* 12, no. 4 [2013]: 597–614).

health. Finally, the content of the phenomenological idea of the future has a plurality of psychological sources. Okonkwo's idea of his future springs partly from reflectively held beliefs about the value of being a leader and warrior and about his ability to achieve such a life. But his idea of the future also springs from psychologically deep fears of being like his father.

Much of the content of the phenomenological idea of the future is a product of habituation. We are, as Hume suggested, habituated to expecting that the future will resemble the past. If you are a college teacher, when you arrive in class, you are unsurprised to find students in their seats, the room basically as you last saw it, and that there is not a cow at the lectern. You are also unsurprised when your lecture neither bores students to tears nor wows them. The students, the room, the so-so lecture, and the absent cow are all part of the content of the idea of the future that you live and act under as you go off for class. The content of the idea of the future is, of course, much richer than this and derives from more than your habituation to the future. The additional sources of content include your predictions; expectations connected to your grasp of causal relations and the enduring nature of objects (like those classroom chairs); normative expectations about how social interactions should go; and expectations about normal life trajectories (such as that you will not die in your fifties), many of which derive from socialization processes (for example, that you will marry and raise a family).

Most of the content of the idea of the future is unreflective, and much of it is not readily available to consciousness. Instead, it operates as a background to propositional states. Some of the content of your idea of the future might strike you as unrealistic or ungrounded were you to bring it to conscious awareness. For example, students may end up in college simply because they have imbibed the idea that this is just what a normal future after high school looks like; a student may later come to see that having had this idea of his future doesn't make much sense, given what he values.[15]

Both particular anticipated bits of the future and one's sense of the future generally have a qualitative character. In this chapter's opening passage from *Things Fall Apart*, Okonkwo previsages with pleasure regaining his place in the clan and his clansmen's esteem, the magnificent new compound he will build, and initiating his sons into *ozo* society. His general sense of the future is of greatness and achievement. His sense of the future changes dramatically once he returns and discovers that the life of a great warrior and leader is no longer a possibility in the changed world of

---

[15] I owe to Alma Barner the observation that our idea of our future is in part the product of our socialization to think that certain kinds of life trajectories are normal and desirable. She suggested that young women often operate under the idea of a future containing marriage and family and may do so even though reflection would reveal that this trajectory is not something they really want for themselves.

his clan. The content and qualitative character of his idea of the future are stripped of what he most values.

Let us call this idea of the future that has both a content, much of which is unreflective, and a qualitative character the *phenomenological idea of the future*. It will be important to what follows to distinguish this idea from the *planning idea of the future*. For planning purposes, we need reflectively held and well-grounded beliefs about what the future will most likely be like.

Basal Hopefulness

The point of observing that we live under a phenomenological idea of the future is that it becomes possible to identify and explain one motivationally important form of hope—basal hopefulness. Basal hopefulness is not hope for this or that outcome but, rather, is what Matthew Ratcliffe describes as a nonpropositional, pre-intentional sense of the future—"a kind of general orientation or sense of how things are with the world"[16] or an "experiential backdrop"[17] against which particular hopes for this or that become intelligible. Basal hopefulness is what is lost in depression. The depressed are not dispirited about this or that bit of the future, but about the future generally. They lose a globally motivating interest in The Future.

In chapter 3, I argued that this basic interest in the future, including in having a future at all, that I call basal hopefulness is critical to agency. Absent an interest in the future, we lose an important motivation for leading the life of an agent: for selecting ends, settling on specific aims, framing intentions and plans, and carrying out those intentions and plans.[18] Basal hopefulness, I suggested, is a sense of the future as sufficiently hospitable to our agential efforts that leading a future-directed life is both an attractive and a productive thing to do.[19]

---

[16] Ratcliffe, "What Is It to Lose Hope?" 602.

[17] Ibid., 600. For additional discussion of pre-intentional states that involve an affectively laden mode of anticipating the future, see also Matthew Ratcliffe, Mark Ruddell, and Benedict Smith, "What Is a 'Sense of Foreshortened Future'? A Phenomenological Study of Trauma, Trust, and Time," *Frontiers in Psychology* 5 (September 17, 2014).

[18] As Victoria McGeer observes in "The Art of Good Hope," hope in the form of "taking an agential interest in the future and the opportunities it may afford" (104) is "a unifying and grounding force of human agency" (101) and "a condition for the possibility of leading a human life."

[19] Many of the items on Aaron Beck's hopelessness scale concern a sense of the hospitableness of the future to one's own agency—e.g., "I might as well give up, because I can't make things better for myself," "I just don't get the breaks, and there's no reason to believe I will in the future," "Things just won't work out the way I want them to," "There's no use in really trying to get something I want because I probably won't get it," "The future seems vague and uncertain to me" (Aaron T. Beck and Arlene Weissman, "The Measurement of Pessimism: The Hopelessness Scale," *Journal of Consulting and Clinical Psychology* 42, no. 6 [1974]: 861–865, 862).

Jonathan Leer's account of Chief Plenty Coup's "radical hope" is one illustration of basal hopefulness.[20] Faced with the destruction of the Crow's way of life as a nomadic, hunting, warrior people, and with a future where the Crow's specific conceptions of meaningful living had no place, Plenty Coup succeeds in retaining basal hopefulness. He retains a sense of a future in which "something good will emerge,"[21] although what exactly that would be was "not yet intelligible" since it would involve a radically different conception of the good than the Crow had at the time.[22] The sustaining source of this phenomenological idea of the future was a highly imagistic dream, which the elders interpreted to mean that the white men would take over, but the Crow, alone among tribes, would survive.

Under unfortunate conditions, however, basal hopefulness can be lost. When that happens, we do not necessarily lose motivating reasons to continue in our practical pursuits. But the motivating force of those reasons ceases to be "seconded" by, or supplemented with, the additional motivational force of taking an interest in the future.

SEARCHING FOR THE MOTIVATIONAL PROBLEM THAT HOPE IS SUPPOSED TO SOLVE

While global motivation is threatened by loss of an interest-sustaining idea of The Future and thus loss of basal hopefulness, the motivation to carry on in a difficult practical pursuit would seem to be threatened by typical features of difficult pursuits themselves. One characterizing feature of difficult pursuits that seems connected to loss of motivation is the agent's belief that the odds of success are low—for example, the cancer patient's belief that her odds of recovering from advanced pancreatic cancer are miniscule. A second characterizing feature of difficult pursuits that seems connected with loss of motivation is the dependency of success on a large number of contingencies falling into place, including the success of multiple subplans. Dependence on many contingencies falling into place renders the odds of success indeterminate but possibly low, as for example, is the case in an attempt to win a close gubernatorial race. A third characterizing feature of difficult pursuits that seems connected with loss of motivation is their being beset by repeated setbacks and obstacles, as was Okonkwo's pursuit of manliness. Setbacks and obstacles may lower the probability of success, render success less determinate than it originally appeared, or significantly raise the cost of the pursuit.

---

[20] Jonathan Leer, *Radical Hope: Ethics in the Face of Cultural Destruction* (Cambridge, MA: Harvard University Press, 2008).
[21] Ibid., 94.
[22] Ibid., 95.

Given these observations, it is tempting to think that whenever pursuits have one or more of these characterizing features, the agent will be vulnerable to loss of motivation and substantial practical hope will play an important sustaining role. It is, in short, tempting to think that the source of the motivational problem that practical hope solves derives simply from the pursuit's perceived low probability of success, dependence on many contingencies, or interruption by setbacks and obstacles. This is not true. Since one of my aims is to identify the source of the motivational problem that hope is supposed to solve, it will be useful to attain greater clarity about when and why these characterizing features have demotivating effects. In what follows, I focus on perceived low probability of success. I suggest that this characterizing feature (and, I assume, the other two as well) has demotivating effects only when the prospect of failure raises the daunting thought, "What a waste! I would have been better off had I not pursued this."[23] We will then need to face the further question of why and how this daunting thought undermines motivation.

Low odds of success are unlikely to have a demotivating effect when redeeming the costs of a pursuit does not depend entirely, or largely, on success. To see why, first consider the fact that the instrumental means to, and constitutive parts of, an end may be valued for their own sake. Aiming to get into a good law school requires, as an instrumental means, engaging in public service activities that will enhance one's application. Aiming to be a successful philosopher involves, as a constitutive part, delivering public lectures. Let's call both of these *entailed pursuits*. Entailed pursuits may be valued solely because they play this instrumental or constitutive role relative to an end, or they may also be valued for their own sake. Now, suppose you embark on a pursuit that has a low probability of success, but whose instrumental or constitutive pursuit you value for its own sake. You are like the athlete who aims to win the Olympics but who enjoys the preparatory training for its own sake.[24] So even if you fail, your efforts have not been all for naught. When entailed pursuits are valued for their own sake, the costs of pursuing those ends are redeemed in the very process of pursuing them. Thus, low probability of success, by itself, doesn't seem to present a motivational problem. After all, whether you succeed or fail, you will have realized something you value for its own sake.

Second, consider the fact that we value not just realizing the ends of practical activities but also *being a certain kind of person* in the process. Among the kinds of person we might value being is someone who is willing to make sacrifices for the sake of a valued end even under low odds of success. You see yourself as a fighter, as someone who

---

[23] In what follows I lean fairly heavily on Douglas W. Portmore's account of redemption in "Welfare, Achievement, and Self-Sacrifice," *Journal of Ethics and Social Philosophy* 2, no. 2 (2007): 1–28.

[24] The example is from Portmore, "Welfare, Achievement, and Self-Sacrifice."

will not abandon the ship of a noble cause even when others would.[25] Being that kind of person is a matter of pride, and whether the pursuit succeeds or fails, you will have been that person. When you value the kind of person that pursuing an end enables you to be, the costs of pursuing that end are redeemed in the very process of pursuing it. Here again, low probability of success, by itself, doesn't seem to present a motivational problem. After all, whether you succeed or fail, you will have realized something you value for its own sake—in this case, being a certain kind of person.

Third, consider the fact that there are, for some people, a single pursuit whose success is the very condition of their being willing to go on in life at all. Recall Okonkwo who was totally invested in becoming a leader and the manliest among men. Even if the odds of success were extremely low, there was for him no acceptable alternative to trying to become such a leader. Success in such a pursuit is, to use Bernard Williams's term, the object of a "categorical desire."[26] Although failure would be an especially bad thing if you have a single categorical desire—you would have no reason to go on—the motivational impact of the prospect of likely failure might be expected to be moot. Success may save your life, but it is unnecessary for redeeming the cost of sacrificing other things you value. There simply is nothing you would have valued doing instead, because the value of everything else is conditional on the satisfaction of this categorical desire.

In none of these cases would the agent be left with significantly unredeemed costs upon failure. In the first two cases, the primary payoff is the pursuit itself, not its success. In the third case, there is no foregone alternative course of action that would have been worth pursuing had you only known that this one would fail.

Low probability of success can enter the motivational scene only when it will be true, if you fail, that you would have been better off had you not embarked on the failed pursuit. These are cases where, projecting yourself into the position of your future self whose pursuit has now failed, you see that your future self will think something like this: "What a lot of wasted effort! All that struggling to make the pursuit succeed, agonizing that it might not, and foregoing things I care about were all for naught. How much better it would have been for me had I done something else instead! Having failed, I have nothing to set against those costs. They are unredeemed." In short, whether thinking about the low odds of success is a daunting thought depends on

---

[25] I owe this point and example to Avery Kolers, who suggested that what matters is that you would continue to endorse your pursuit from the future, even if it fails, because you endorse the kind of person that engaging in that pursuit enabled you to be.

[26] Bernard Williams, "The Makropulos Case: Reflections on the Tedium of Immortality," in his *Problems of the Self: Philosophical Papers 1956-1972* (Cambridge: Cambridge University Press, 1973).

what one believes the view-from-then—the view of one's future self confronting how the pursuit turned out—will look like.[27]

The view from the failed then is not necessarily a view about one's decision to embark on a pursuit and stick to it. Sometimes, of course, one kicks oneself in retrospect for having been so stupid. But your future self may also look back at the choice you made under uncertainty and think it was a good one. If you had to do it again, you would make the same choice because it was worth taking the chance of success. Better to try and fail than never to try at all!

It's important, then, to be clear that there are two different senses in which we talk about wasted and nonwasted effort. First, there is *deliberation-related* wasted effort. So long as you deliberated correctly about the probability of success and about what you value, it is not a wasted effort to try to bring about a desired future. Even if you fail, the effort is not wasted because you couldn't know in advance that you would fail. But if you deliberate incorrectly and fail, your having tried to bring about that future *is* wasted effort. You didn't have a sufficiently good reason for paying the costs of that pursuit in the first place, and you would have seen that had you deliberated more carefully.

Second, there is *failure-related* wasted effort. From your improved epistemic position in the future, you can see that what you were doing all along is paying costs that would not be redeemed. What is not wasted effort under conditions of uncertainty (Who knows? Maybe I'll succeed!) is wasted effort under conditions of certainty about failure. That's exactly the kind of certainty one has when a pursuit has in fact failed. Thus, from your improved epistemic position in the future, even if you have no reason to regret the decision, you do have reason to regret that something didn't occur earlier that would have bumped you off course: the acquisition of some decision-relevant bit of information (Had I only known that!), some disablement (Had I only had less energy!), some interference by others (Had she only stopped me from doing this!).

And now here's the truly daunting thought. Once you take the view-from-then, by previsaging failure, you can see that it isn't as though everything proceeded swimmingly until you hit the future when the project fails, at which point all that effort

---

[27] When you are deliberating under conditions of low probability of success, it is important to keep in mind the view from (the failed) then. Doing so makes vivid exactly what is at stake. Your future failed self is not going to be distracted by rosy thoughts about how wonderful it would be to succeed. You are instead going to be painfully alive to what costs you have paid and now have to live with. And you are going to be painfully alive to what else you might have been doing with all of that time, emotional energy, money, and the like that you have spent on this failed pursuit. These are clarifying thoughts that typically improve the chances of deliberative success. They help us to settle in advance on a plan for what to do next if we do fail. And they help us make appropriate precautionary plans against the risk of failure.

magically converts into wasted effort. Taking the view from the failed then, you see that *what you are doing now is wasted effort.* So why do what you're doing?

UNSATISFACTORY ACCOUNTS OF HOW HOPE SOLVES THE MOTIVATIONAL PROBLEM

We have now gotten a lot closer to locating the source of the motivational problem that substantial, practical hope is supposed to solve: in taking up the viewpoint of one's future self whose pursuit has failed, one sees one's current activity as wasted effort whose costs will not be redeemed. While in the grip of that daunting thought, continuing efforts seem futile and irredeemably costly—hence, the demotivating effects of the daunting thought. But of, course, in the present you don't know that your pursuit will in fact fail. So, we need an explanation of how that daunting thought gets a grip on us, creating a motivational problem. Until we have that, we will not have fully identified the source of the motivational problem. Doing so, as I suggested earlier, will guide us toward the correct account of how practical hope solves the motivational problem.

What *seems* initially most plausible is that those daunting thoughts about wasted effort and unredeemed costs get a motivational grip on us precisely because we believe the odds of success are low, and thus the view from the failed then is most likely correct. Hope would then be needed, as Philip Pettit puts it, to guard against "the danger that the confidence level will be so low that the agent loses heart and ceases to exercise agency effectively. If the agent assigns a relatively low probability to the desired prospect, then that may cause him or her to make no effort to bring it about, thereby ensuring that he or she certainly does not bring it about."[28] Were the agent's subjective probability assessment high, she wouldn't be thinking about potentially wasted effort and thus would have no difficulty motivating herself to take the steps she thinks necessary to bring about the desired end. As it is, the agent is motivationally defeated by her own low probability assessment. Hope's motivational work, on this line of thinking, will be to somehow render that assessment motivationally inert. There are a number of options for how hope might do that.

Three Accounts of Hope: Eyes-on-the- Prize Hope, Optimistic Hope, "As If" Hope

Perhaps hope is, in part, a disposition to ignore one's own probability assessment and focus exclusively on the desirability of one's end. After all, emotions and emotional attitudes are, in part, distinctive patterns of salience. Danger is salient in fear, offenses and

[28] Pettit, "Hope and Its Place in Mind," 157.

wrongs in resentment. Perhaps hope does double duty, making psychologically salient the desirability of the end and at the same time suppressing attention to what we actually believe about the odds. Hope would then consist in a *belief* that a future outcome is possible, a *preference* for that outcome, and *a disposition not to think about the low probability of the outcome* but instead to keep one's eyes on the prize.

Alternatively, perhaps hope is an epistemic disposition to believe that the odds are better than in fact it would be reasonable to believe they are. Hope is thus a form of optimism. This disposition to believe in higher odds might amount to a disposition to delusionally inflate the odds: rather than disposing us to ignore our own probability assessment, hope disposes us to make probability assessments that are not fully responsive to evidence. More charitably, the disposition might be to believe the highest odds within a range of reasonable probability assessments. When the odds are not entirely determinate, the hopeful believe the most attractive option. In short, perhaps hope consists in a *belief* that a future outcome is possible, a *preference* for that outcome, and *a disposition either to falsely inflate the odds or to choose the most favorable among reasonable options for what the odds are.*

Neither of these accounts of hope is particularly attractive. The first option—the eyes only on the prize—would, sure enough, keep us from being demotivated by thoughts about the dismal odds. But sustaining motivation would come at the cost of being disposed not to notice the very things one needs to notice in order to engage in rational planning. Under low odds, backup plans are in order in case the pursuit fails. Furthermore, when success depends on a lot of contingencies falling into place or unanticipated obstacles and setbacks not arising, one ought to be prepared to reconsider the pursuit if contingencies do not fall into place and obstacles and setbacks arise. A disposition to ignore discouraging news will interfere with rational reconsideration. Thus, the very feature of hope, so construed, that supports agency by sustaining motivation also undermines rational agency by keeping out of view facts relevant to making backup plans and rationally reconsidering in light of new evidence.

Hope construed as optimism is an unattractive account for the same reason. Delusionally inflating the odds, like ignoring the odds, may indeed motivate in ways that a realistic odds assessment would not. But again, the very feature that sustains motivation threatens to undermine backup planning and rational reconsideration. Hope construed as a bias toward believing the most favorable among a range of reasonable odds looks more promising. But it's not going to be motivationally helpful in exactly the kinds of cases where motivational help is most needed—namely, where all the options for reasonable odds are depressingly low.

Perhaps hope is instead what Philip Pettit suggests it is.[29] Hope is a *belief* that a prospect is possible, a *preference* for that prospect, and *a strategic decision in the face*

[29] Ibid.

of the demotivating effects of a low probability assessment to adopt an "as if" view of the prospect—namely, as one that is going to obtain or has a good chance of doing so.

In defending this account of hope, Pettit starts from an analogy between hope and precautionary thinking. In situations where there is some probability, even if not a high probability, of an undesired state-of-affairs materializing, there is a danger of finding ourselves unprepared if all our planning is based on what we reasonably believe is most likely to occur. The person who plans to build a house, using his confident assessment that he can do so for $100,000, risks being unprepared for cost overruns. What he needs to do is set his probability belief off-line and reason *as if* the building costs will in fact be somewhat more. Just as precautionary thinking guards against the danger of being unprepared, hope guards against the danger that we will lose heart and fail to do what we need to do for our practical pursuits to succeed. To guard against that danger, we once again need to put our actual probability belief off-line and make decisions and form attitudes "as if the desired prospect is going to obtain or has a good chance of obtaining."[30] In doing so, one forms attitudes and performs actions of the kind that a good chance of the hoped-for possibility would make intelligible.[31] "To hope that something is the case or that you can make it the case, then, is to form an overall outlook akin to that which would be appropriate in the event of the hoped-for scenario's being a *firm or a good prospect*."[32] Replacing one's actual probability assessment with an "as if" assessment in one's planning idea of the future is, in his view, strategically rational: the payoff is better planning and higher motivation.

I share Adrienne Martin's criticisms of this view. Martin observes that if hope were like this, hope would be at odds with the precautionary planning that Pettit rightly insists agents need to engage in. If the cancer patient who is unlikely to survive "truly acted as if there were a good chance she would receive the 'miracle cure,' then she would not do significant planning for the likely event that her cancer kills her in the near future."[33] The "as if" assessment may indeed incentivize better planning for how to realize one's end, but it will also deincentivize both backup planning and rational reconsideration if the odds dip even lower. Martin also points out that, although Pettit denies that such "as if" planning involves self-deception, it's hard to see how it would not do so. Hope-inspired confidence in success is made possible only by keeping out of sight and out of mind one's actual, dismally low probability assessment. Finally, Martin points out that this construction of hope doesn't seem to fit the phenomena very well. "The person who takes 1 percent as a reasonable basis for hoping against hope doesn't

---

[30] Ibid., 158.
[31] Ibid.
[32] Ibid. (emphasis mine).
[33] Adrienne Martin, *How We Hope* (Princeton, NJ: Princeton University Press, 2014), 22.

thereby think of 1 percent as 25 percent, or anything like that—she simply sees 1 percent as enough to go forward."[34]

In sum, under all three options for how hope solves the motivational problem, the price of hope's motivational benefits is diminished realism in our planning idea of the future.

Failure to Explain the Motivational Problem

There is a second, quite different reason for rejecting all three options: *they fail to explain why a belief in low probability of success would pose any motivational obstacle in the first place.*

Consider this example: a while ago, I had to decide whether or not to try to reactivate our Ph.D. program, which the Arizona Board of Regents had suspended. Trying to do so would take a lot of work over a year and half. If I did nothing, we stood no chance at all of having Ph.D. students. If I took on the project, we would have a small chance; but there was a large chance that the project would fail, and I would be left with a lot of unredeemed costs. The deliberative question was: "Would it be better to act so as to increase the probability of having the desired future than to avoid the risk of unredeemed costs?" My answer was yes, it would be better to actively increase the probability of having Ph.D. students. The deliberative process led me to see that I had sufficient motivating reasons to take on and carry on in the pursuit. So it's a mystery why, later, considering the same low odds of success would be demotivating and why substantial practical hope would need to be enlisted.

That mystery is intensified if one also keeps in mind that deliberative processes are not just about whether to embark on a pursuit. They are also about what level of commitment to make for seeing it through and thus about how motivated one is to do so. When you settle on an intention to pursue an end, you are not settling on an intention to pursue it no matter what. If you are thinking clearly, you are also deciding where you are going to set the bar for the number and severity of setbacks and obstacles you are willing to treat as "to be solved" rather than as "reasons to reconsider." In short, intentions to do X come with varying possible degrees of commitment. You can *take a shot* at X. When you take a shot, you embark on a practical pursuit with the intent of discovering whether or not it is worth continuing. You treat setbacks, obstacles, feelings of disenchantment, and the like as providing prima facie evidence against continuing commitment to this pursuit. You prepare yourself in advance to give it up once a fairly low threshold of obstacles and setbacks is reached. Alternatively, you can *endeavor* at X. To endeavor is to commit yourself to continuing on in a pursuit in

[34] Ibid., 23.

spite of setbacks, obstacles, and feelings of disenchantment—though not in an unlimited way. In endeavoring, you are simply more resistant to unfavorable evidence than you would be if you were merely taking a shot. Because the bar for what counts as too many or too great a setback is set higher than in merely taking a shot, endeavorers resist more failures of their subplans than shot takers. Alternatively, one can *totally invest* in *X*, as Okonkwo did. Those who totally invest themselves in a practical pursuit typically think that no future is acceptable other than one where the pursuit succeeds. Total investors are thus highly inflexible about changing courses even in the face of numerous and severe obstacles and setbacks.[35] I decided to set the reconsideration bar for pursuing the Ph.D. program higher than merely taking a shot but lower than being totally invested.

In short, deliberating about whether a pursuit is worth the risk and where to set the reconsideration bar would seem to establish the motivation in advance. If deliberation provides clarity about what one, really, is motivated to do and just how motivated one is, it's then an utter mystery why, later, thinking about the low odds of success would have any motivational impact. Perhaps it does because one loses sight of why one ever thought this was a good idea in the first place. But *that* problem is to be solved by recalling one's original reasons. It's not to be solved by enlisting some special attitude—practical hope.

The puzzle here is not just about why one would need to draw on supplemental motivation, given that deliberation is already about what one has motivating reason to do. The puzzle is also about how hope could supplement one's existing motivation to succeed. In the case of other emotions, it is easy to see how those emotions might provide additional motivation for a practical pursuit beyond one's initial motivating reasons. Suppose, for example, you are involved in a sports competition—say, a tennis match that you desire to win. In the course of the match, your opponent makes derogatory remarks about your playing, and this makes you angry enough that you now want to show up your opponent and put him in his place. Anger provides motivational fuel in the form of new motivating reasons to win—namely, to put your opponent in his place and show him up. By contrast, hoping for success in a practical pursuit does not seem to provide a new motivating reason beyond your original reasons for desiring success and thinking it possible. The only option appears to be the unacceptable one that hope involves a distortion of the probability assessment one would have had, had one not been so hopeful.

Not only does deliberation establish the motivating reasons in advance of the pursuit, it also, as I suggested, establishes one's degree of commitment by setting the bar

---

[35] Victoria McGeer's insightful discussion of the defective nature of willful hope, in her "The Art of Good Hope," applies, I suspect, to many total investors.

for when obstacles and setbacks will be treated as "to be solved" and when they will be treated as reasons to reconsider. As a result, some of the motivational effects claimed for practical hope would seem instead to be motivational effects of commitment. Pettit, for example, argues that hope is important because it provides "stability across the ups and downs of evidence" and guards against the demoralization that those ups and (especially) downs might produce.[36] Nancy Snow argues that hope provides resilience in the face of difficulties, as well as flexibility and openness in finding and pursuing creative new means of pursuing ends.[37] But these are just the kinds of effects that one would expect commitment to produce. Setting the reconsideration bar provides stability against the ebb and flow of evidence and determines when resilience and flexibility in meeting obstacles and setbacks is called for; and effectively treating problems as "to be solved" would involve being open to creative strategies for doing so. There is thus a second puzzle here about what pursuit-sustaining motivational effects might be claimed for hope that commitment doesn't already provide.

THE MOTIVATIONAL PROBLEM RECONSIDERED, AND THE NATURE OF SUBSTANTIAL PRACTICAL HOPE

Here's what has gone wrong with our thinking about hope and motivation: we have implicitly been working from two assumptions:

(1) that all motivation-relevant mental states are states that are also eligible to play a role in our deliberative reasoning; and
(2) that the crucial motivation-relevant mental state that undermines motivation to pursue ends under low odds of success is the belief that the odds are low.

We thus concluded that hope must somehow involve removing the belief in low odds from the planning idea of the future used in deliberation. This solved the supposed motivational problem, but at the price of introducing distortion in our deliberative reasoning: the hopeful ignore or inflate the odds or regard them "as if" good ones. In addition, given that the low probability assessment was already factored into deliberation about whether risking failure is acceptable, we were left wondering why a belief in the low probability of success would subsequently pose a motivational problem.

I think we should give up both assumptions. In describing basal hopefulness, I suggested that motivation comes both from our motivating reasons—say, the reasons we

---

[36] Pettit, "Hope and Its Place in Mind," 158.
[37] Nancy E. Snow, "Hope as an Intellectual Virtue," in *Virtues in Action: New Essays in Applied Virtue Ethics*, ed. Michael W. Austin (New York: Palgrave MacMillan Publishing, 2013).

have to get out of bed and get dressed in the morning—and from the phenomeno-logical idea of the future under which we live. Depressed people can have motivating reasons to get out of bed and get dressed. They have jobs they want to retain and chores they need to do, and so they have reason to get up. What they lack is the motivation that comes from an idea of the future as hospitable to agency. Perhaps they experience the future as closed to meaningful activities, or as so uncontrollable as to make instru-mental reasoning largely pointless. Having lost an interest in the future, they find get-ting up and getting dressed very hard to do.

I suggest something similar in cases of pursuing ends under low odds where redeem-ing costs hinges on success. Those who pursue ends under low odds have motivating reasons to do so. They have settled for themselves the question of whether doing so is worth it and how worth it the pursuit is. The belief that the odds are low is not in itself demotivating.

But this is not the end of the story about motivation. The problem with the accounts of hope considered so far is that they take insufficient stock of what living temporally amounts to. It is not just a matter of having beliefs *about* and desires, intentions, and plans *for* the future. Living temporally is also a matter of living under an idea *of* the future. Contemplating low odds inclines us to do something besides just hold a belief. It inclines us to live under the idea of a future that has failed. We are so inclined because we understand that, despite the apparent openness of the future at the time of choice and pursuit, the future will at some point be closed. Only one thing will have happened. We will have succeeded or failed. This is what taking the view-from-then makes salient. In taking the view-from-then, we project ourselves into a determinate future—a successful or failed one. Low odds pull us toward the idea of a failed future. The pull is similar to the pull of habituation to a future. It is not reason that leads us to imagine that the future *will be* one determinate way. Low odds do not rationally warrant living under the idea that in the future the pursuit will have failed.

On the contrary, under low odds, other ideas of the future remain eligible. We can take a different view-from-then, projecting ourselves into the successful future. And if we're lucky, that becomes the idea of the future under which we live in the present. Those who hope, despair, and merely fret may differ not in their probability assessments of what the future will be but, rather, in how they fill in the content of the determinate future that they previsage in reflective imagination and that operates as a background idea of the future. Those who hope use the desired successful future to fill in the content of the determinate future. Okonkwo, for example, imagines a magnifi-cently rebuilt compound and the high esteem he will receive. Those who despair use the undesired unsuccessful future. And those who merely fret fill in the content of the future with the obstacles and setbacks of things going wrong.

Both Pettit and Martin are right that in hope we live under some kind of "as if" idea of the future. Pettit suggests *as if* the prospect has a good chance of obtaining. Martin suggests *as if* the prospect is simply *possible* (rather than *as if* it is unlikely). Both of these are views from now of a still-open future. I am suggesting that the "as if" idea of the future is the view-from-then idea of the determinate future. Hope, I propose, is a *belief* that success in a pursuit is possible, a *preference* that success is what actually materializes in the temporal unfolding of events, and a *phenomenological idea of the determinate future whose content includes success*. That phenomenological idea of the future has motivational effects independent of the agent's motivating reasons. Substantial practical hope thus "seconds" the existing motivating reasons.

So far, I have been arguing that the second assumption is false. That assumption was that the motivation-relevant mental state that undermines motivation to pursue ends under low odds of success is the belief that the odds are low. The mental state that undermines motivation to pursue ends under low odds is, instead, the phenomenological idea of a failed future.

Let us turn now to the first assumption: that all motivation-relevant mental states are states that are also eligible to play a role in our deliberative reasoning. In discussing basal hopefulness, I said that we should keep distinct the phenomenological idea of the future and the planning idea of the future. For planning purposes, what matters are evidence-based beliefs about the probability of success, what costs might be unredeemed if the pursuit fails, and the value of the end.

The phenomenological idea of the future is not a belief. Living under the idea of a determinate, successful future is not the same as believing or expecting that one will succeed or is likely to succeed. It is simply a matter of one of the eligible futures— the successful one—dominating one's sense of the determinate future. This idea of the future is thus not the right sort of state to figure in deliberative reasoning. It is also not a fully reasons-responsive state. As I suggested earlier, the content of the idea of the future has multiple sources. One possible source is the "cognitive resolve" that Pettit suggests. Because the idea of the future has motivating effects, it is strategically rational to try to live under the idea of a successful future. But that idea has other nonrational sources as well. Some people, for example, have the good fortune to have had their low-odds pursuits regularly succeed. They become habituated to a successful future. Others are not so fortunate, becoming habituated instead to failure. Okonkwo's inhabitation of a successful manly future appears driven by the psychological unbearability of ending up like his father. Being neither a belief nor a fully reasons-responsive state, the phenomenological idea of the future is not eligible to play a role in deliberative reasoning. So, our first assumption was also false.

That the state that is central to substantial practical hope is neither a belief about the likely future nor a fully reasons-responsive idea of a particular future explains why the rational warrant for hope must be partly strategic. Usually, the rational warrant for an emotion is the fact that the person has good reasons to believe the emotion-grounding factual and evaluative beliefs are true. Resentment is rationally warranted, for example, when you have good reasons to think you have been wronged. Hope is indeed partially rationally warranted by one's having good reasons to believe success is within the realm of possibility and the pursuit is valuable enough to assume risks of unredeemed costs. We can indeed criticize people for hoping irrationally insofar as those beliefs are unwarranted—for example, for deluding themselves about the odds of success. As McGeer observes, that delusion may spring from unresponsiveness to real-world constraints on pursing one's ends. The wishful hopers she describes fail to take the necessary steps on which the possibility of realizing their ends depend, because they operate from a kind of "abracadabra" sense of their own agency.[38] As she also points out, we can sometimes criticize the "meaning and value they have invested in particular hopes."[39] One might wonder, for example, whether the supreme value Okonkwo places on becoming the manliest of men isn't more the product of pathological fears of becoming his father than reflection on the value of manliness. Even if the rational warrant for the belief and desire constitutive of hope are open to assessment, substantial practical hope is not a fully rationally warrantable emotional attitude, because the phenomenological idea of the future is not a fully reasons-responsive state. If there is any rational warrant to be had for (the correctness of) one's idea of the future, it is that it is an eligible idea—one that is not ruled out by its impossibility.

Adrienne Martin's appeal to how those who hope and those who despair *gestalt* their situations differently under identical probability assessments is helpful in explaining the idea that there are multiple eligible ideas of the future.[40] What low-probability assessments provide us with are two thoughts: the prospect is *possible,* and the prospect is *unlikely.* Given this, we have two options for gestalting the uncertain future: acknowledge the unlikelihood of success but emphasize its *possibility,* or acknowledge the possibility but emphasize its *unlikelihood.* The options are like those presented by the duck–rabbit illusion. We may see it as a duck while acknowledging that it is also a rabbit, or we may see it as a rabbit while acknowledging that it is also a duck. In seeing a pursuit's success as possible, or the figure as a duck, we are not latching onto the one and only correct description—simply an eligible description. The central difference between Martin's and my view is that she takes the eligible ideas of the future to be those connected with the view from *now* (where, for all one knows, success is possible),

[38] McGeer, "The Art of Good Hope," 113.

[39] Ibid., 123.

[40] Martin, *How We Hope.* See especially the discussion of her core view in chap. 2, "Incorporation."

whereas I take them to be connected with the view-from-*then* of what one's current efforts will amount to.[41]

Because the phenomenological idea of the future has psychological sources other than our reasons-based beliefs, it is no surprise that we employ all sorts of nonrational means to manipulate our idea of the future. We try not to think about our probability assessments and instead keep our eye on the prize, or we inflate the probability assessment. We focus on thinking positively, steer clear of naysayers, remind ourselves that others have succeeded under similar odds, give ourselves pep talks, tack up a picture of the desired prize, and the like. In all of this, what we are trying to manipulate—or at least what we should be trying to manipulate—is our phenomenological idea of the future, not the probability assessment that figures in our planning idea of the future. As should be obvious, there is an inherent risk in these strategic efforts to manipulate the phenomenological idea of the future. The risk is that we may inadvertently eliminate from our planning idea of the future an assessment of the odds of success or may replace an accurate probability assessment with an unduly rosy one.

Substantial practical hope may thus be not only an emotional attitude worth cultivating but also an emotional attitude worth guarding against. The danger of inhabiting a successful future is not only that we risk distorting the planning idea of the future but also that we open ourselves to crushing disappointment when the temporal unfolding of events ends in failure. Had Okonkwo's idea of the future not been so dominated by the successful redemption of years of paying costs, he might have survived his pursuit's failure.

I have argued that there are two kinds of hope that are motivationally important, and thus important to our leading our lives as agents: basal hopefulness and substantial practical hope. I have suggested that in order to understand how either form of hope could have motivational effects, we need to keep in mind that our temporality consists not just in having future-oriented intentional states but also in living and acting under a phenomenological idea of the future. My primary interest has been in understanding how substantial practical hope could supply motivation that is distinct from our motivating reasons for undertaking a pursuit with a particular degree of commitment and that does not involve introducing distortion into our planning idea of the future.

[41] A second central difference is that I deny the appropriateness of the hopeful idea of the future's playing any role in deliberation about what to do or subsequent justification of what we have done. Martin argues, as do Pettit and I, that it can be strategically rational to adopt a hopeful idea of the future if doing so would promote one's ends. But she also argues that to do so is to adopt a "licensing stance." Seeing future success as possible (rather than unlikely) licenses—in the sense of providing a justification for—further activities, such as fantasizing about success, treating one's desire for the outcome as a motivating reason, and relying on a positive sense of anticipation in one's plans. I have argued that the license comes not from hope but from deliberation about whether the risk of ending up with unredeemed costs is worth it.

We can see how hope might do this if we locate the motivational problem not in our probability assessment but, rather, in our adopting the view from the failed then as part of our phenomenological idea of the future. The substantial practical hope I proposed has a three-part structure: a belief that success in a pursuit is possible, a preference that success materialize in the temporal unfolding of events, and a phenomenological idea of a determinate future that includes success. In different ways, both basal hopefulness and substantial practical hope "second" the deliberation-based motivating reasons.

5

What Good Is Commitment?

One of the central ways we connect ourselves to our futures is by making commitments. So far, I have made only passing reference to commitment. In chapter 1, I suggested that we lead our lives in the "narrow" sense by making and acting on choices about the characterizing features of a whole life that give it a shape and a narrative storyline. But giving one's life such an overall shape would apparently require making long-term commitments of the sort that Mother Teresa and Okonkwo made. It might be thought that leading a life in this narrow sense, and the commitments upon which such a life depends, plays a particularly critical role in living a meaningful life. The normative outlook conception of meaningful living that I developed in chapter 2, however, makes no mention of the importance of commitment to meaningful living. The aim of this chapter is to explain and defend that omission by taking a closer look at what commitments are and then exploring how best to answer the question, "What good is commitment?"

That human beings make commitments of various sorts might seem so obviously a good thing that the question "What good is commitment?" could be thought to ask merely after the kind of good that commitment affords. To that question, one might respond that commitment is good in a variety of ways. Promises and contracts—two prominent types of commitment—have obvious utility as devices of social coordination. The affirmation of one's commitment to another, or to bringing about some feature of her welfare, promotes trust—something that has both social and moral value. Even personal commitments, such as a commitment to learning or to doing one's job well, may enhance both the moral good of trust and the social goods of reliance and coordinated planning. Many commitments are good because they are morally required, strongly morally recommended, or constitutive of good moral character, as are, for example, commitment to our children's education and to lovingly caring for them or commitment to acting with integrity. Finally, the social world is often so arranged as to quasi-force locking in our future via making commitments, even when we would not otherwise have chosen to so firmly commit our future. Others may be unwilling to embark on joint ventures with us on the basis of anything less than a promissory or contractual commitment; and the penalties for change of plans may be sufficiently steep as to make lack of commitment to a plan unwise, as is the case when costly airline tickets are nonrefundable. In short, commitments have social, moral, and prudential value.

In asking "What good is commitment?" I do not deny that commitment can be good in these ways. My interest, instead, is in a particular range of commitments that are often thought to be good because they contribute to a life's being well lived. The commitments I have in mind are ones whose objects are the sorts of things that are candidates for inclusion in a life plan, or could give shape to a life, or define an identity, or answer the question of what one's life is about. Intuitively, sexual, ethnic, and religious identities; places of geographic residence, avocation, and career; and friendships and intimate relationships would count as such candidates. I call these *substantive commitments* to distinguish them from, among other things, *normative commitments* to particular values and practical principles and *guidance commitments* (for example, to looking before one leaps or to make decisions only in a cool hour). The commitments that give shape to a life are typically long term, but not necessarily so. Substantive commitments might include acquiring skills that can be learned fairly quickly (for example, the basics of ballroom dancing) and time-limited activities (such as a three-year stint of military service). By contrast, a long-term commitment to making one's bed every day or riding the number 30 bus to work would not likely, absent some story about their place within more significant projects, count as commitments that give a shape or a plan to a life.

Deeply embedded in popular cultural portrayals of admirable lives, and in the kinds of life advice we offer to younger and older adults, is the idea that making commitments of the sort I've just described is a good thing *for the individual.* The idea here is that a life whose plan is provisional—and thus whose shape is not just revisable in extremis but also readily open to revision and frequent change—is not as good a life for its protagonist as is a life whose contours have been fixed by commitment. Children who lack the experience and knowledge to make commitments, young adults who need to prepare for adulthood by experimenting with options, and elderly adults who live with a shortened time frame are exempt from such advice to commit. But adults who fail to commit open themselves to criticism and pity; they are "unable to settle down," "aimless," "undisciplined," "lazy," or "immature."

Here, the good of commitment is not just its social utility, moral value, or instrumental value under particular social arrangements (like that of nonrefundable airline tickets). The good of commitment consists in the quality of life it enables. Such a life might variously be described as healthy, mature, meaningful, or conducive to success or satisfaction.

Much philosophical literature implicitly shares the cultural assumption that a committed life is a better-lived life: the limits of the will are set by one's love-based commitments; one's deep identity is defined by one's fundamental commitments to projects and relationships; flourishing, meaningful lives are ones committed to worthy projects. The life plans that figure prominently in Rawlsian-inspired political theory are typically described as having either the force of reason or the force of cultural attachment so firmly behind them as to suggest that what is valued is not the capacity to frame sequences of provisional life plans but, rather, to commit oneself to a life plan that, though revisable, typically resists revision.

Setting aside considerations connected to the fact that we live our lives among other people—that is, setting aside considerations of the social utility and moral value of commitment and the rationality of making particular commitments given particular social arrangements—what is the normative justification for recommending that people shape their lives around commitments? Why think that, for their own sakes, individuals should commit?

In aiming to trouble this normative assumption, I do not intend to argue for the severely skeptical conclusion that lives go worse in virtue of being shaped around commitments, and that commitment is thus a bad thing.[1] I do intend to argue for the modestly skeptical conclusion that shaping one's life around some set of commitments is not obviously a better strategy for making one's life go well than not doing so; and this is true quite apart from the worthiness or unworthiness of the particular objects of commitment.[2] Shaping one's life around commitments is thus better regarded as an optional style for managing one's diachronic existence.

I begin by examining the terrain of commitment. What are the distinctive features of commitment? I then turn to critiquing the principal philosophical defenses of the value of committing one's life. In the last section, I explain what makes shaping one's life around commitments attractive to many persons, if not universally so.

---

[1] Charles Larmore argues that lives are not properly regarded as the subject of a plan, and lives do arguably go worse when so seen. The life plans he has in mind are the sort that I think are implicitly assumed in much liberal political theory—namely, plans to which we are committed. So, one might read Larmore's essay as spelling out an argument for the severely skeptical conclusion (Charles Larmore, "The Idea of a Life Plan," *Social Philosophy and Policy* 16, no. 1 [1999]: 96–112).

[2] The modest skepticism involves two claims: first, that commitment isn't universally *necessary* for making one's life go well; second, that while for those with a particular style of managing their future, commitment is a good *strategy* for making their life go well, for others it is a poor strategy.

COMMITMENT

Commitment is a species of intention. Within that species, it may be philosophically useful to distinguish significant subspecies of commitment: promise, contract, resolution, vow, attitudinal commitment, and the kind of life-shaping commitment that is the subject of the present inquiry.[3] Two subspecies of commitment have gotten the most philosophical attention: the kind of commitment to future performance constitutive of promising and contracting, and the kind grounded in identity-defining feelings of love or categorical desire, which I call *attitudinal commitment*. Very shortly, I will set aside promises, contracts, and resolutions, since the normative pressure to commit that interests me is the pressure to commit in ways that contribute to having something like a life plan or ongoing identity. Attitudinal commitments, however, figure prominently later in the discussion, since some, though not all, life-shaping commitments are grounded in identity-defining feelings.

One initially plausible way of organizing the various subspecies of commitment, and one that tracks the contrast between promise-based commitments and attitudinal commitments (though I will suggest reasons for *not* sorting commitments this way), is to see commitment as taking two basic forms: active and passive.[4] *Active commitments* are ones that we take on by making a decision to commit and often by using a commitment convention—promising to others, contracting, pledging, enlisting, volunteering, signing up for, officially adopting, promising ourselves, or making a resolution. Active commitments bring about a connection to a particular kind of future.

Passive commitments, by contrast, are ones that we find ourselves with and that, independently of deliberative decision making and subsequent employment of commitment conventions, already connect us to a particular kind of future. Unlike active commitments, passive commitments are not voluntaristic. The avowing of a passive commitment does not, as Stanley van Hooft observes, bring about a new state of affairs but, rather, expresses a prior "inchoate commitment which we find ourselves with and which it would be constitutive of our integrity to acknowledge."[5]

---

[3] I don't mean to suggest that these subspecies are distinguished from one another along some single dimension (vows might differ from the other subspecies in the degree to which they lock in the future), nor that these subspecies do not sometimes overlap in various ways (so we might say that some promises are vows). So, the metaphor of "subspecies" should not be taken too strictly.

[4] I take the terms, though not the precise meanings she gives them, from Nancy Schauber, "Integrity, Commitment and the Concept of a Person," *American Philosophical Quarterly* 33 (January 1996): 119–129. Schauber limits active commitments to commitments to other persons that make use of conventions such as the convention of promising.

[5] Stanley van Hooft, "Commitment and the Bond of Love," *Australasian Journal of Philosophy* 74 no. 3 (1996): 454–466, 465.

Though intuitively attractive, this contrast between active and the passive "commitments" does not clearly capture two kinds of *commitment*. On the one hand, if we take passive commitments to be nonvoluntaristic in the strong sense that we in no way control either the having of them or their persistence[6]—they are simply, and without choice, what one finds one's life bound up with[7]—passive commitments do not look much like commitments at all. They are simply deep psychological attractions. Being moved on the basis of such involuntary psychological attractions to pursue a project, maintain a relationship, care for the well-being of some entity, and the like is not yet to be committed. On the contrary, such passive "commitments" function in our psychological economy as alternatives to commitment. The stability of carings over time does the same work as commitment insofar as it locks in one's future. Thus, if we can rely on the stability—in the sense of both endurance and unwavering motivational strength—of our carings, there is no functional purpose to also making a commitment. We need not, for example, make a commitment to prepare for a marathon or to be a patient person or to maintain a relationship if we are already so strongly and stably disposed toward these things that there is no risk that, over time, temptations, the cooling of love, boredom, loss of self-control, the emergence of competing carings, and the like might dislodge that marathon preparation, patience, or maintenance of a relationship from our future. By contrast, commitments *safeguard* one's future against psychological vicissitudes. (I turn to just how they safeguard the future in a moment.) The contrast between active and passive commitments, in this case, seems to capture not two different kinds of commitment but, rather, two kinds of motivations for connecting oneself to a particular future: voluntary, reasons-based motivations and motivation originating entirely from involuntary psychological attractions.

On the other hand, if we take passive commitments to be nonvoluntaristic in the weaker sense of deciding, without being aware of it, to take on a commitment for reasons that are articulable if not articulated, and in a way that safeguards one's future against psychological vicissitudes, then passive commitments are commitments, but not of a clearly different kind. Decision making simply occurs at varying levels of self-conscious awareness.

All genuine commitments are active in the sense that they are made, not merely discovered as facts about one's psychology; and they persist through being sustained,

[6] Schauber, "Integrity, Commitment and the Concept of a Person," 121; van Hooft, "Commitment and the Bond of Love," 455; Harry G. Frankfurt, *The Reasons of Love* (Princeton, NJ: Princeton University Press, 2004), 46, 55, 66.

[7] Two notable discussions of these kinds of commitments are Bernard Williams, "Persons, Character, and Morality," in his *Moral Luck* (Cambridge: Cambridge University Press, 1981), 1–19; and Harry G. Frankfurt, *Taking Ourselves Seriously, and Getting it Right* (Stanford, CA: Stanford University Press, 2006) and his *The Reasons of Love*.

not through being persistently suffered. Some commitments surely are grounded in wholehearted, stable carings. They are grounded in caring, not by being caused by caring; rather, one reason for making a commitment is one's present and expected future psychological investment in the very things to which one commits. Indeed, we expect people to make some major life decisions on the basis of their wholehearted, stable carings—choice of a partner, for example, or of career. But caring is not the only reason for committing oneself, and other reasons may trump carings in one's deliberation about what to commit to. So, for example, young adults are often advised to consult their hearts in committing to a career path, but also to be realistic about their chances of success, to be economically practical, and to be mindful of the other things they might want to do and have in life.

Thus, commitments are active, in part, because they are authored. They are also active because it is up to us to sustain a commitment rather than a continued commitment's being a matter of psychological fortune. Constitutive of any commitment is a stance of being prepared to sustain that commitment. That is, a commitment is both an intention to engage with something (a person, relationship, goal, activity, identity, etc.) and a preparedness to see to it that the intention to engage persists.[8] Seeing to the persistence of an intention comes in degrees, however. People may be prepared to do more or less to sustain their intention to engage. We measure depth of commitment by what the person is prepared to do or resist in order to see to it that the intention to engage persists. Someone prepared to do very little to see to it that her intention to engage persists has made only a shallow commitment or a "commitment" more accurately described as a *mere intention* or a *provisional plan*, rather than a commitment.[9] So, we might say that a student who gave up her biology major because she wasn't getting As in all of her classes wasn't committed to majoring in biology. Were she committed, she would take steps to see to it that her disappointing grades did not deter her from proceeding with her biology major.

---

[8] Mike Martin emphasizes this connection between commitment and seeing to the persistence of one's commitment (Martin, "Love's Constancy," *Philosophy* 68, no. 263 [1993]: 63–77, 65). The term "preparedness" is admittedly vague. It is tempting to say instead that one *intends* to see to it that one's intention to engage persists. But what kind of intention is this? A *mere intention* is too weak to capture what is involved in a commitment; and positing a *commitment* to see to it that one's intention to engage persists would make the definition circular. I take it that if one is genuinely prepared, some set of counterfactuals about what one would do under circumstances of new information or temptation are true.

[9] I will say more about the distinctions between mere intentions, provisional plans, and commitments in the next section. My aim, both here and in the next section, is not to set up criteria for definitively determining which intentions count as mere intentions, which count as provisional plans, and which count as commitments. I'm not convinced that one *could* do so. Here, I only want to roughly outline features we would want to examine more closely in determining whether someone is committed at all, and if so, how committed.

Being prepared to see to it that one's intention to engage persists means being prepared to take steps to revive one's motivation to carry through on the commitment should one's interest fade. Harry Frankfurt's description of the way that carings entail a commitment to sustain the caring itself applies generally to commitments: "When a person cares about something . . . he is willingly committed to his desire. . . . He is therefore prepared to intervene, should that be necessary, in order to ensure that it continues. If the desire tends to fade or to falter, he is disposed to refresh it and to reinforce whatever degree of influence he wishes it to exert upon his attitudes and upon his behavior."[10] Committed but burned-out teachers, for example, are disposed to try to rekindle their interest in teaching and in their students rather than quit. Committed partners are disposed to "spice things up" when boredom sets in rather than part ways. The motivation to follow through on simple promissory commitments is often sustained simply by reminding oneself "I promised." And in many cases reminding oneself both of one's original reasons for making a commitment and of new reasons acquired over time may renew the motivational basis of one's commitment.[11]

Seeing to the persistence of one's commitment also involves refraining from putting oneself in the way of temptation; refraining from cultivating activities, attitudes, and ways of life that are incompatible with sustaining one's commitment; repressing commitment-threatening emotions and desires; and resisting the live option of reconsidering the reasons for having the commitment. That is, commitment entails readiness to engage in a set of refusals.

That commitments involve a high degree of resistance to reconsideration distinguishes being committed from both merely intending and having a provisional plan.[12] Mere intentions, provisional plans, and commitments all bind the future self insofar as they involve taking reconsideration off the table unless there is some deliberation-relevant change—for example, a change in one's situation, the acquisition of information one wasn't aware of before, or a change in one's values or desires.[13] I take it that

---

[10] Frankfurt, *The Reasons of Love*, 16.

[11] Vanya Kovach and John Fitzpatrick, "Resolutions," *Australasian Journal of Philosophy* 77 no. 2 (1999): 161–173; Monika Betzler, "Sources of Practical Conflicts and Reasons for Regret," in *Practical Conflicts: New Philosophical Essays*, ed. Peter Baumann and Monika Betzler (Cambridge: Cambridge University Press, 2004), 197–222.

[12] I don't mean to say that commitments aren't intentions. They are. The contrast here is between commitment intentions, provisional plans, and mere intentions. I also don't mean to suggest that one can't be committed to a plan. But one can have a plan that one is perfectly willing to give up should a better one be suggested. People often say things like, "That's my plan, though I'm not wedded to it" (as opposed to, "That's my plan and I'm sticking to it!").

[13] Just as framing an intention, adopting a provisional plan, or making a commitment may be done consciously or unconsciously, so taking reconsideration off the table is sometimes a reflective, conscious decision and sometimes it is an unreflective, unconscious response to one's articulable but not articulated reasons for intending, provisionally planning, or committing.

what distinguishes commitments from mere intentions, as well as from provisional plans, is that commitments are intentions to follow through despite or in the face of developments that would, in the absence of commitment, make it rational to reconsider one's mere intentions or provisional plans.

This feature is especially obvious if one considers quite long-term commitments. People who make long-term commitments often can predict that in the future they will have relevantly different desires and values, the circumstances of action will have changed, they will have substantially more and better information, and they may be better practical reasoners. The paradigm case of this is marital commitment. Reasonably observant first-time marriers and, even more so, second- and third-time marriers typically know that the circumstances of deliberation will change, perhaps dramatically, over time; and the marriage vow itself reminds spouses of the main changes that they are to disregard—for better or worse, in sickness or in health, for richer or poorer.

In short, to be committed, one must be prepared to weather circumstantial and informational changes that would provide sufficient reason to alter mere intentions and provisional plans. Just how committed one is depends on how much one is prepared to weather. At the far end are vows that, in paradigm cases of traditional marriage vows and religious vows, require being prepared to weather virtually any possible circumstantial, epistemic, or attitudinal and value changes.

That commitments consist, in part, in a refusal to alter one's original choice under the same conditions that would make it reasonable to revise mere intentions or provisional plans does not mean that commitments depend on either deliberate blindness to reasons or irrationally discounting their force. Some people do, of course, see to it that their commitments persist by using various irrational mechanisms of not noticing, not thinking about, repressing, wishful thinking, and underestimating. But the committed may also be fully aware of the range and gravity of unanticipated problems that now beset their course, yet they rationally refuse to change course even though, under the same conditions, it would be irrational for a mere intender or provisional planner to so refuse. How could that be?

First, that there are (or may be) unanticipated problems in pursing an aim often underdetermines how one should regard those problems—in particular, whether one should regard them as weighing against one's original intention or as problems to be dealt with. As I suggested in the last chapter, to commit is to adopt a different policy toward unanticipated problems from the policy one would have adopted had one instead provisionally planned or merely intended. In particular, it is to adopt the policy of regarding a greater quantity and greater severity of unanticipated problems as to be dealt with by working to surmount them, rather than as triggering reconsideration. In short, the rationality of staying the course in the face of unanticipated problems is not simply a function of how highly one values or strongly desires a particular end. It is also a function of the problem-handling policy one has adopted.

Second, what makes it reasonable to stay the course in the face of the same factors—say, boredom—that would make it reasonable for a mere intender or provisional planner to reconsider is the fact that whether or not there are sufficient reasons in favor of pursuing an aim is partly up to us. Commitment involves being prepared to seek new motivations and new reasons for sustaining one's commitment when old ones fail. Again, the marriage commitment is a paradigm case. The reasons of romantic love that might originally have grounded a marital commitment are highly unlikely to be available decades later. What will more likely be available is a quite different set of reasons; and whether we become the kind of person who has those reasons or not will be at least partially up to us. In short, mere intenders rationally stay the course when they have sufficient reasons on hand for doing so; the committed reasonably stay the course on the basis of reasons they intend to generate (and intend to generate in part by staying the course).

Seeing to the persistence of one's commitment by finding new reasons that support one's commitment is one of a variety of positive forms that "seeing-to" can take. Seeing-to in some cases is a matter of positive planning and active efforts to reorganize habitual patterns of action and habitual priorities. Consider, for example, the resolution to stop smoking or to lose weight.[14] Although seeing to the persistence of one's resolve in part means finding ways to tie one's hands—for example, removing temptations from your home or setting yourself up for shaming if you backslide—seeing to the persistence of one's resolve may also be more a matter of "setting one's mind" to it through intensified planning, as a resolution to lose weight might involve buying dieting books, setting up an exercise schedule, joining a health club, and keeping a record of caloric intake. Setting up occasions to revisit one's reasons for having a particular commitment—what Kovach and Fitzpatrick call "recapitulative" processes[15]—is another method of seeing to the persistence of a commitment. Some occasions for revisiting the reasons for commitment are socially conventionalized, for example, celebrations of wedding and other anniversaries, renewal of vows, Independence Day celebrations, religious and work retreats, and Alcoholics Anonymous meetings.

In sum, commitments are authored rather than passively suffered; they are a species of intention, but they differ from mere intentions insofar as they involve a strong

---

[14] I take resolutions to be a subspecies of commitment distinguished by the fact that they are made in order to overcome some internal obstacle to doing or becoming what one wishes to do or become.

[15] Kovach and Fitzpatrick, "Resolutions," 170.

resistance to reconsideration; and they involve a preparedness to see to it that one's intention to engage persists.

WHAT GOOD IS COMMITMENT?
THE PRAGMATIC ARGUMENT

One might approach the question "What good is commitment?" purely pragmatically. Is commitment necessary for setting and achieving aims? It would seem so. First, people typically find themselves attracted to a plurality of options for what to do with their lives. Many of those attractive options involve time-extended activities, such as pursuing a veterinary medicine degree or a Ph.D. in philosophy, making one's home in Maine or Mexico, or adopting children or seizing as many opportunities for travel as one can. Human lives are mortal and resources and energy are finite. In addition, some valued options will not be available later in life if passed up earlier. This is especially evident where the option requires physical abilities that one might expect to have earlier but not later. That we desire many things and that our lives are limited in the ways just mentioned constitute what Connie Rosati has called "the circumstances of the good."[16] Under these conditions, if we hope to have any of our desires for temporally distant or temporally extended options satisfied, we must make up our minds which valuable options to pursue. Thus, finitude of time, resources, and energy, as well as availability of options forces a choice between life options. We must commit. Or so it seems.

Second, one might note that the very nature of some aims also puts pressure on us to make up our minds whether we intend to commit to the aim or not. And this is true even in the absence of competing desires to do other things. Where aims can be achieved only by taking a series of temporally ordered and coordinated steps over a period of time—as, say, getting a college degree or renovating a kitchen—we will not be able to achieve the aim in the future unless we commit now to pursuing that aim, a commitment on the basis of which it will then make sense to formulate and execute a complex temporally extended plan for achieving that aim.[17] Getting some of the things

---

[16] Connie S. Rosati does not offer a pragmatic argument (or any other argument) for commitment; her own development of the notion of the circumstances of the good that I draw on here occurs in the quite different context of an investigation of agent regret. Connie S. Rosati, "Mortality, Agency, and Regret," in *New Trends in Philosophy: Moral Psychology*, Poznan Studies in the Philosophy of the Sciences and the Humanities, vol. 94, ed. Sergio Tenenbaum (Amsterdam: Rodopi, 2007), 231–260.

[17] Michael E. Bratman, *Intention, Plans, and Practical Reason* (Cambridge, MA: Harvard University Press, 1987); Michael E. Bratman, "Reflection, Planning, and Temporally Extended Agency," *Philosophical Review* 109 (2000): 35–61.

we want out of life requires planning and the execution of that plan over time. Rational planning, however, depends on a prior commitment to the plan's aim.

Putting both pragmatic considerations together—the need to decide between competing aims and the need to form and execute a plan for achieving aims—we might conclude that if we are going to do anything at all with our lives other than live from moment to moment, we will need to make some commitments.[18] And so commitment is a pragmatically good thing.

But is it really *commitment* that is necessary? That conclusion, I want to suggest, depends on making one of two dubious assumptions: (1) that framing intentions for our future always involves committing ourselves, or (2) that the only (reliable) way of settling the future sufficiently to undertake temporally extended activities or achieve temporally remote aims is by making commitments.

Consider the first assumption: It might seem that in framing any kind of intention one is necessarily making a commitment, since all intentions involve the present agent coming to a decision about what to do in the future. That decision settles the deliberative question about what to do in the sense that the agent does not continue deliberating once the intention is framed and does not reopen deliberation except under a limited array of conditions.[19] Intentions thus have, to use Michael Bratman's term, "inertia"; and, again using his phrasing, they "resist reconsideration."[20] By taking the issue of what to do at a later point in time off the deliberative table, intentions have the apparent effect of committing the agent to future performance.

As long as intentions are contrasted with either mere wishes (where an agent settles on a goal but fails or refuses to adopt and execute a plan for reaching it) or with the absence of intentions for one's future, all intentions seem aptly described as commitments to future performance. But these are not the only contrasts we need to make in describing agents' relations to their future actions, and it is unhelpful to that end to collapse the different species of intention: mere intention, provisional plan, and commitment. Nor does ordinary language support that collapse. We do say things like, "I had intended to do . . . " and then add ". . . but I'm not committed to doing so."

To see the difference between mere intentions and commitments, consider the different modalities in which one might, in the morning, plan to take a bike ride in the afternoon. Between framing the intention and executing the plan, something may come up—say, a friend calls with an attractive invitation to see a movie that is only showing in the afternoon. If the plan to bike were framed under the modality "mere intention," this newly presented and attractive option to see a movie instead is just the

[18] Bratman, "Reflection, Planning, and Temporally Extended Agency," 40.
[19] Bratman, *Intention, Plans, and Practical Reason*, 16, 67.
[20] Ibid., 17.

sort of new information that makes redeliberation about one's afternoon plans reasonable. Why stick to a plan crafted in ignorance of all the attractive options for the afternoon? By contrast, if the plan to bike is framed under the modality "commitment," learning of a new attractive option for the afternoon does not automatically make redeliberation reasonable; depending on the depth of the commitment, the movie option may be excluded from the range of new information that could even raise the question "Shall I reconsider?"

We get a more helpful taxonomy of decisions regarding the future by noticing that the degree to which different intentions settle the question of future performance is scalar.[21] At one end are mere intentions, which set a sufficiently weak barrier to reconsideration that they are not well described as *resisting* reconsideration. Indeed, a mere intention—say, a mere intention to see a movie on Friday—can settle the question of future performance without there being any resistance to reconsideration. Typically, having settled what to do Friday evening, one simply stops deliberating and doesn't look for new information that might reopen the question of what to do on Friday. Mere intentions have inertia because one doesn't bother to look for possibly more attractive options or potential problems with carrying through on the intentions. But of course, something may come up to change one's mind—someone points out a terrible review of the movie, or one receives a party invitation for Friday. Much of the inertia of mere intentions results from nothing in fact coming up, not on resistance to redeliberation.[22]

Although in deciding to do something in the mode of merely intending, one does not adopt an attitude of resistance to redeliberation; reasons to resist reconsideration may emerge after, and as a result of, settling on a plan. Intending to go to a movie on Friday, you buy a nonrefundable ticket, hire a babysitter, and agree to meet up with friends at the theater. Changing your mind at this point means wasting an investment and letting others down. But notice that it is not the intention—the fact of having made up your mind—that erects the barrier to reconsideration but, rather, the fact that you have executed enough of the plan to go to the movies to make reconsideration now not worth it. Had something only come up earlier, you might have happily reconsidered.

[21] Because that degree is scalar, there will inevitably be some arbitrariness or indefiniteness in sorting out distinct species of intentions, as I plan to do, on the basis of differences in the degree to which they settle the future.

[22] This is not to say that mere intentions do not set up *some* barrier to reconsideration. Even if I just merely intend to go to the movies on Friday, that mere intention will place some range of factors off-limits for triggering reconsideration; and in that sense even mere intentions involve a "resistance" to reconsideration. However, since mere intentions, provisional plans, and commitments settle the future to different degrees, it is more helpful to use the description *resisting reconsideration* to pick out the especially high threshold for triggering reconsideration that is characteristic of commitments and not mere intentions.

By contrast, to intend in the mode of being committed is to erect a strong barrier to reconsideration via the sole fact of having made up one's mind. As I suggested earlier, to be committed is to resist reconsidering despite new information or change of desire that, had one merely intended but not committed to doing something, would have been reason to redeliberate. The committed moviegoer, for example, goes ahead and hires the babysitter and buys the ticket even though she realizes, after having decided to go, that she is going to be exhausted on Friday.

The pragmatic argument—that given the circumstances of the good and the fact that achieving aims typically depends on executing complex temporally extended plans, one must make up one's mind which among the desirable options is the one to pursue—at most shows that one must frame *some* intentions that settle the future to *some* degree. It is not, by itself, a reason to think that commitment is necessary.

But, you might think, surely there will be a good deal of wasted effort, time, and resources in a life that remains open to a change of plan should something else come up. A student who merely intends or provisionally plans to major in X may find, as time passes, new reasons to major in Y, and then in Z. A person who merely intends or provisionally plans to pursue a relationship with A unless something else comes up may find herself dropping A for B, and later B for C. More important, a life that remains as open to plan revision as mere intentions and provisional plans allow will not settle the future sufficiently for time-extended activities to be (reliably) completed or temporally remote aims to be (reliably) achieved. Commitment is needed.

But this concern that there will be a great deal of wasted time, effort, and resources, and that temporally extended and remote aims won't be realized absent commitment, gets much of its force from what we are invited to imagine a life without commitment to be like. The uncommitted person will flit from one thing to the next, starting projects only to drop them in midstream, hopping from one relationship to another, never seeing any plan to completion. That image, however, blurs the distinction between merely intending and having no intentions at all, and it ignores the option of provisional planning. Merely intending and provisional planning settle the future unless something comes up. Real-life choice contexts are often quite stable, so that the considerations available for deliberative decision making persist over time as the only available considerations. That is, often nothing comes up. One can stick with a plan or a relationship for a very long time simply because no problems or more attractive options emerge. In addition, it's important to keep in mind that the sunk costs and prospective costs created once one has partially executed a plan or spent time conducting a relationship create reasons for resisting reconsideration even when one is not committed to the plan's aim or to the relationship.

Finally, in those cases where agents confront new options and face no significant costs to changing course, it's unclear why changing course, even changing course frequently, should be regarded as a waste of time, energy, and resources to be avoided, rather than as wisely seizing the opportunity for trading up. Nor is it obviously more pragmatically rational to adopt the committed's policy toward even large problems, treating them as problems to be dealt with, rather than to adopt the mere intender's or the provisional planner's lower thresholds for taking problems as reconsideration triggers rather than as to be dealt with. Whether merely intending, provisional planning, or commitment is the best strategy would seem to depend on what one's present and anticipated future options are.

WHAT GOOD IS COMMITMENT?
THE BETTER-LIFE ARGUMENT

A central defect of the pragmatic argument is precisely that it defends commitment on purely pragmatic grounds. On that view, we are in essence forced to commit by the realities of human life—namely, that we can't do everything and that getting the things we want takes time and planning. One might think, however, that commitment is necessary for a well-lived life and, in particular, for a life that is meaningful to the protagonist of that life. Thus, there is something to be said for the value of commitment quite apart from the empirical realities that might seem to necessitate commitment.

First, commitments, especially long-term commitments, seem necessary for a life well lived because they are the basis for a life's having a chosen, as opposed to merely accidental, coherence, unity, and stability over time. We make our life a coherent whole by having projects, relationships, identities, and ways of life to which we are deeply committed and which we are unwilling to abandon even in the face of many or serious obstacles or the temptations of attractive alternatives. The committed person's life has an integrity—in the sense of a crafted integration of its temporal parts—that the uncommitted person's life lacks. His life as a whole adds up to something, and his life trajectory has a narrative unity in virtue of that life's being shaped by enduring commitments.

When a life has diachronic unity and coherence, the person is able to say what he and his life are about. Making and sustaining long-term commitments that are highly resistant to reconsideration is the primary mechanism for such self-definition. What makes us a single identifiable agent over time is precisely the fact that we have willingly bound our life to a set of projects, relationships, social identities, geographical locations, and so on. Absent such long-term commitments, we cannot say either what our life is about or what defines our ongoing identity. As Marya Schechtman notes, "it is not an unfamiliar thought that a person needs activities to provide shape and unity to her life, and that a life with no plans, projects, or goals would quickly lose coherence."[23]

---

[23] Marya Schechtman, "Diversity in Unity: Practical Unity and Personal Boundaries," *Synthese* 162 (2008): 405–423, 415.

Thus, a life is made better precisely by having a unified trajectory and by expressing a clearly defined, stable identity.

Among the better-life arguments, I find this one the least persuasive. Commitment is not the only vehicle for securing narrative unity and integrity. A life can easily have narrative unity, and the temporal parts can easily be well integrated, quite apart from that life's being guided by one or more long-term commitments. Indeed, lives marked by many changes in careers, relationships, ways of life, and social identities can have a high degree of narrative unity and integrity. What matters is that the protagonist has some account (a narrative or set of principled reasons) that makes intelligible how she, as the author of her life, got from point A to point B to point C.[24] Agents' lives are unified and integrated not by the *fact* of being centered around some single choice or set of choices that persists across time but, rather, by the unifying and integrating *activities* of agents themselves who make intelligible decisions about if, when, and why to alter their life trajectories.

Of course, a person whose life trajectory is not governed by some long-term commitments will not, in the end, be able to identify what her life as a whole was about and who she has been by pointing to some identity-defining project, relationship, social identity, or way of life that dominated her life. And that may seem a strike against an uncommitted life. However, that a person cannot point to the object of a long-term commitment as constituting what her life was about or who she is hardly leaves her with nothing to say. Her life may have been one of overcoming adversity, seeing the light, making the most of every new opportunity, or experiencing as much as she could of what life had to offer. These kinds of whole-life accounts do not depend on making long-term commitments, and indeed some are possible only because the person does not lock in her life trajectory by making long-term commitments.[25]

Even if the narrative unity of a life doesn't depend upon making commitments, one might still think that a life devoid of commitments will lack a different kind of unity—namely, the kind of unity of agency that depends on having a normative (rather than narrative) identity. Someone who does not make any commitments, even relatively simple commitments to some time-extended projects, relationships, social identities,

---

[24] As Christine Korsgaard observes of personal identity, "authorial psychological connectedness is consistent with drastic changes, provided those changes are the result of actions by the person herself or reactions for which she is responsible" ("Personal Identity and the Unity of Agency: A Kantian Response to Parfit," *Philosophy and Public Affairs* 18, no. 2 [Spring 1989]: 101–132, 123). The same point applies to narrative unity and integrity.

[25] Margaret Walker argues that philosophical attachments to a life's having a life plan, being driven by categorical desires, or fitting the form of a quest, may say more about the historical and social location of the philosopher and philosophical audience than about any necessary quality of good lives (*Moral Understandings: A Feminist Study in Ethics*, 2nd ed. [New York: Oxford University Press, 2007]).

and the like, will appear not to have made up her mind about what she really values. Having no commitments that unify her agency across time, she will not have anything convincing to say to others about what she cares about and about who she is as an agent—that is, as someone who chooses and acts on the basis of what she values. Thus, having an identifiable normative identity appears to go hand in hand with making commitments.

On closer scrutiny, this particular defense of commitment, however compelling at first glance, just isn't going to get us what we want. That is because it is really an argument for the agentic importance of making *normative* commitments. Unified agency is a matter of making up one's mind about what one values and what one's evaluative priorities are—that is, forming a normative outlook—so that one can establish for oneself practical principles and their rank-ordering. In acting on those values and principles, one leads a life rather than having a life happen to one. That unified agency depends on making normative commitments is, I think, quite right.

Nothing, however, follows from this about the necessity of making *substantive* commitments—namely, commitments to particular projects, relationships, social identities, ways of life, and so on. And that is because unified agency depends only on making up one's mind what one's guiding practical principles will be, not on those principles having any particular content. Some practical principles not only are consistent with failure to make substantive commitments but also are likely to require not doing so. As Christine Korsgaard notes, "To act on whatever desire is strongest at the moment" is a practical principle.[26] Someone who deliberately chooses courses of action because she values, above all, satisfying her immediate, strongest desire is surely leading a life and differs from the person who, not having made up his mind about what he wants, is caused to act by whatever desire is strongest at the moment. "To act on whatever desire is strongest at the moment" rationally entails not making substantive commitments. There are plenty of other practical principles similarly at odds with substantive commitment, ones that are less far-fetched as examples of what might guide real-life agents' choices about how to lead their lives. Persons with very low self-esteem, persons who have been severely traumatized, persons with deep psychological needs to be socially accepted, to name just a few personality types, might adopt principles like "To do whatever will make me feel good about myself," "To do whatever will secure my safety," or "To do whatever will make people like me." It may be that, for example, securing one's safety is best done by making some substantive

---

[26] That this *is* a possible practical principle is a point that Korsgaard has repeatedly made. See, for example, Christine M. Korsgaard, "Kant's Analysis of Obligation: The Argument of *Groundwork I*," in her *Creating the Kingdom of Ends* (Cambridge, MA: Harvard University Press, 1996), 43–76, 57; Korsgaard, "Self-Constitution in the Ethics of Plato and Kant," *Journal of Ethics* 3, no. 1 (1999): 1–29, 16–17.

commitment—for example, committedly developing self-defense skills or entering a committed relationship with someone who makes one feel emotionally or physically safe. The point, however, is that practical principles like the ones just mentioned do not entail making some substantive commitments. Individuals who place sufficiently high priority on adventure or novelty might even adopt the normative principle, "To make no substantive commitments" (either at all or in a particular domain, as a Don Juan might commit himself to making no commitments to any intimate relationships). Thus, unified agency will not necessarily manifest itself in the making of time-extended commitments to some projects, persons, ways of life, or social identities.

Imagining the sorts of normative commitments that would not naturally issue in making at least some substantive commitments is, however, instructive. Lives devoted to the pursuit of safety, gratification of the strongest present desire, social acceptance, or sheer novelty seem shallow. These are not the sorts of normative commitments whose pursuit is likely to contribute to a good, flourishing, or excellent life—and thus a meaningful one on agent-independent conceptions of meaningfulness. Nor will persons with such commitments have readily available reasons-for-anyone to offer either others or themselves to make sense of why they value what they do—and thus why their life is valuable on a normative outlook conception of meaningfulness. So, perhaps substantive commitment is instead a good because it makes a life more meaningful than it otherwise would have been, or at least increases the odds that one will lead a more meaningful life.

In his later work, Frankfurt argues that this is so.[27] In his view, there is a kind of love, or caring, that is "volitionally necessitating" in the sense that we cannot avoid giving the objects of caring priority in our normative commitments, and therefore we cannot act against the objects of what we care about without feeling that we have done the unthinkable and betrayed ourselves. Such deep carings are, in his view, what make life meaningful: "The function of love is not to make people good. Its function is just to make their lives meaningful, and thus to help make their lives in that way good for them to live."[28] And, he says, "The fact that we cannot help loving, and that we there-fore cannot help being guided by the interests of what we love, helps to ensure that we neither flounder aimlessly nor hold ourselves back from definitive adherence to a meaningful practical course."[29] He elaborates:

> By providing us with final ends, which we value for their own sakes and to which our commitment is not merely voluntary, love saves us both from being

---

[27] Although Frankfurt has long argued for the significance of caring, his claims about the dependence of meaningfulness on care—and care of a particular sort—are especially strong in his *Taking Ourselves Seriously*.

[28] Frankfurt, *Taking Ourselves Seriously*, 99.

[29] Ibid., 66.

inconclusively arbitrary and from squandering our lives in vacuous activity that is fundamentally pointless because, having no definite goal, it aims at nothing that we really want. Love makes it possible, in other words, for us to engage wholeheartedly in activity that is meaningful.[30]

One of the advantages of this particular defense of commitment is that it puts at center stage a kind of commitment often taken to be paradigmatic. These are the attitudinal commitments that I mentioned at the outset of this chapter.

Attitudinal commitments are grounded in the emotions and desires of the agent, particularly in feelings of love, of relatively intense caring, of being called-to, and what Bernard Williams has called "categorical desires"—namely, desires that answer for the agent the question of why to go on in life at all.[31] Such attitudes are the basis of one's being, in Susan Wolf's terms, "actively engaged" with particular projects or relationships in one's life.[32] They explain why one experiences particular projects or relationships as deeply satisfying and personally fulfilling. Mother Teresa's love of Christ appears to have grounded an attitudinal commitment to her work in India, and Okonkwo's ruling passion to become the manliest of men grounded his total investment in becoming such a man. Marital commitments, commitments to one's children, and religious commitments are, in paradigm cases, also attitudinal commitments.

Attitudinal commitments differ from other sorts of commitments—for example, promissory commitments and resolutions—in originating from identity-defining loves and desires, and in the typical absence of conflicting motivations. To be attitudinally committed to some aim, for example, is to be disposed to act on that commitment unstintingly and ungrudgingly—dispositions that are not constitutive of either promissory commitments or, even less so, resolutions. Being grounded in psychologically deep features of the self, attitudinal commitments typically have longevity and are uniquely suited to answer the question "Who am I?" They might also seem, as they apparently did to Frankfurt, to be what makes life meaningful. For Frankfurt, however, attitudinal commitments come to seem critical to a meaningful life only because he assumes that the only meaning-supplying carings are ones that are "volitionally necessitating" and thus are ones that naturally issue in substantive commitments.

In chapter 2, I proposed a quite different conception of meaningful living. Meaningful living involves expending your life's time on ends that in your best

---

[30] Ibid., 90.

[31] Williams, "Persons, Character, and Morality," in *Moral Luck*, 11.

[32] Susan Wolf, "Happiness and Meaning: Two Aspects of the Good Life," *Social Philosophy & Policy* 14, no. 1 (1997): 207–225, 209; Wolf, "Meanings of Lives," paper presented at New York University School of Law, Colloquium in Legal, Political and Social Philosophy, New York, October 23, 2003, pp. 9–10, www1.law.nyu.edu/clppt/program2003/readings/wolf.pdf.

judgment you have reason to value and thus reason to use yourself up on. Because you have reasons-for-anyone, reasons-for-the-initiated, and reasons-for-me to adopt the ends you do, you "care" about your ends in the sense that you adopt a *valuing attitude* toward them. You might also "care" about your ends in the sense that your *feelings* of love or attachment figure among your reasons-for-me for choosing the ends you do. Caring in either of these senses—valuing attitude and feeling of love—is a scalar phenomenon. Nothing one cares about in these senses need be volitionally necessitating.[33]

So while I agree with Frankfurt that caring is connected with meaningful living, it is caring as valuing attitude that matters; and love sometimes figures among one's reasons-for me for having that valuing attitude. What is necessary for meaningful living is that one's life allows space for the pursuit of what one cares about in these more ordinary senses of "caring." Such carings might be strong enough to ground an attitudinal commitment, as in Okonkwo's case. Or, they might not. Instead, one might remain open to reconsidering and revising how one expends one's time (in light of new information, new opportunities, or the realization that a highly ranked but time-consuming end is crowding out time for other pursuits one values).

It might still be objected that a life devoted to something one values so much that one is willing to make an attitudinal commitment to it—as Mother Teresa and Okonkwo did—will be a more meaningful life than one devoted to things less strongly valued. But meaningful living, I have argued, is not just a function of how highly one values particular ends. It is also a function of how much of one's life is occupied in primary time expenditures. It will depend on empirical circumstances whether the cultivation of a ruling passion and the making of an attitudinal commitment are a better or worse strategy for increasing meaningful living. A person who has many, varied, and easily pursued objects of lesser care may end her life having spent more of its days and hours in meaningful activities than her more single-minded, passionate counterpart.[34]

Even if volitionally necessitating attitudinal commitments aren't essential to meaningful living, one might still think the person who lives meaningfully will need to make some commitments. In chapter 2, I argued that reasons-for-anyone are a particularly important class of reasons. They figure prominently in justifications of the

---

[33] Michael E. Bratman expresses skepticism that there are any volitionally necessitating carings in his "A Thoughtful and Reasonable Stability," in Frankfurt, *Taking Ourselves Seriously*, 77–90.
[34] It's worth bearing in mind that deep carings are not a matter of voluntary choice, even if we can sometimes contribute to their cultivation. Not everyone will be so fortunately situated that life presents suitable objects of ruling passions. No star-crossed loves or gripping vocations and avocations present themselves. It seems odd to regard such lives as necessarily devoid of meaning.

choiceworthiness of one's ends, both to other people and to oneself.[35] Choiceworthy life occupations are typically time extended by their nature—pursuit of a career, involvement in a relationship, service to a charitable organization, development of a valuable skill, acquisition of or contribution to knowledge of some important subject, and the like. Given the time-extended nature of such choiceworthy pursuits, commitment might well be thought a necessary condition for leading a meaningful life, since absent commitment the person will not stick to these pursuits long enough to realize the goods that make them choiceworthy. Indeed, paradigm examples of choiceworthy lives are typically also highly committed lives.

But recall, first, that making a commitment is not to be contrasted with having no intentions whatsoever. Commitments are to be contrasted with provisional plans and mere intentions. All three involve making decisions that settle the future to some degree by establishing thresholds for what new information or change of desire will be sufficient to trigger reconsideration, and thus thresholds beyond which problems are not problems to be dealt with but reasons for reconsideration. If one uses "commitment" loosely to refer indiscriminately to all decisions that close the future to some degree or another, then it is certainly true that developing one's talents, acquiring knowledge, and the like require commitment in that loose sense. You could not learn ballroom dancing without at least framing a mere intention to take the classes. Using "commitment" in this loose way, however, obscures the scalar nature of closing the future. The question at issue is whether it is unquestionably better to develop one's talents, acquire knowledge, make social contributions, and pursue enriching social interactions via commitments, rather than provisional plans or mere intentions.

My claim is that it is not. It is true that someone who forms a mere intention or a provisional plan to, say, learn Spanish or help out with a political campaign is less likely to learn as much Spanish or help a campaign in as many ways or for as long a time as would the committed person. But, again, it's important not to exaggerate the temporal instability of these intentions. Decision-making contexts are often highly stable over time, so that reconsideration is never triggered; and a wide variety of factors other than a decision to foreclose future reconsideration keep people in time-extended activities once initiated, including the need to stave off boredom, economic necessity, the absence of attractive alternatives, social pressures, a lack of imagination, psychological needs, and habit, to mention only a few. Where those circumstantial stabilizing factors are absent, mere intenders and provisional planners

---

[35] Agent-independent and agent-independent-plus theorists about meaningfulness will prefer to talk about the objective or agent-independent value of activities. The following argument against the necessity of commitment to meaningful living is intended to apply to those conceptions of meaningful living as well.

will change course more frequently than the committed will. It does not follow from this, however, that they do less to develop their talents or contribute to the social good, even if they do less to develop a particular talent or to contribute to the social good in a particular way. As I argued earlier, *normative* commitments, including a commitment to develop one's talents or contribute to the social good, do not entail *substantive* commitments to this or that activity. The individual who merely intends to help by fostering kittens may reconsider and change course after the first experience with the high mortality rate of kittens, and the provisional planner may change course only after her house becomes infested with fleas; the committed person whose policy is to treat these as problems to be dealt with stays the course, instead. A normative commitment to contributing to the social good would require that the mere intender and the provisional planner in this case select some other avenue of social contribution. It may, of course, be better for the welfare of others that there are committed persons. My aim has only been to argue that it is not clearly better for the individual that she make her life meaningful via the mechanism of commitment rather than via mere intentions or provisional plans.

The view that leading a meaningful life depends on commitment gets much of its persuasive force, I believe, from the assumption that meaningful lives are about something—something that underwrites a single narrative story, that is the object of a ruling passion, and that makes long stretches of one's life or one's life as a whole choice-worthy. If lives can have meaning without being about something, then meaningful lives need not include pursuits that are so very time extended as to virtually necessitate commitment.

In his essay on well-being and time, David Velleman argues that, given that persons have both a synchronic and a diachronic identity, they care both how their lives are going *at a particular moment* in time relative to alternative possibilities and how their lives *as a whole* are going relative to alternative possibilities.[36] It is thus a mistake to think that there is a single answer to questions about a person's well-being. How one answers the question "Did this contribute to my well-being?" depends on whether one is taking a more temporally local or more temporally global perspective.[37] From a temporally local perspective, a romantic evening out with a new love interest may contribute positively to one's well-being. From a temporally more global perspective, however, the romantic evening may contribute little to one's well-being if that evening

[36] J. David Velleman, "Well-Being and Time," in his *The Possibility of Practical Reason* (Oxford: Oxford University Press, 2000), 56–84.
[37] Velleman uses the terminology "momentary" well-being and "lifetime" well-being rather than "local" and "global" (ibid.).

sparks what proves to be a disastrous affair. In Velleman's view, the more global perspective on well-being does not trump the more local one. As he says,

> the value something has for someone in a restricted context of a single moment in his life is a value that genuinely accrues to him as the subject of that moment, even if interactions with events at other times result in its delivering a different value to him in his capacity as the protagonist of an entire life. The good that something does you now is not just the phantom of a restricted method of accounting; it's an autonomous mode of value.[38]

A similar point about the irreducible difference between synchronic and diachronic perspectives applies to questions of whether what one is doing with one's life is meaningful. Observing that your life has been occupied with one or more time-extended pursuits that, in your best judgment, you have reason to value for their own sake answers the question of whether your life is meaningful from a more temporally global, diachronic perspective. Your life has been about something, and that something was a valued end. Accepting only references to relationships, careers, avocations, and the like as answering the question "Is my life meaningful?" ignores the temporally local question "Is what I am doing *now* meaningful?" And in this case, the temporally global perspective doesn't just ignore the local perspective, it quite often requires that it be ignored.

Consider the average life of a philosopher. While participating in academic philosophy may make her life as a whole more meaningful than alternative options would, an enormous amount of her more temporally local activities will have been spent doing things that aren't valued for their own sake. Grading a hundred exams answering the same question, tracking down footnotes, sitting through tedious committee meetings, and evaluating hundreds of job applications may just be entailed rather than primary time expenditures. The average intimate relationship is similarly not dominated, at the local level, by high-quality moments of intimacy but, rather, with vastly more mundane interactions that may be trivial, boring, or irritating. The difference in temporal perspective on the meaningfulness of a person's life explains, I think, why she may feel that her daily life is largely meaningless even while, and indeed in virtue of, pursuing time-extended activities that make her life as a whole (or longish stretches of it) meaningful. It also may explain why retirement—a moment in time when a person typically finishes making something meaningful of her life—is also anticipated as a time when she can now do meaningful things.

In short, if the answer to "What makes life meaningful?" is "Doing something that, in my best judgment, I have reason to value for its own sake," there will be at least two

---

[38] Ibid., 80.

different strategies for putting meaning in life. One may opt for a temporally global strategy, aiming to make one's life about something that is valued for its own sake, and to do so by making commitments. Or, one may opt for a temporally local strategy, aiming to pack one's hours and days with meaningful pursuits and interactions, and to do so by not making the sort of time-extended commitments that promise to reduce the options for local meaning. For the reasons given earlier, such a life need not be devoid of contributions to the social good, enriching personal interactions, the development of skills, and the acquisition of knowledge, even if one is not committed to making one's life about such things.

THE ATTRACTION OF COMMITMENT

None of my arguments so far have been meant to suggest that commitment is a bad thing. My aim has been to trouble the normative assumption that it is better for agents to shape their lives around some set of commitments than not to do so; I've done this by providing reasons to be skeptical that commitment is either pragmatically required or a necessary condition for a well-lived life.

Suppose there are no compelling reasons why persons ought, for their own sakes, to lead lives that include commitments. There might nevertheless be reasons why a life that includes commitments is an attractive life, and thus why people would be drawn to committing their futures rather than simply to making more readily revisable plans. Attitudinal commitment, I suggest, is attractive to those whose normative style includes *prizing* things. Commitment in general, I suggest, is attractive to those who have a *familiarity-seeking* style of managing their futures. In both cases, there are reasons to expect these styles to be widespread, even if they are not universal.[39]

Normative Style

It is one thing to think that something is valuable, even of utmost value, and it is another thing to prize it. Prizing is a normative attitude toward what one takes to be not only valuable but also special in a way that cannot be fully accounted for by showing what makes the thing, or person, or activity valuable. Kantian prizing of

---

[39] I here adopt a strategy employed by Galen Strawson in "Against Narrativity," *The Self?* ed. Galen Strawson (Malden, MA: Blackwell, 2005), 63–86. Strawson argues that rather than thinking most lives are, and that all lives ought to be, experienced as a narrative, we are better off thinking of there being different *temporal styles*; figuring one's life as a narrative has appeal for those whose temporal style is nonepisodic. Similarly, I suggest that rather than thinking most lives are, and all lives ought to be, organized around commitment, we are better off thinking there are different normative and temporal styles. Some styles make commitment attractive and others do not.

the humanity in persons is perhaps like this. Whatever valuable-making qualities or capacities of persons we point to invite us to assign a mere price (perhaps a very high price) to humanity, so that the prizing of humanity as special in a way beyond price may seem to outrun the available reasons. Or, consider prizing, regarding as special, Beanie Babies or the Red Sox. While grounded in some specifiable, value-conferring features of Beanie Babies and the Red Sox that Beanie Baby collectors and Red Sox fans might be quick to point out, the prizing outruns the bases for valuing. Though prizing involves a personal attitude, to prize is not to see oneself as willfully making up some special additional value. It is, rather, to appreciate or to see something in the prized object that makes it potentially prizable by others (though perhaps only by a very special sort of other, as in the saying "Only a mother could love . . . "), even if one cannot point to prize-making features in the way one can to valuable-making features, and thus cannot communicate why it is prizeworthy. To love a particular person or animal, for example, is to see one's love as both grounded in some valuable features and responsive to a specialness that is not fully explained by appeal to what are, after all, repeatable (and thus not special-making) valuable features.[40]

Prizing, then, has two features: (1) a value judgment about the prized object (or person, activity, way of life, identity, etc.) based on intersubjectively available reasons for assigning that particular value; and (2) a personal attitude of regarding the object as special and as worthy of behavioral and attitudinal responses that treat it as special. These two features of prizing give prizers reasons to think that others may also prize what they do (for example, a Red Sox fan expects to find other fans, or a lover isn't surprised that her beloved has other admirers), but also to recognize that the resources for persuading others to prize what they do are highly limited.

The principal practical expression of prizing something, of one's regarding it as special, is commitment—commitment to living one's life as an X, to collecting X, to taking care of X, to cheering for X, to striving to achieve X, and so on. Attitudinal commitment, then, is an attractive feature of life for those whose normative style includes prizing. Prizers might predictably find their lives diminished by the absence of suitable objects of prizing and of attitudinal commitments, and find themselves moved to seek out new objects for prizing, to cultivate prizing attitudes, and thus to create the basis for new attitudinal commitments. (Personal ads looking for that special someone often provide good examples of prizers at work.)

Prizing does not seem to me to be a basic capacity of any evaluator but, rather, an optional extra—a normative style. One can imagine persons who are excellent

[40] Martha C. Nussbaum, "Love and the Individual: Romantic Rightness and Platonic Aspiration," in *Reconstructing Individualism: Autonomy, Individuality, and the Self in Western Thought*, ed. Thomas C. Heller et al. (Stanford, CA: Stanford University Press, 1986), 253–277.

evaluators and practical reasoners, but who are unable to prize anything. One can even more readily imagine persons who differ in the degree to which they have or exercise this normative style, some being chary prizers, others promiscuous prizers. To describe prizing as a normative style is to underscore not only its being optional in a being with evaluative capacities, but also that it is an approach to valuing that may or may not find suitable objects.

That prizing is a pervasive normative style is not a brute fact about persons. Prizers can be made, not just born. Contemporary capitalist culture encourages people to be prizers through the marketing and advertising of objects to be prized (for example, Beanie Babies), the resources for enacting one's prizing (biking equipment, red roses and diamonds, stamp-collecting albums), and paraphernalia for announcing one's prizing (message-laden wall plaques, throw pillows, T-shirts, and "I love ___" bumper stickers). The culture of authenticity encourages people to find jobs, relationships, and avocations that can be prized as truly self-expressive. Various religions, political rhetoric, and sometimes the law encourage people to be prizers of families. Activist groups encourage us to be prizers of the environment, fetal life, and peace. As cultural participants, we learn to be prizers and to cultivate this normative style in ourselves.

What shapes us into prizers who find making attitudinal commitments attractive may be more than our culture. Prizing both connects us to others through activities of shared prizing and distinguishes us as individuals through our distinctive patterns of prizing. To the extent that we are evolutionarily designed to be both social beings and beings who have needs to be recognized as individuals, there may also be an evolutionary basis for this normative style that explains the pervasive attraction of prizing and its attendant, attitudinal commitment.

Temporal Style

Not all commitments are attitudinal commitments having their source either in what I've called prizings or in what Frankfurt calls volitionally necessitating carings. What all commitments do have in common is that they lock in the future in a way that mere intentions and provisional plans do not. What could be attractive about that? If social arrangements don't require commitment as the precondition for getting or doing what one wants or being in a relationship with whom one wants—that is, if commitment isn't quasi-forced—prudential rationality would seem to favor more provisional plans that are intended to remain in place only until something else comes along and that are compatible with putting oneself in the way of temptation, keeping a lookout for information that would occasion redeliberation, not trying to resuscitate flagging interest, and the like. Why not live life with an eye to opportunities for trading up that are good enough to outweigh the sunk and prospective costs of abandoning a plan under way? Why tie oneself to a future more strongly than these cost considerations already do?

I said at the beginning of this chapter that the attraction to commitment might be a function of a particular style of managing one's diachronic existence. It is time to talk about time. What I suggest is that the attraction of locking in one's future lies in the way that doing so enables persons to take up residence in time, much the way that settling geographically enables one to take up residence in space. For some, this will be attractive, and for others, not.

Humans conduct their lives in space and through time; and they fill their lives, both spatially and temporally, with other persons, animals, material objects, green and built environments, activities, interactions, rituals, sounds, smells, and so on. One knows where one is in space not by being familiar with the contents of a particular point in space—say, a hotel room—but by knowing what spaces surround one's location. For example, one knows where hotel corridors go, what part of the city the hotel is located in, what roads are nearby, or the city's surrounding geography. Knowing where one is in space is also a matter of knowing how to navigate that space, because one knows the tracks through space that will get one from here to the there one wants to go to. One also knows where one is in space by knowing what the surrounding spaces contain. I am not just here, in my home, but also in a place within whose surrounding geography I can locate the grocery and movie theater, friends, parks, highway noise, and roosting bats. The more extensive one's knowledge of the surrounding spatial horizon and the richer one's knowledge of the contents of that horizon, the more one might be said to know where one is and to not be lost.

Similarly, one knows where one is in time, not by knowing (or not just by knowing) what hour or day it is or the temporal horizon of future days and times, but more importantly by knowing the contents of that temporal horizon. To know the day of the week is to know very little about one's place in time. To know what will fill that day and those to come, where one will live, what places one will go to, with whom one will interact, what deadlines will come due, what activities will engage one's time, what one will smell, and how the weather will feel at various distances on the temporal horizon is to know where one is in time and to not be lost.

Knowing one's place in time is also a matter of knowing how to navigate from the present to the future, including what events beyond one's control will need to happen and what actions within one's control one will need to take to get from the present here to the future there. Mere intentions, provisional plans, and commitments are ways of laying down tracks through time in much the way selecting routine travel routes is a way of laying down tracks in space. And just as tracks through space determine not only how one gets from point A to point B but also the contents of one's spatial experience—what landmarks one will pass, whether one will see wild turkeys or smell hamburgers grilling along the way—so agential tracks through time determine more than what one will be doing.[41] They determine the contents of one's temporal experience across and at different moments of time. A policy of going home for Thanksgiving enables me to know both what I will be intentionally doing—taking a plane, eating dinner, talking with family—and what richer context I will find myself in that includes others' conversations and activities, the smell of turkey, furniture familiar from childhood, and so on. Knowing both what I will do and the richer context of action, I can imaginatively inhabit the future (with pleasure or anxiety); and even if not imagined beforehand, the future, when it arrives, will be unsurprising.

People, it seems to me, have different spatial and temporal dispositions. Some like open horizons, not knowing what comes next, with opportunities for explorations and novelty. Others prefer more closed horizons, knowing where they are in space and time, and finding what comes next familiar and unsurprising. That is, some prefer to live in the present under an idea of the future whose content is richly filled in, while others prefer to live under an idea of the future whose content is not so thoroughly specified. If this is so, one might expect to find some people more attracted to provisional planning and others more to commitment. One can, of course, use commitment to render the future familiar to varying degrees—shorter- versus longer-term commitments, fewer versus more commitments, commitments to one-off goals versus commitments to repetitions (such as annual Thanksgivings with family or daily exercise), commitments to identities, and to ongoing relationships, and commitments to achieving the unlikely or to persons who are unreliable versus commitments to goals that are easily achieved and to trustworthy persons.

In short, the attraction to commitment may reflect only one style of managing the geography of one's future—a style that involves taking up permanent residences in time and making the future one's home. For creatures who share with their animal kin a sense of comfort in returning to the familiar and a disposition to adopt habitual routines that reduce surprises, one might expect commitment to be widely attractive. But as creatures who also share with their animal kin a vulnerability to boredom and a curiosity about the new, one might also expect that attraction to have its limits.

[41] J. David Velleman has argued that humans have an impulse to know what they are doing and thus they have an incentive to make and carry through on intentions (in "From Self Psychology to Moral Psychology" and "The Centered Self" in his *Self to Self: Selected Essays* [Cambridge: Cambridge University Press, 2005], 224–283). "I can avoid puzzlement by first framing an idea of the creature's [i.e., one's own] next action and then enacting that idea," he writes (261). I think the cognitive needs are larger than this. It's not just puzzlement about what one is doing, but also puzzlement about one's entire surroundings—the richer context in which doings take place—that creatures like us typically want to avoid.

6

Living with Boredom

Boredom is worth exploring partly because it is so hard to look at, so much taken for granted as an aspect of life.[1]

It is like dust. You go about and never notice . . .. But stand still for an instant and there it is, coating your face and hands.[2]

There is, one might think, an intimate connection between living meaningfully and absence of boredom. Harry Frankfurt, whose work on meaningfulness strongly influenced my normative outlook conception of meaningfulness, offers one account of that connection.[3] In his view, to have what he calls "final ends" (and what I call simply "ends")—things that we care about and value for their own sake—is important because it is by orienting our activity toward final ends that what we do comes to seem important, interesting, and not a matter of indifference. A life without final ends would not just fail to be meaningful to the person who lives it. "Anyone who lived that life would be indifferent and unengaged with respect to whatever it might be that he did. Furthermore, he would be bored."[4] His life would lack the very features that could attract his attention and "responsiveness to conscious stimuli" and generate "psychic liveliness."[5]

Although there is clearly something right in the idea that living meaningfully plays a role in staving off boredom, meaningful living may play neither as positive a role nor as a singular in making our lives less boring. To begin, living meaningfully may contribute to boredom. Throughout this book, I've emphasized the importance of paying attention to actual time expenditures at the temporally local level, rather than focusing exclusively on temporally global and abstractly described characterizing features of one's life. Primary time expenditures on the pursuit of ends we value for their own sake

---

[1] Patricia Meyer Spacks, *Boredom: The Literary History of a State of Mind* (Chicago: University of Chicago Press, 1995), 27.

[2] George Bernanos, quoted in Jon Winokur, *Ennui to Go: The Art of Boredom* (Seattle, WA: Sasquatch Books, 2005), 18.

[3] Harry G. Frankfurt, "On the Usefulness of Final Ends," in *Necessity, Volition, and Love* (Cambridge: Cambridge University Press, 1999), 82–94.

[4] Ibid., 88–89.

[5] Ibid., 89.

typically come with entailed time expenditures on both instrumental means and constitutive activities, neither one of which we may value for its own sake. Think back to Friedan's housewife mentioned in chapter 1. Frankfurt himself appears sensitive to the possibility that ends might have these (locally) meaning-reducing costs. "The activity that is required in order to attain a certain final end of great value," he observes, "may be, after all, extremely meager; and insofar as a person devotes his life to pursuing that final end, his life would be nearly empty."[6] It is thus important, Frankfurt argues, that in adopting an end to pursue, one considers the network of activities that pursuit of that end will involve. Of course, one might, as perhaps Friedan's housewife did, decide that the end is sufficiently valuable to be worth paying the temporal costs of entailed time expenditures on things one does not value and engagement with which is unlikely to generate "psychic liveliness." But this is just to say that the effort to live meaningfully may itself be the source of boredom.

In his response to Frankfurt's view, Elijah Millgram suggests a different reason why activities instrumental to pursuing ends may fail to generate interest: they may become entirely routinized.[7] Consider Friedan's housewife again. When motherhood was new, how to go about mothering required consideration and choice. Once those activities are routinized, Millgram observes, the connection between daily activity and the valued end typically drops below the radar of attention.[8] The enlivening sense of the importance of the end ceases to be transmitted to entailed pursuits. I would add that sheer routinization—that is, repetitiveness—even if one remains alive to the means–end connection, would also seem in itself to be boring. If repetition simply bores, then even a sense of the importance of what one is doing may fail to stave off boredom. (I have something to say about why repetition bores a bit later in the chapter.)

I suggested at the beginning that not only may meaningful living not play as positive a role in forestalling boredom as assumed, it may also not play as singular a role in making our lives less boring. Millgram's central aim in critiquing Frankfurt is to suggest that being interested rather than bored is not wholly dependent, in the way Frankfurt suggests, on one's ends. Indeed, ends themselves may become boring, and it is the possibility of finding other things interesting that enables us to reset those ends. So, the account of what enables us to be interested and the account of why we may find ourselves bored need to be detached, at least partly, from the account of meaningful living. I agree.

---

[6] Ibid., 87.
[7] Elijah Millgram, "On Being Bored Out of Your Mind," *Proceedings of the Aristotelian Society* 104 (January 2004): 165–186.
[8] Ibid., 171.

My aim in this chapter is to explore what such accounts of interest and boredom should look like. I do not pursue Millgram's laudatory depiction of boredom—its function in reshaping the contours of agency by helping us reset ends. Nor is the focus exclusively on the relation between boredom and setting ends. I instead argue that vulnerability to boredom is connected, in a variety of different ways, to our being evaluators who lead our lives through time. Boredom is an inescapable consequence of being the kind of being who evaluates, engages temporally with value qualities, and decides how to expend time. It is, in part, this constitutive vulnerability to boredom that makes being a temporal evaluator so difficult. Although not forwarding a laudatory account of boredom, I argue against the contrasting view: that boredom is always problematic, signaling some deficiency in the bored person or in her circumstances.

That boredom is a problem is the leitmotiv of philosophical and psychological literature on boredom. The *prevalence* of boredom—either in the lives of particular boredom-prone individuals or in postmodern culture generally—is a problem. And what bored people *do* is a problem: they pursue meaningless diversions and indulge in normative delinquencies ranging from goofing off instead of working, to overeating, to crime. The implicit message of this boredom-as-problem literature is that the human capacity for boredom is not itself interesting or important. Boredom becomes so only when it causes or signals trouble.

By contrast, I think that boredom itself is interesting—in part because it is puzzling. Why, for example, would the bored be especially disposed to remedy their boredom via meaningless diversions like playing solitaire or Internet surfing, as well as "normative delinquencies" like goofing off at work, when they have options for making more productive or meaningful use of their time? And why does repetition bore? This fact is typically taken as an obvious truism requiring no further explanation. But when what repeats is something that initially interested us, why would repetition over time produce boredom, as opposed to, say, contentment or a longer period of interest?

More significantly, the human capacity for boredom—not just some problematic cause or consequence of boredom—is important because it illuminates the difficulties inherent in leading the life of an evaluator. Attending to boredom shifts our philosophical gaze from the *ranking* and *end-setting* activities of evaluators to the *temporal lives* of evaluators who seek out, meet up with, spend time with, and act with respect to value qualities. Boredom, I argue, is virtually inevitable, not because the world itself is boring but because the kinds of lives that evaluators typically live create the conditions for boredom—hence, the title of this chapter, "Living with Boredom." It is boredom's connection with the difficulties involved in leading the life of an evaluator, and the special vulnerability of some evaluators to boredom, that makes understanding boredom illuminating.

Not taking a boredom-as-problem approach is considerably at odds with the literature on boredom (in psychology, sociology, philosophy, and literary criticism). I begin, then, by describing three main boredom-as-problem approaches and by offering reasons for not approaching boredom this way. Those approaches, however, inadvertently expose puzzling features of boredom which an adequate analysis of boredom needs to explain. I then examine principal life circumstances that invite boredom: stalled lives, normative constraints, value disappointment, value satiety, and leisure. The aim here is to bring into view the different shapes that boredom takes and their connections to different sorts of difficulties that evaluators face.

THE BOREDOM-AS-PROBLEM VIEW

Boredom may seem an unlikely place to look for significant insights about evaluators, even if we take "evaluator" quite broadly to refer to beings who appreciate a wide spectrum of value qualities; who rate objects, actions, and character traits; who set and pursue ends and assess instrumental means; who grasp, comply with, and assess their own and others' responsibility for violating norms; and who are appropriate subjects of moral critique. First, rather than the activation of capacities linked with evaluation, boredom appears to be the inactivation of those capacities. Typically, boredom is marked by the absence of either desire or aversion. It is a state of indifference, disengagement, inability to pay attention, and lack of motivation—what Frankfurt describes as the absence of "psychic liveliness." Evaluation appears to go off-line insofar as the bored find nothing worthy of positive or negative evaluation and often are at a loss to say what would not be boring. Boredom is, in Elizabeth Goodstein's words, an "experience without qualities," or more precisely, an experience of a world whose qualities do not invite evaluative differentiation.[9]

Second, while virtually anything can be the object of boredom, much of what bores us is trivial—television shows, the dinner conversation, one's hairstyle, waiting in line. Boredom in this respect is like embarrassment: to the extent that it is an evaluative attitude, boredom's orientation is not typically toward important value qualities (such as injustice, harm, benevolence, suffering, loss of status, threat).

Almost any emotion one could name, other than boredom, bears some interesting connection to the capacities, concerns, and actions of evaluators. It is perhaps no surprise, then, that those who theorize about boredom generally do not take as their subject matter boredom as such but, rather, something that is only contingently connected

[9] Elizabeth S. Goodstein, *Experience without Qualities: Boredom and Modernity* (Stanford, CA: Stanford University Press, 2005).

with boredom, and in particular, something that makes some types or some quantities of boredom look like an important problem worth reflecting on.

Boredom Causes Problematic Behavior

One strategy is to focus on the personally and socially harmful things that people do out of boredom. Boredom is, for example, causally connected with gambling, drinking, drug abuse, overeating, crime, dropping out of school, juvenile delinquency, risk-taking (for example, adolescent train surfing, which is often lethal), poor task performance including shoddy workmanship, and social conflict.

In its focus on the social and personal ills caused by boredom, this boredom-as-problem view ignores the fact that people put their boredom to many uses other than socially or personally harmful ones. Some of these are relatively innocent: gossiping, shopping, Internet surfing and channel surfing, cleaning the house, doodling, and napping, to mention a few. Others are salutary. Boredom is sometimes credited with being a stimulus to creativity, invention, and positive life changes.[10] Elijah Millgram, as we've seen, argues that all final ends are bound to become boring after a time, and that this is not regrettable. Rather, we should see the capacities for interest and boredom as "among the top-level components of rationality. . . . Their function is not to stabilize the self, but to push you past the structures of final ends that you might have taken for your personal that-without-which-not."[11]

That boredom can be put to bad, innocent, and good uses, suggests that boredom is not a distinctively problematic emotion, since the same might be said of the uses to which people put any other emotion. But perhaps there is something about boredom itself, as opposed to the limited opportunities or misguided imagination of some bored people, that produces a tendency to relieve boredom with bad behavior rather than through innocent or creative outlets. If it turned out, for example, that many seemingly innocent escapes from boredom in fact involve normative delinquencies (for example, the bored grad student balances her checkbook instead of working on her dissertation, or the bored faculty member doodles instead of preparing a question for the guest lecturer), and if we had some account of why escaping boredom through normative delinquencies made sense given what boredom itself is like, then an analysis of boredom might give us some insight into both the distinctive nature of boredom and the lives of evaluators. I think there is a reason why bored evaluators often indulge in normative delinquencies, but the first strategy takes this for granted rather than explaining it. An

---

[10] One author attributes the student protest movement of the '60s to boredom (Haskell E. Bernstein, "Boredom and the Ready-Made Life," *Social Research* 42 [Autumn 1975]: 512–537, 524).

[11] Millgram, "On Being Bored Out of Your Mind," 183.

adequate account of boredom should shed some light on the puzzling attraction of the bored to normative delinquencies.

Chronic Boredom Is a Problem but Situational Boredom Is Not

Some evaluative attitudes point primarily outward from the evaluating subject toward the qualities of objects. Disgust, admiration, and resentment are like this. Here, the language of feeling is part of the language of criticism and appraisal. Other evaluative attitudes point primarily inward toward the subjective inclinations of the individual. Loving, liking, being pleased by are like this. While individuals often have reasons for loving or being pleased—reasons having to do with the qualities of the things loved and the things that please—"loving" and "being pleased by" are part of the language of subjective self-revelation. Boredom points both outward toward the qualities of the world that are boring *and* inward toward some feature of the bored person that prevents engagement. We are bored both from without and from within.[12]

It is tempting to try to accommodate this feature of boredom by sorting boredoms into two different types. Indeed, psychoanalytically inspired literature on boredom does just that.[13] On the one hand, there is "normal," "situational," and "responsive" boredom. Such boredom points outward, responding to what is reasonably regarded as boring—the boring lecturer who has nothing interesting to say or the boring psycho-analysis patient who says nothing the analyst hasn't heard before. On the other hand, there is "chronic," "pathological" boredom, which points inward toward an internal source. On the conventional psychoanalytic account, chronic boredom stems from early repression of unacceptable impulses that leave the individual in a state of tension but unaware of how to discharge it, and wanting help from the external world but unable to find it. In Otto Fenichel's words, "the person who is bored can be compared to someone who has forgotten a name and inquires about it from others."[14] Offering another psychoanalytic account, Haskell Bernstein suggests that the training of children for success that has started at younger and younger ages since the 1950s, and the practice of taking children along on adult outings where they are required not to get excited, results in children learning to cope with parental demands for obedience

---

[12] Jerome Neu, "Boring from Within: Endogenous versus Reactive Boredom," in *A Tear is an Intellectual Thing: The Meanings of Emotion* (New York: Oxford University Press, 2000), 95–107.
[13] Otto Fenichel, "On the Psychology of Boredom," in *The Collected Papers of Otto Fenichel*, 1st series (New York: W.W. Norton, 1953), 292–302; Hilde Lewinsky, "Boredom," *British Journal of Educational Psychology* 13 (1943): 147–152; Bernstein, "Boredom and the Ready-Made Life."
[14] Fenichel, "On the Psychology of Boredom," 293.

through massive repression of feeling.[15] Once in adolescence or adulthood, the incapacity to feel spells chronic boredom.

A philosophical version of this chronic-boredom-as-problem approach, developed in greatest detail by Lars Svendsen, distinguishes ordinary episodes of being bored with the boring from a more chronic existential or profound boredom.[16] Existential boredom originates, however, not in psychological pathology but in the absence of a theological guarantee of value and meaning, as well as in a loss of confidence in the authority of traditions to bestow meaning on life activities. Existential boredom might fairly be described as an encounter with the absurdity of human life—that is, with the absence of any ultimate basis for thinking that how we spend our lives is grounded in anything other than sheer choice. From this more philosophical viewpoint, human life is essentially boring; it is not worth taking an interest in, since it lacks agent-independent value and meaning.

Because the psychoanalytic and philosophic analyses of chronic boredom set aside what they take to be unproblematic, situational boredom, they implicitly deny that there is anything significant about either the human capacity for boredom or the vast majority of boring moments experienced by the vast majority of people. To set aside situational boredom in favor of its more exotic cousin on the grounds that, after all, some things just are boring, period, is to miss the way that warranted boredom differs from other warranted emotions.

Things aren't boring in the way they are pitiful or enraging or enviable. In these latter cases, the warrant, if there is one, is entirely within the objects themselves—the suffering of some being, the extremity of a wrong, the greater good fortune of another. By contrast, things can become boring without any change in the things themselves. The psychotherapy patient's narrative isn't boring on first hearing, but ten sessions in, the same narrative is boring. Our ends, if Millgram is right, are not boring when we choose them; they become boring over time simply in virtue of continuing to be our same ends, not in virtue of any change in the worthiness of those ends. Or consider Bernard Williams's assessment of why immortality would be boring. He takes up the fictional character, Elina Makropulos, whose biological age has been frozen at forty-two and whose character remains the same. In Williams's view, what makes immortality unlivable for her, and what explains her refusal, after 342 years of life, to keep taking the drug that keeps her alive is that "everything that could happen and make sense to one particular human being of 42 [of a certain sort of character] had already

[15] Bernstein, "Boredom and the Ready-Made Life," 528–29, 531.
[16] Lars Svendsen, A Philosophy of Boredom, trans. John Irons (London: Reaktion, 2005). See also Sean Desmond Healy, Boredom, Self, and Culture (Cranbury, NJ: Fairleigh Dickinson University Press, 1984); and Goodstein, Experience Without Qualities.

happened to her."[17] In these cases, it is the repetition of more of the same that warrants boredom. But why would more of the same be so unwelcome? It won't do to say that repetitiveness, monotony, and lack of novelty just are boring, and if extended eternally, are unbearably boring. One wants to know how sheer repetition could have this effect on evaluators. There is surely a place where explanation runs out, but to stop at "repetition is boring" is to stop too soon. One wants to know what this says about the way evaluators engage with value qualities. An adequate analysis of boredom should shed light on the puzzling transformation of the interesting into the boring via repetition.

The Amount of Postmodern Boredom Is a Problem

A third strategy for rendering boredom interesting enough to warrant theoretical reflection depends not on singling out an especially dramatic (because pathological or existential) form of boredom but, rather, in locating the drama in the historical emergence and proliferation of boredom. Boredom is a problem because the world didn't used to be so boring. It is now, and is increasingly so. The principal basis for the claim that the premodern world was not so boring is etymological. *Bore* enters the English vocabulary in mid-eighteenth century and *boring* in mid-nineteenth century. Different authors cite different complexes of causal factors for the modern origin and postmodern escalation of boredom.[18] Included on the roster are: the loss of a theological or tradition-based ground for attributing meaning and value to activities; a shift in the conception of time from meaningful natural and cultural rhythms to a sequence of identical quantifiable moments; the Industrial Revolution's separation of work from leisure and the regimentation of the workday, which increases boredom at work and introduces the problem of what to do with leisure time; and the expansion of affluence and leisure time that places the problem of free time at the doorstep of more people.

Those more interested in contemporary contributions to the veritable plague of boredom cite the blandness and repetitiveness of urban design (including housing developments and strip malls); the American quest for certainty and predictability; a decline in the difficulty, discomfort, and inconvenience of life; mass produced and disposable goods; multitasking; and the accelerated tempo of modern life.[19]

[17] Bernard Williams, "The Makropulos Case: Reflections on the Tedium of Immortality," in his *Problems of the Self: Philosophical Papers 1956–1972* (Cambridge: Cambridge University Press, 1973), 82–100.
[18] Healy, *Boredom, Self, and Culture*; Svendsen, *Philosophy of Boredom*; Goodstein, *Experience Without Qualities*; Spacks, *Boredom: The Literary History*; Yasmine Musharbash, "Boredom, Time, and Modernity: An Example from Aboriginal Australia," *American Anthropologist* 109, no. 2 (2007): 307–317.
[19] See, for example, Dennis Brissett and Robert P. Snow, "Boredom: Where the Future Isn't," *Symbolic Interaction* 16, no. 3 (1993): 237–256.

This boredom-as-problem approach comes closer than the previous two approaches to illuminating a connection between boredom and the lives of evaluators, or at least the lives of postmodern evaluators. If the world itself has become more boring, evaluators today will have a much tougher time escaping boredom than did evaluators in earlier eras.

One might wonder, however, about the truth of the claim that the world is more boring. The principal bit of evidence—that the word *boring* came into use in the mid-nineteenth century—might indicate that premodern people were less bored. But that etymological fact is compatible with two other hypotheses. First, premodern people might have felt bored but simply lacked the label "boredom" for that feeling. While leisure may bore *us*, so we have more of *that* kind of boredom than premoderns, there may well have been other aspects of the premodern world that would have made premodern life equally, though differently, boring—say, hours-long Masses in a language one doesn't understand, or potatoes for dinner every day. Perhaps they lacked the label "boring" for those long, incomprehensible Masses or those all-too-familiar potatoes because they organized their psychological space differently—for example, in terms of *boredom*'s and the *boring*'s historical predecessors, *ennui* and *acedia*, and *tiresome* and *wearisome*. Or perhaps it is because, as Patricia Spacks suggests, they had other terms of appraisal that, for them, adequately did the work of our "it's boring."[20] In short, premoderns could have been bored in the absence of a label, in just the same way that they might have had diabetes or suffered posttraumatic stress disorder in the absence of the labels "diabetes" or "PTSD."

A second, compatible hypothesis is that while premodern people did not feel bored, the world in fact had just as many boring features then as it does now. Here, the case would be similar to that of other recently constructed notions such as *human right* and *childhood*; while premoderns lacked such concepts and found neither human rights violations nor childhoods in their world, we might nevertheless think that such terms had application—for example, that women's human rights were violated when they were burned as witches or that children in premodern eras were typically deprived of their childhoods. If so, the proliferation of boredom is to be credited to a modern

---

[20] "That the word has not always existed, has not even existed for long, suggests not necessarily that the experience is new but at least that the concept has not always been necessary" (Spacks, *Boredom*, 23). Spacks observes that there might well have been just as many occasions for boredom in pre-"boredom" eras, but that other terms of interpretation and criticism did the needed work—ones, for example, that did not depend on attunement to inner psychic states or evaluative weight placed on the importance of individual happiness (9–10). What changes in the modern era is a new focus on the individual, including the interior states of the individual—her pleasures, pains, happiness, unhappiness—as well as a sense of a right not only to pursue happiness but also to be happy. "The inner life comes to be seen as consequential; therefore its inadequacies invite attention. The concept of boredom serves as an all-purpose register of inadequacy" (23).

discovery about the way the world is, not to a special problem with the modern and postmodern worlds.

Even granting the hypothesis that the world has become more boring, the specific features of modern and postmodern life cited to explain the emergence of boredom as a problem worthy of a name are puzzling. How could both regimented workdays *and* leisure be principal causes of boredom? If what is boring about regimented workdays is that one is told what to do, when to do it, how to do it, and when to stop doing it, one would think that unregimented leisure would be a principal source of relief from boredom. What are evaluators thinking when they complain that being told what to do with their time *and* that being free to decide for themselves what to do with their time produce boredom? An adequate account of boredom should shed some light on why both regimented and leisure time bore.

Boredom and the Loss of Evaluative Meaning

The claim that boredom has proliferated since the modern period is based not only on an etymological fact and facts about changes in the organization of human life activities. It is also based on observations about how our thinking about the world has changed. The most often cited difference is the loss of a theological grounding of value and meaning. The world bores because everything is, ultimately, meaningless and without value. But surely this is neither a correct description of how value and meaning are now understood nor a correct description of what the bored usually mean when they complain that what they do with their lives lacks meaning.

Rather than evacuating the world of meaning and value, skepticism about an external grounding of meaning and value occasioned a shift toward connecting value and meaning to human valuing activities, valuing activities reflected in individuals' feelings, and a human sense of what matters. Tighter connections between value, valuing activities, and a human sense of what matters opened up a space for thinking not only about what might be valuable or meaningful from an impersonal or divine standpoint but also what might be personally meaningful to individual evaluators—a meaning for which individual feelings might seem an especially reliable indicator. The subjects in Richard Bargdill's study of life boredom, for example, did not complain of there being no ultimate reason to value one thing over another; theirs is not an existential boredom. Rather, they complained of being stuck in lives that are not the ones they want for themselves and that they ended up with after having "compromised their personal goals for less desirable projects."[21] In short, while granting that boredom is

[21] Richard W. Bargdill, "The Study of Life Boredom," *Journal of Phenomenological Psychology* 31, no. 2 (2000): 188–219, 200.

an evaluative attitude that sometimes registers the lack of value in or meaninglessness of what one spends time with, one might doubt that most boredom can be traced to a modern crisis of value and meaning.

Analyses that connect boredom tightly to absence of meaning face two further difficulties. First, as Millgram noted, what individuals find meaningful sometimes bores. Lars Svendsen confesses at the beginning of his book on boredom, "I have never been so bored as when I was in the process of completing a large dissertation after several years of work. The work bored me so much that I had to mobilize all my will in order to continue, and all that I felt in doing so was a tremendous tiredness."[22] Perhaps he had come to find the project worthless or no longer personally meaningful; he doesn't say. But it's also common for people involved in long-term projects to forge ahead through boredom precisely because they regard their projects as worthwhile and personally meaningful; they're simply bored with it at the moment. And this suggests that an adequate account of boredom may need to specify a plurality of sources of boredom rather than reducing it to a single source—loss of the specific sort of meaning that comes from doing what one takes to be worthwhile.

Second, boredom often motivates indulgence in meaningless activities. This is puzzling if what the bored suffer from and wish to escape is loss of meaning. Consider this confession: "When I get real bored, I like to drive downtown and get a great parking spot, then sit in my car and count how many people ask me if I'm leaving."[23] Or, this confession from a grad student bored with working on her dissertation:

> Whenever I forced myself to go to school, instead of working, I would sit there and get on the internet and read *inane* chat groups that were going on. I read so many newsgroups: I knew what was going on in the Simpson's group and would talk to these people for an hour, sometimes six hours a day. How ridiculous is that? . . .
>
> I thought it was ridiculous that I did that. I still think I sort of wasted time; four to eight hours a day reading these stupid little comments on the computer screen. There's no meaning in that. I thought it was stupid. My time would have been much better spent reading a book.[24]

If the problem is absence of meaning, it's hard to see why these particular choices of escape—along with gambling, delinquency, crime, social conflict, overeating, alcohol

---

[22] Svendsen, *Philosophy of Boredom*, 35.

[23] Steven Wright, quoted in Jon Winokur, *Ennui to Go: The Art of Boredom* (Seattle, WA: Sasquatch Books), 133.

[24] Bargdill, "Study of Life Boredom," 210–211 (italics in the original).

and drug abuse, risk-taking, horseplay, gossiping, doodling, and daydreaming—would be such common responses to boredom. One might respond that those who turn to meaningless diversions are those who have no other options or who mistakenly opt for "*ersatz* meaning."[25] But this is not universally true, and I suspect not even commonly true. The grad student is well aware that what she does is meaningless and that she has the option of doing something more meaningful, like reading a book. Even for those who have no other options, there remains the question of why things like doodling and eating answer boredom *at all*. Why not instead do nothing, rather than something else that's just as meaningless? Or, why not just go to sleep? An adequate account of boredom needs to explain both boredom with what one takes to be a worthwhile project and the attraction of meaningless diversions.

We now have a set of puzzles to address, in addition to our original question, "How might attention to boredom illuminate the difficulties inherent in leading the life of an evaluator?" Those puzzles include: "Why might normative delinquencies be an especially attractive method of escaping boredom?" "Why is more of the same boring?" "If meaningless activities are boring, then why do the bored try to escape boredom through meaningless activities?" "Why do both regimented and leisure time often bore?"

Without claiming to offer an exhaustive typology of boredom, I think that answers to these particular questions emerge from a focus on some of the prime boring circumstances: a stalled life, normative constraints on action, satiety and disappointment with value experiences, and leisure.

THE CIRCUMSTANCES OF BOREDOM

Stalled Lives

One kind of meaning whose absence bores is *temporal* meaning. And one kind of "more of the same" that bores is more of the same going nowhere in a life or part of a life one expected or hoped would go somewhere. That is, stalled lives bore. When a person's life stalls, what actually happens in that life is incompatible with its having the trajectory the person assumed or hoped her life would have. Sometimes the best option for escape from the boredom of "more of the same going nowhere" is wasting time in meaningless activities that are not supposed to go anywhere.

Temporal meaning differs from evaluative meaning. *Kinds* of activities or projects have evaluative meaning when judged to be worthwhile, valuable kinds of things to do. So, we might say that getting an education or reading a morally rich book like

[25] Svendsen, *Philosophy of Boredom*, 26.

J. M. Coetzee's *Disgrace* has evaluative meaning.[26] Specific *activities in the present* have temporal meaning when they are constituent parts of a temporal trajectory. To see one's life as having a trajectory is to see present doings and experiences as pointing toward a desired future and deriving their meaningfulness from, as Karen Jones puts it, what happens "elsewhen."[27] Located on a trajectory, present doings and happenings take on such temporal meanings as being "a present actualization of . . . ," "causally instrumental to . . . ," "a necessary waiting period before . . . ," "a temporary setback from . . . ," and "the next in the sequence of. . . ." Some trajectories are goal-directed— for example, earning a degree; others are progressive—for example, improving one's Spanish; still others are continuations— for example, enjoying retirement. Some trajectories are life trajectories; others are not, either because their temporal span is too limited to characterize what a life (or even a phase of a life) is about or because the trajectory is not sufficiently dominant (for example, it is just one among a plurality of long-range trajectories of similar importance).

Trajectories stall in a variety of ways. Some stall when the agent exhausts her resources for effecting the trajectory. Margaret, the math graduate student, for example, takes herself to be on a goal-directed trajectory in which she proceeds from research, to solving the theoretical problem posed by her dissertation, to receiving a Ph.D. At a point early on, she exhausts her resources for effecting that trajectory and instead spends day after day reading and rereading the same source material, hoping for miraculous inspiration. Or, consider another of Bargdill's subjects, a woman who spends her adult life raising children, which she finds unsatisfying, and remaining married to a man she describes as an emotionally abusive "beast" who undermines all her efforts to be happy. One might imagine she hopes to be on a progressivist "things will get better" trajectory—the children will grow up, her marital problems will be resolved, she will find ways of being happy. Located on a progressivist trajectory, present unhappiness acquires temporal meaning as merely a stage in a trajectory toward a better future. Over the course of time, however, this woman exhausts her resources for effecting that trajectory, as well as her hopes that something will change. She says of her life, "It's like you take a train, and you have a long ride, and you come to the end, and where do you go? There's nothing for you, nobody for you. It's like a big empty room. What do you do? Lay down and die."[28]

Some trajectories stall because the person sets a trajectory that exceeds any resources he has or might develop; or because his life circumstances preclude envisioning his life

---

[26] J. M. Coetzee, *Disgrace* (New York: Viking, 1999).

[27] Karen Jones, "How to Change the Past," in *Practical Identity and Narrative Agency*, ed. Catriona MacKenzie and Kim Atkins (New York: Routledge, 2008), 269–287.

[28] Bargdill, "Study of Life Boredom," 199.

on a trajectory in the first place. One of Aaron Esman's adolescent patients, Jonathan, sets a trajectory for himself that so far outstrips his abilities that it stalls out immediately. Jonathan "imagined himself the modern successor and rival of Joyce, Yeats, and Pound," but he is utterly unwilling to expend the time and effort to learn the craft of writing.[29] Unwilling to give up his idea of his life's trajectory, he stalls out in a present that is in fact going nowhere.

Stalled lives promise to go on as more of the same that isn't going anywhere. Decisions and actions—such as Margaret's deciding sometimes to struggle with her dissertation and sometimes to avoid it—come to have less the character of moving oneself into the future than of prolonging the present. Present actions and happenings lose their temporal meaning. Describing his subjects, Bargdill says, "they could no longer see themselves making progress toward their futures";[30] "they were no longer throwing forward possibilities."[31] Feeling trapped in a persistent present that is divorced from a trajectory into the future, Bargdill's subjects responded to their life boredom by avoiding doing anything to change their circumstances, absorbing themselves in the immediate present, and passively hoping that something would just happen to change things. Brissett and Snow nicely sum up the hopelessness of this sort of boredom: "Boredom is the preoccupation, non-appreciation, and or disinterest in what one already has and the loss of a sense of future possibilities for intention and choice and a leaning into the future."[32]

At one level, escaping the boredom of a stalled life via meaningless diversions makes sense. Reading chat room comments and counting how many people ask if one intends to leave one's parking space aren't supposed to go anywhere. So, too, cruising, wandering, and "indulging in vast amounts of amorphous unstructured time" such as playing cards, as the Walpiri Aborigines do in apparent efforts to escape life boredom, restructures time in terms of activities that aren't supposed to go anywhere and whose significance is wholly complete within the present moment.[33] Lacking a temporal meaning that could be lost, these seem perfect escapes for the bored who are burdened by the experience of their lives as more of the same failure to move forward. "When I lose my vision," says a Bargdill subject, "I lose any idea or projection of what I want to do in the future. I don't have any distinct plans, or even an idea of what I want to do and so I want to immerse myself more in the present rather than projecting myself in the future."

[29] Aaron H. Esman, "Some Reflections on Boredom," *Journal of the American Psychoanalytic Association* 27, no. 2 (1979): 423–439, 429.
[30] Bargdill, "Study of Life Boredom," 197.
[31] Ibid., 199.
[32] Brissett and Snow, "Boredom: Where the Future Isn't," 240.
[33] Musharbash, "Boredom, Time, and Modernity."

For those unwilling or unable to reorient their lives on a trajectory that could go somewhere, shifting to present-bound activities may be the best route out of boredom. Unfortunately, present-bound activities remain open to temporal redescription as occurring within a life trajectory that has stalled: one surfs the Internet as part of a stalled trajectory. So, as Bargdill discovered, boredom with a stalled life trajectory tends to infect trajectory-independent activities. "Presently, I am bored with my whole life. None of the old things I used to do bring enjoyment to me anymore. Nothing. [Boredom] covers my social life. It covers school. It covers work. It covers going to the grocery store. . . . It covers a lot of things. My hair."[34]

It is tempting to lay the fault for life boredom at the doorstep of the bored: sticking with a stalled trajectory appears to be a form of practical irrationality. Margaret could change her dissertation topic rather than hide from her advisers and waste time in chat rooms. The married woman could disentangle herself from the "beast." Jonathan could set his sights more realistically or work harder at the craft of writing.

Possibly. But "fault" may reside instead with the fact that there is no guarantee all the demands of practical rationality can be met simultaneously. One of the difficulties evaluators face is that they must select ends that are both evaluatively worth having and prudentially advisable (because the ends match their competencies, make good use of their resources, and are ones for which the person is willing to take the necessary instrumental means). Prudential considerations may narrow the range of reasonable ends to ones not sufficiently worth having to count as one's life going somewhere. Worthwhileness considerations may narrow the range of ends that would make one's life go somewhere acceptable to ends beyond one's abilities to achieve. Attending either choice is the risk one's life will stall. Margaret prioritizes prudence at the expense of worthwhileness. She adjusts her sights downward from a preferred topic that she finds personally worthwhile to one both she and her advisers believe she is well suited for.[35] Disengaged from the subject, her life stalls. Jonathan prioritizes worthwhileness at the expense of prudence. He sets an end he finds worth having, but it is well beyond his present competences and motivational resources; his life stalls. Moreover, whether such stalled lives are best handled by cutting one's losses or by sticking it out is often underdetermined by the available evidence. In short, boredom with a stalled life need not originate in some failure of practical rationality.

[34] Bargdill, "Study of Life Boredom," 198.
[35] Her dissertation was on a topic that extended a project she had worked on for a year prior as a research assistant; her work on that earlier project proceeded quickly and successfully; her dissertation project involved writing computer code that she was good at; she had done well in the classes most related to her dissertation; and although she stalled on her dissertation project, if she changed topics she would lose a lot of time.

Among those most vulnerable to losing the temporal meaning of their present activities, and thus to suffering stalled-life boredom, are persons who structure and understand their lives in terms of dominant, long-term aims. (They are even more vulnerable if having those aims involves risky dependencies on favorable turns of events, others' cooperation, and uncertain competencies and motivational resources.) Less vulnerable to loss of temporal meaning are those who structure and understand their lives in terms of a plurality of minor aims that individually and collectively are not construed as one's life trajectory. Also less vulnerable are those whose aims are easily met and for whom "more of the same" signifies "having arrived" rather than "going nowhere," and is thus a source of contentment rather than boredom.

Normative Constraint

Attending to the specific kind of boredom produced by stalled lives gives us one set of answers to the questions, "Why does more of the same bore?" "Why might those engaged in evaluatively meaningful projects nevertheless be bored?" and "How can meaningless diversions answer the needs of the bored?" Attending to the specific kind of boredom that arises in contexts of normative constraint suggests an explanation for a different, puzzling feature of boredom: "Why would normative delinquencies serve as an especially attractive escape from boredom?"

Otto Fenichel, the psychoanalyst whose observations on boredom heavily influenced subsequent psychoanalytic and psychological accounts of pathological boredom, observed that normal boredom "arises when we must not do what we want to do, or must do what we do not want to do."[36] While not all boredom arises this way, Fenichel is surely right that a great deal of ordinary boredom originates in contexts of normative constraint. Norms of etiquette require that we patiently and attentively listen to boring conversation partners. Work requirements include attending boring meetings and doing boring tasks. Schoolchildren often complain of being bored by what they are required to study in school. While what comes most readily to mind are times when we feel forced by externally imposed normative constraints to do what we don't want to do, we also bring about our own boredom through our willing compliance with self-imposed norms. Because we accept norms of instrumental rationality, we willingly choose to do what, while useful in getting us what we want, is in itself boring. We wait in lines for cappuccinos, floss our teeth, and memorize the driver's handbook for the licensing exam. Accepting norms of self-discipline and self-improvement, we practice scales, do daily workout routines, and spend time repeating simple-minded sentences on foreign language tapes. Because we accept norms of beneficence, we choose to do

[36] Fenichel, "On the Psychology of Boredom," 301.

good deeds that involve boring things, like inventorying donated clothes or baking 500 samosas for a cultural event. And our own commitments to participating in valued projects, relationships, and ways of life may entail extended or frequent periods of "compulsory" boredom. Recall, for example, Lars Svendsen's confession that he had never been so bored as while he was completing a large dissertation project.

Psychoanalytic and psychoanalytically influenced work on boredom sometimes defines boredom as a stressor, in the same league with anxiety,[37] which is connected to both frustration and rage. If one focuses on, say, leisure-time boredom when the boredom is often connected to not knowing what one wants to do and not being particularly attracted to anything, it's hard to see how boredom could be a stressor or connected with anxiety or rage. Boredom in contexts of normative constraint—especially when the constraints are externally imposed (through, say, threats of penalties for noncompliance) rather than self-imposed—however, does fit this description. When one is compelled to do what one doesn't want to do, especially when what one is compelled to do serves no apparent good purpose or when those imposing the constraint lack legitimate authority to do so, frustration and anger—and hence, stress—would seem natural responses. Toward the end of her narrative of her own life boredom, Margaret shifts from narrating her own reasons for imposing her particular thesis topic on herself to a narrative of external imposition: "I sort of felt like I had been forced into the situation [by her dissertation advisors]—like it wasn't of my own choosing to work on this problem. In fact, I think I felt resentment toward them because I felt that they sort of pushed me into this problem and it was easier for them and they wanted someone to work on it. So they picked me and why did they have to pick me?"[38]

One source of frustration when boredom arises under conditions of normative constraint is that one knows what one would rather be doing. The many bumper stickers that proclaim "I'd rather be ___ing" are perhaps testimony to how much boredom is suffered by people who experience what they have to do as depriving them of time to expend on what they want to do.[39] Even when the boredom-generating normative constraints are self-imposed, one may feel that one's life is being used up rather than lived (for example, by all the tasks one dutifully volunteers to do in order to be a workplace good citizen). This, I think, explains the attraction of normative delinquencies.

For those whose boredom is engendered by the "have to dos" and the "ought to dos" in their lives, rebellion against boredom might naturally find its outlet in normative delinquencies that violate the specific normative constraints engendering boredom.

---

[37] J. M. Barbalet says that "there is broad agreement that boredom is a type of anxiety." Barbalet, "Boredom and Social Meaning," *British Journal of Sociology* 50, no. 4 (December 1999): 631–646, 636.

[38] Bargdill, "Study of Life Boredom," 217.

[39] I confess, I have a bumper sticker in this genre: "Born to ride, forced to go to school."

Recall Margaret who sounded a bit puzzled about why she chose to escape boredom by reading inane chat room comments rather than reading a book. Her boredom stems, in part, from her feeling that she has to read dissertation-related material: "If I finished this [thesis] I could enjoy the things I used to enjoy. I would be free to study other things that interested me. I certainly felt like I wasn't free, freed from this obligation, free from thinking that I had to work on this all the time or else I'd have to feel guilty about it."[40] Reading a good but wrong book would violate the normative constraint that chains her to her dissertation; reading something totally noneducational and utterly inane violates it better.

Escaping boredom by refusing the terms of boredom—namely, the externally and self-imposed "have to dos" and "ought to dos"—may also explain the attraction of criminality, alcohol and drug abuse, gambling, overeating, and social conflict. One needn't search normative delinquencies for something that makes them evaluatively or temporally meaningful activities in order to explain their being satisfying escapes.[41] More plausibly, the satisfaction of the escape resides in one's refusing to do (at least temporarily) the "has to be done" that bores.

As in the case of stalled-life boredom, one might be tempted to lay the fault for boredom under conditions of normative constraint at the doorstop of the bored. First, many conflicts between complying with normative constraints and doing what interests one are avoidable. Students can often choose to fulfill educational requirements in ways that are likely to interest them. Workers can choose career paths and jobs in which the regimentation of the workday is more, rather than less, likely to involve tasks the worker finds interesting. The beneficent can elect to discharge their duty of beneficence in more, rather than less, interesting ways. And those who find that their commitments are producing considerable boredom can reset their commitments in more interesting directions (this was Millgram's assumption about what boredom would motivate those bored with their final ends to do).

Although people sometimes do bear responsibility for making their lives more boring than they need be, boredom is also a normal hazard of leading a life that is normatively constrained in all sorts of ways. One of the common difficulties that evaluators face is that in choosing to comply with moral and nonmoral normative requirements, as well as choosing to commit themselves to valuable projects, relationships, and ways of life, they create the very conditions that engender boredom—namely, the paucity of anything here and now that engages an evaluator's attention. Hence, the feeling that

---

[40] Bargdill, "Study of Life Boredom," 217.
[41] Barbalet ("Boredom and Social Meaning"), for example, tries to read gambling and social conflict as attempts to introduce meaning into one's life.

one isn't really living one's life at the present moment but, rather, postponing real life until some future, more engaging moment.

The difficulty here is not a problem to be solved through better practical reasoning. To be an evaluator is to have the capacity to set aside the pursuit of what engages an evaluator's attention in favor of complying with prudential, moral, and social norms. To be an evaluator is also to have the capacity to steer one's life in accord with values attaching to temporally extended activities and temporally remote aims—values that by their nature are not given in present experience and activity. Both compliance with norms and pursuit of temporally extended activities or temporally remote aims are compatible with the paucity of anything here and now that engages an evaluator's attention, interest, and concern. Boredom, as I suggest in the next section, registers the absence of value qualities *in the present* that are worthy of an evaluator's attention.

Prolonged submission to normative constraints—for example, to the constraints imposed by commitment to career success—may increase one's vulnerability to boredom. Worse, prolonged deferment of questions about what would be engaging if free of such constraints may render one unfit for later answering them. Aaron Esman, for example, observes of one of his patients, a former businessman who now finds his retirement boring, that "[h]is monolithic life of work did not permit him—or the legions of those like him—to develop interests and skills needed to cope with endless leisure," or as I would say, to cope with freedom from normative constraints.[42] A similar fate may be in store for those for whom the practical questions "What do I need to do?" "What do I have to do?" and "What ought I to do?" dominate their planning, crowding out questions like "What would be interesting to do?" In light of this, Brissett and Snow's advice for the bored sounds like good advice:

> Surely people can change their consciousness and thus their experience and appreciation of the dance of life. But it seems to us that the best bet is behavior: doing things differently; on some occasions not doing anything at all; doing things that do not appear to count for much; doing things where the outcome is uncertain if not unpredictable. Perhaps the best antidote for boredom is what Georg Simmel (1991 [sic]) called "the adventure."[43]

---

[42] Esman, "Some Reflections on Boredom," 432.

[43] Brissett and Snow, "Boredom: Where the Future Isn't," 252. They offer this advice because they believe that *certainty* about the future produces boredom. They may be right. But the advice applies also to the forms of certainty about the future that are the result of the normative dominating—indeed, consuming—one's thinking about how to live one's life. The reference to Georg Simmel is to his essay "The Adventure," in *Georg Simmel: On Individuality and Social Forms*, ed. Donald N. Levine (Chicago: University of Chicago Press, 1971)

Value Disappointment

Examining the boredom created by stalled lives and suffered under normative constraints suggests a general account of boredom: to be bored is to find present activities and experiences not worth an evaluator's attention. This is not simply the platitude that the uninteresting bores. Boredom responds to the insufficiency of temporally indexed value qualities—qualities attaching to present activities and experiences. That insufficiency is not simple demerits on some scale of value. What is outrageously bad, disgusting, or appallingly unfair is typically not boring. Nor is it simply a failure to generate a specific psychological attitude called "being interested." Rather, the insufficiency is specifically *insufficiency for engaging a person's evaluation-related capacities*. Evaluation-related capacities include desire and aversion, attentiveness, close inspection, positive or negative value ranking, storing in memory, acting upon, deciding how to deal with, assessing the degree of relevance to one's ends or instrumental resources, and so on.[44] Finding their present insufficient to engage them as evaluators, the bored find themselves unable both to pay attention and to be fully in the here and now.

Because boredom is only one of a plurality of temporal attitudes that evaluators can adopt toward their activities and experiences, the insufficiency of present value qualities to engage one's attention isn't inevitably boring. Past- or future-oriented temporal attitudes enable disattention to the present in favor of those of the past's or future's value qualities. The despairing, the fretful, the regretful, the guilt-ridden, the eagerly or hopefully anticipatory, the goal-directed planners, and the task-oriented project themselves into futures or relive pasts, disattending the present.

That evaluators have past- and future-directed temporal attitudes by which to avoid present boredom does not mean they ought to make use of those attitudes to escape boredom. Evaluators who properly care about the quality of their lives and how they are leading them will care not just about where to head their lives and where their lives have been but also about how to fill the present. A significant amount of everyday decision making concerns what sorts of value qualities to spend time with and how best to ensure one does so. Consider accepting a party invitation, planning a trip to the natural history museum, or selecting library books to check out. Unlike decisions and plans that aim to achieve something of value—say, the completion of home repairs—these decisions and plans aim at spending time with particular value qualities. The goal of planning a trip to a museum is to put oneself in a position to participate in a variety of activities that share the same value quality.

---

[44] Barbalet usefully describes boredom as "a feeling of not being involved in or engaged by events or activities" ("Boredom and Social Meaning," 634).

At the museum, you will see the dinosaur skeletons, look at the bird exhibits, examine trays of insects, and peruse the North American mammals diorama. The entire museum outing is aimed at spending time with what is cognitively enriching and perhaps also wondrous.

However, in choosing which value qualities to spend time with in the present, evaluators run the risk of creating the very boredom they hope to avoid. Indeed, much of what bores does so precisely because we bring to our present experience expectations about what we will find. That is, in choosing to spend time with anticipated value qualities, we set ourselves up for disappointment.

Part of what we are doing in choosing to spend time with a value isn't just predicting what will engage our attention but also stipulating in advance the value qualities (for example, the quality of "spiritually uplifting" in a sermon) and their degrees (for example, what could be expected of this pastor) that the experience or activity must have in order to engage our attention. That we find things interesting or boring is thus in part a function of what we decide in advance to invest our interest in. Such decisions set the conditions under which we will allow ourselves to be interested. The sermon, for example, turns out to be disappointingly boring in comparison with what we anticipated. It is no surprise, then, that on any plausible list of what people complain that they've been bored by, there will be the very things they chose to spend time with in the expectation that these things will engage their attention: parties, movies, novels, television shows, sports matches, dates, sex, vacations, classes, sermons, and historical tours, to mention only a few. (Expectation frames play an important role in chapter 7's exploration of contentment and discontentment.)

Snobs make themselves especially vulnerable to boredom, in part by setting the bar very high for what they are willing to take an interest in and in part by narrowly circumscribing the range of value qualities with which they are willing to engage. Those who set the bar lower or with less specificity do less to set themselves up for boredom. But even here, the expectation of finding something engaging may invite disappointment, engendering boredom. Least vulnerable to boredom are those with extremely low or nonexistent value expectations, who leave themselves open to engagement with whatever presents itself.

Again, as in the other circumstances of boredom, the difficulty here is not necessarily a practical problem to be solved. Part of leading the life of an evaluator is making decisions about what to invest one's interest in. The snob whose standards are high, rather than misguided, may not make a worse choice than the person with low or unspecific standards, even if high standards make boredom more difficult to avoid. Moreover, any evaluator who makes plans to spend time with and anticipates engaging with value qualities runs the risk of disappointed boredom.

Value Satiety

But what about monotony and repetition? Surely, the largest share of boredom is generated not by disappointed expectations but by one's having done, seen, heard, read, felt, or otherwise experienced something so many times that it now bores. This was Williams's worry about immortality. If you have a character at all, this will limit your range of choices and responses; and given endless time, your life will eventually repeat itself, and repeat itself too many times not to be boring. The course of your relationships, for example, will lose the character of adventure and surprise and "take on a character of being inescapable"—a sure recipe for boredom.[45] The boredom of repetition was also Millgram's prognosis for everyone's ends and was his reason for rejecting Frankfurt's identification of the agent with her present constellation of ends: "One is bound to get bored with whatever ends, ideas, or concerns one now has."[46] Refashioning oneself by selectioning new ends is a good way of forestalling boredom. And on a more mundane level, one might think that a sure sign of cognitive development is that countless repetitions of the same story or same movie cease to entertain, the way they do entertain children, and come to be boring.

Why does repetition bore? The best explanation is that value qualities are *consumable* items in the life of evaluators. The fact that evaluators consume value qualities remains out of philosophical sight so long as concern focuses on the value-ranking and end-setting activities of evaluators, rather than on those evaluators' temporal experience of value qualities. The former philosophical concerns largely skirt the question of what it is like to be an evaluator who conducts her life in time.[47] In spending time with a value quality, one may use it up.

"Using up," of course, does not mean that the activity in question has any fewer value qualities at the end of one's time with it than it did at the beginning. A museum exhibit has the same educational value, measured in terms of the quality of its displays and informational signs, when boredom sets in as it did pre-boredom. Learning Spanish is just as worthy an end after one has become bored with the endeavor as when one chose to learn the language. A thing's bearing value qualities and an evaluator's "making use" of those value qualities are two different things. Evaluators make use of—in the sense of doing something with or engaging with—value qualities when they rate, appreciate, investigate, contemplate, fantasize about, think what to do with, hope for, worry about, take seriously as calling for action, plan for how to realize, and aim at

---

[45] Williams, "The Makropulos Case," 90.
[46] Millgram, "On Being Bored Out of Your Mind," 179.
[47] One notable exception is the observation that evaluative judgments commit the agent to cross-temporal policies about what to count as a deliberative consideration and how to rank that consideration against others.

value qualities (to mention only some of the things evaluators do with value qualities). Making plans to see a sunset, contemplating the atmospheric conditions that produce its colors, appreciating its beauty, and telling others about its splendid colors are ways of doing something with the sunset's value qualities.

Evaluators, however, rarely if ever have inexhaustible capacities for doing something with the value qualities they encounter. They get done with the doing. They come to the end, for example, of their capacity to appreciate, or they run out of things they can think of to do with this thing. Elina Makropulos runs out of things she can think of to do with personal relationships. She still might judge relationships to have value, even to be personally valuable to her (she'd like to have personal relationships in her life, if she's going to have a life). But she's exhausted her capacities as an evaluator to do something with the value qualities of relationships.

What gets used up, then, isn't the value quality itself but the capacity to engage with it as an evaluator—sometimes only temporarily, sometimes permanently. This is to say that one doesn't get bored just because one has lost interest. One loses interest because the object of boredom does not satisfy one's basic interest as an evaluator. To be an evaluator is to want to do something with value qualities. A machine that is programmed to generate what we would regard as reasonably accurate value assessments on the basis of descriptive information is not an evaluator. Evaluators have, in addition to ranking abilities, a basic drive to do something with value qualities. Sometimes the world disappoints, failing to present value qualities worth our doing something with. At other times, the difficulty is that we have used up our capacity to engage with a value quality. Repetition then bores.

When their ends bore them, what ought evaluators to do? They might take the ability to engage with some things but not with others as a brute, inalterable fact about themselves. They simply find that they care about some things; and they simply find that they have ceased so to care about others. If our being interested in some things but bored by others were just a brute fact, then interest and boredom would provide the foundation for selecting and revising ends.. Boredom with ends means, as Millgram implies, that it's time to select new ones.

I think this is false. Engagement often depends on a scaffolding of prior learning and experience that prepares us to take an interest in what initially was not interesting. Whether the appropriate scaffolding is in place or not is, at least in part, up to us. The uninitiated who find watching the Olympic dressage events comparable to watching paint dry are not without options for learning how to engage with the sport. "Be patient; stick with it; give it a chance" is standard advice for those trying out worthwhile activities that initially bore. The scaffolding that prepares us to engage at all may also prepare us to adopt as an end what we've learned to engage with. And when an end later comes to bore us, updating the scaffolding is an option. The point here is that while there are evidently limits to our ability to engineer engagement, voluntary choice and fortuitous experience have an appreciable influence on what we find ourselves capable of engaging with.

One difficulty faced by evaluators bored with their ends is epistemic: one cannot say for sure whether boredom is permanent, temporary, or remediable with additional scaffolding. What, for example, does Elina Makropulos's boredom with relationships signify? That she has fully consumed the possible value qualities of relationships? That, having fully consumed the possible value qualities of the kinds of relationships she has had to date, she might nevertheless be fortuitously surprised by her experiences in the next one? That additional scaffolding—say, a new perspective provided by therapy—could remedy her boredom? That her boredom is only temporary and remediable by taking a vacation from romance, perhaps a long one (after all, she has time)?

A second difficulty faced by evaluators bored with their ends is normative: the objects of ends are also typically objects of commitment. That is, they are fixed as ends not simply in virtue of a contingent yet deep and persistent caring but also as a matter of chosen policy to resist redeliberation and to treat various obstacles and setbacks to pursuit of those ends as problems to be dealt with, rather than as evidence against retaining those ends. If one's ends are indeed objects of commitment, then boredom, even persistent boredom, does not provide obvious grounds for revisiting one's commitment in the same way that persistent boredom would provide grounds for reassessing more provisionally adopted ends.

As I argued in chapter 5, people might reasonably have different temporal styles of managing their own futures, some pursuing ends as only provisional plans, open to revision in light of setbacks and obstacles, and others by making commitments that resist revision. What evaluators ought to do when their ends persistently bore them depends in large measure on what temporal style they have adopted for managing their futures. For those attracted to commitment, persistent boredom is clearly not a good reason for abandoning an end rather than living with boredom.

Leisure

I turn now to one last principal life circumstance that generates boredom: leisure. One of the more commonly cited explanations of postmodern boredom is the emergence of a cultural distinction between work and leisure, as well as, for some individuals, increasing quantities of leisure time. The distinction between work and leisure in modern life is structural—life activities are organized into on-the-job labor, typically for defined periods of time, and less well-defined periods of domestic labor; and free time or leisure. Structured leisure includes work breaks, evenings at home, weekends, and vacation time.

The distinction is also conceptual and normative. Conceptually, we define what leisure is in contrast to our conception of work. Unlike work activities, leisure activities are noncompulsory—they are chosen by the leisured agent independently of externally or self-imposed mandates. They are thus not aimed at completing what needs or has to be done, and instead are activities one finds intrinsically rewarding or enjoyable. Being opposite to work, leisure activities afford relaxation, rejuvenation, and freedom from effort, challenge, and problem solving. Unlike work, leisure activities are temporally unregimented.

The norms for "doing" leisure also, in part, rest on a distinction between leisure and work. Leisure time is supposed to be used for leisure activities, not work. Those who use their leisure time for work or worklike activities are criticizable by others as workaholics who are unable to relax. And, to the extent that we value leisure and are mindful of its scarcity, we come to have normative expectations about our own leisure performance. Should we fritter away our leisure time in what wasn't in fact rewarding or in work or worklike activities, we open ourselves to self-criticism for wasting leisure time.

The conceptual opposition between work and leisure, and our acceptance of a normative injunction to use leisure well by avoiding worklike activities, and instead pursuing intrinsically rewarding ones, however, makes leisure-time boredom puzzling. If the regimentation of the workday, under externally imposed requirements that leave the worker without the option of choosing activities that engage her attention, is what makes work boring, then freedom from those boredom-causing conditions would seem to spell relief from boredom. Given free time to do as one pleases, and the happy normative expectation that one will use that time for activities that are rewarding and enjoyable, how could leisure activities fail to engage the evaluator's attention? In short, why would leisure so often bore us?

Having looked at different sources of boredom, we are now in a position to answer that question. Leisure often exaggerates some of the factors that produce boredom in other circumstances. Consider, first, an absence of temporal meaning. Typically, jobs involve at least short-term trajectories in the form of tasks to be completed and goals to be reached. Some involve long-term trajectories in the form of extended work projects or career ladders. That means that, however unengaging the particular tasks might be in themselves, they are likely to be seen as temporally meaningful. Leisure, however, is typically conceived not just as time away from paid labor but also as time during which one ought not to engage in worklike activities. Running household errands, preparing for a certification exam, repairing the lawn mower, and the like during leisure time constitute yet more work, rather than leisure. The normative ideal for leisure is *not* working—as it were, stopping and smelling the roses, and just relaxing. To use one's leisure well comes to be equated with *not* engaging in activities that have a temporal trajectory. However restorative that may be, it also means avoiding activities that have temporal meaning—a prime setup for boredom.

The risk of value satiety may also be exacerbated by leisure time. Among the kinds of activities that the conceptual and normative opposition of leisure to work may encourage us to exclude from leisure time are what Mihalyi Csikszentmihalyi calls "autotelic" activities that enable individuals to enter the "flow" state.[48] Autotelic activities are intrinsically rewarding because they involve use of skills that are well matched to the ongoing physical or intellectual challenges posed by the activity and thus give the person a sense of control over what comes next. They also present the most opportunity for entering what he terms the "flow" state.

> In the flow state, action follows upon action according to an internal logic that seems to need no conscious intervention by the actor. He experiences it as a unified flowing from one moment to the next, in which he is in control of his actions, and in which there is little distinction between self and environment, between stimulus and response, or between past, present, and future.[49]

Flow activities are, as Csikszentmihalyi observes, activities in which there is no time to get bored. That is in part because they are activities that, in my terms, are ones where the capacities of an evaluator are fully engaged. They are also 'deep' enough to present ever more difficult opportunities for action, so that the level of skill one can attain is in "principle inexhaustible."[50] Thus value satiety has little opportunity to set in.

Csikszentmihalyi argues that the essential difference between boredom-producing and non-boredom-producing activities is not between work and play, as we culturally understand those, but between activities that afford the flow experience and those that do not.[51] While Csikszentmihalyi thinks flow experiences typically occur in play, although they are possible in work, subsequent studies have suggested that most flow experiences happen at work.[52] One reason they do is that the activities that most engage our attention by demanding skilled action take effort; and external compulsion, a feeling of obligation, or long-term commitment may be needed to motivate individuals to embark on them—all forms of motivation that jobs and domestic duties may supply.[53]

---

[48] Mihalyi Csikszentmihalyi, *Beyond Boredom and Anxiety: The Experience of Play in Work and Games* (San Francisco, CA: Jossey-Bass, 1975).

[49] Ibid., 36.

[50] Ibid., 192.

[51] Ibid., 185.

[52] John T. Haworth, *Work, Leisure, and Well-Being* (New York: Routledge, 1997), 94.

[53] Roger C. Mannell, Jiri Zuzanek, and Reed Larson, "Leisure States and 'Flow' Experiences: Testing Perceived Freedom and Intrinsic Motivation Hypothesis," *Journal of Leisure Research* 20 no. 4 (1988): 289–304.

To make matters worse, the expectation—one that can easily rise to the level of a normative requirement—that leisure activities will not resemble work means that we often approach leisure time with a resistance to doing anything, let alone autotelic activities, that looks like work. And that includes not working at having fun. Unfortunately, many of the engaging things we could do with leisure time in fact take some work to set up—planning and hosting a party, taking a vacation, getting supplies and setting up a new project. As Al Gini observes, "most of us get very little time off from the job. And when we do, we want to do something different, something special. We want an interesting interlude. We want to escape the tyranny and tedium of the everyday. We want to have fun, and we don't want to work at planning or preparing for it either. We already do enough work."[54] Thus, when left free to choose activities to do in leisure time, the ones individuals are internally motivated to do may not offer enough challenge to ward off value satiety for very long.

For those for whom leisure means time alone or time with inadequate social partners, there are additional risks of boredom. No matter how resourceful or motivated they are to find engaging activities, evaluators do not have inexhaustible capacities for doing something with the value qualities they encounter. As I suggested earlier, evaluators may simply run out of things they can think of to do with the value qualities on hand. One reason boredom is correlated with loneliness is, I suspect, that other people are a resource for engaging with value qualities we would not otherwise have noticed or for engaging with them in ways we would not have thought of. Reading a novel on one's own may offer plenty of opportunities to engage with its value qualities; but reading it with a book group whose members can point out alternative interpretations and draw attention to what one overlooked increases the avenues for engagement. In addition, evaluators do not have inexhaustible capacities for thinking up things to do with their leisure. Other people help us answer the question "What shall I do with my time?" and often with things we wouldn't have thought of or have been motivated to attempt absent the social reinforcement.

Leisure may increase the likelihood not only of value satiety but of value disappointment as well. One reason we find ourselves bored is that we bring to an experience standards for what that experience must be like in order for us to invest interest in it. The higher the standards, the more likely the experience will disappoint. Both the scarcity of leisure and the uninteresting or unsatisfying nature of many jobs may easily lead one to have high expectations about one's leisure time experience. So people who work long hours in jobs that offer little that engages their attention may have much higher expectations for their leisure time.

---

[54] Al Gini, *The Importance of Being Lazy: In Praise of Play, Leisure, and Vacations* (New York: Routledge, 2003), 157.

Moreover, when leisure time is scarce in comparison to externally regimented work time, the importance of spending one's leisure time well—that is, in activities that are themselves valuable, meaningful, or enjoyable—intensifies: Am I enjoying my weekend? Vacation? Evening off? Patricia Spacks suggests that the modern era's focus on the individual and the individual's happiness partially explains the emergence of a discourse on boredom. "To consider human existence as an arena for seeking happiness virtually guarantees heightened consciousness of how little happiness daily routine necessarily provides. . . . Given constant assessment of degrees of pleasure, boredom becomes an essential category of experience."[55]

Perhaps the most obvious source of leisure time boredom, however, is simply that one can't think of anything interesting to do. This is the boredom that children complain of ("There's nothing to do!"); that parents resist in their children ("Go find something to do! What's wrong with your toys [friends, books, etc.]?"); and which adults learn to conceal because to be bored in this way is shameful. Being bored because one can't think of anything to do looks suspiciously culpable. It seems to indicate laziness, a lack of inner resources, a lack of imagination, and dependence on being passively entertained rather than on actively entertaining oneself.

So here, finally, do we have a place where the fault for boredom can be laid entirely at the doorstep of the bored? I am dubious. We as philosophers attach a great deal of importance to making choices, setting ends, framing intentions, and making plans. What we virtually never attend to is the fact that there are a *lot* of hours in a day, a week, a month that agents have to figure out what to do with. Happily, for most of us, what to do with all that time isn't a matter of much choice. Our jobs present us with tasks to be done, our home lives greet us with chores to be gotten through and pets to walk, our friends suggest outings to go on, our educational goals call for classes to take, and so on. By contrast, in *true* leisure, everything is optional, since nothing has to be done. And our cultural norms for doing leisure well enjoin us *not* to fill leisure time with work or worklike activities, on pain of being criticized for being workaholics. Norms for using leisure well thus tend to rule out complex, goal-directed activities that would fill up lots of time.

Boredom is a predictable result of having entire weekends, weeks of vacation, months of unemployment, or years of retirement that are entirely up to us to fill. The more the expenditure of time is not preset by work, family duties, complex time-extended projects, and the like, the more an agent is tasked with continuously deciding what to do with herself. Evaluators do not have inexhaustible capacities for thinking up things to do to fill their time. Living with boredom is sometimes the unavoidable cost of being an evaluator with time on her hands.

[55] Spacks, *Boredom*, 23.

7

On Being Content with Imperfection

We are temporal beings. We are conscious of the temporal unfolding of actual events; we have expectations about how events will or ought to unfold; and we can imagine how counterfactually they might have unfolded. We are also evaluators. We assess the good and bad aspects of our present condition, as well as the present we might have had, had things turned out differently. It is part of being an evaluator that we can imagine what would have been (even) better. For such beings, the present persistently offers a plethora of opportunities for discontent.

Given that basic aspects of our nature make us susceptible to discontent, it is no surprise that contentment is often elusive. And it might seem that there is not much we can do about that. However, while susceptibility to discontent comes with the territory of being human, individuals have a hand in the degree to which discontentment pervades their life experiences.[1] Being disposed to be contented, as opposed to being discontented, with what the present offers is, I suggest, a virtue.

However odd this may seem, there is historical precedent for the view. Eighteenth-century Christian moralists took a lively interest in the "art of contentment."[2] To

---

[1] As happiness researcher Sonya Lyubomirsky points out, almost a century of research indicates that objective features, such as level of wealth, social status, and kinds of life events account for only eight to fifteen percent of the variance in happiness ("Why Are Some People Happier than Others? The Role of Cognitive and Motivational Processes in Well-Being," *American Psychologist* 56, no. 3 [2001]: 239–249, 240). She proposes that the difference between happy and unhappy people has much more to do with the way each construes events. "[H]appy people perceive, evaluate, and think about the same events in more positive ways than do unhappy ones" (243). As a result, "happy and unhappy individuals appear to experience—indeed, to reside in—different subjective worlds" (244). I argue that these particular points apply to discontentment and contentment. The general relationship between contentment and happiness is a large topic and not the focus of this chapter, which aims to get a fix on two contrasting emotional attitudes we might have toward imperfect conditions. *One* meaning of subjective happiness might be equivalent to the contentment with perfect conditions I mention shortly.

[2] See, for example, Rev. Mr. Smith, *The Great Duty of Contentment and Resignation to the Will of God* (London: self-published, 1777); John Leland, John Rogers, and Thomas Amory, *Three Short Discourses on the Manner of Christ's Teaching, the Fear of God, and Christian Contentment*, abridged from Leland, Rogers, and Amory by a member of the Society for Promoting Christian

be discontent with the earthly life God provides, and to be so despite the promise of eternal, perfect contentment in the afterlife, was, they thought, a vice and a sin. Contentment with one's present, earthly condition, whatever it happens to be, is both a virtue and a religious duty, a view that continues to have contemporary appeal.[3]

As might be expected, a main reason offered for there being a duty of contentment is that discontent rests on the mistaken view "that things might have been better ordained,"[4] and "that some other Situation or Circumstances would have been better or happier for us."[5] If, however, we bear in mind that the God who permits us to be afflicted in this life is the same God who, out of his goodness and benevolence, will provide us with everlasting contentment, we will realize that present afflictions must also be aspects of his goodness and benevolence. Central to the art of contentment is reflection on both the "awful and adorable excellencies and perfections"[6] of God and on the way justly inflicted woes and iniquities "improve us in the exercise of virtue,"[7] thereby qualifying us for the next life. The force of these observations is to suggest that all apparent bads are in fact goods. There are no genuine misfortunes, so we have no warrant for discontent.

This is not the view I endorse. On the contrary, I begin from the assumption that our present condition is almost always an imperfect one. It is part of being an evaluator that we are capable—and often quite correctly so—of imagining what, counterfactually, would have made our present circumstances (even) better. Thus, we often take ourselves to have reason both to discontentedly lament unimprovable circumstances and to strive to improve those circumstances that are improvable.

It is tempting to think that being discontented rather than contented with imperfect conditions is the sensible response. Indeed, it might seem that one could only manage to be content in the face of genuine bads by somehow evading their significance. Perhaps the contented are unable to or refuse to acknowledge the negative facts; they are inappropriately—and perhaps dangerously—unresponsive to reasons. Perhaps they distort the evaluative facts, inflating the goods and dismissing the bads as merely apparent. Or, perhaps they have pragmatic reasons for studiously ignoring imperfections and dwelling exclusively on what's good; that might be a psychological

Knowledge (Newark: S. & I. Ridge, ca. 1800); William Webster, *The New Art of Contentment; Contained in an Essay upon Philippians IV: 11* (London: J. Everingham & T. Reynolds, 1754); A Gentleman of Glasgow, *An Essay on Contentment. In which this Important Subject is Treated after a New Manner* (London: J. Davison, 1749).

[3] Witness the fact that Puritan preacher Jeremiah Burroughs's 1648 *The Rare Jewel of Christian Contentment* is available on Amazon.com.

[4] Leland, *Three Short Discourses on the Manner of Christ's Teaching*, 25.

[5] Ibid., 26.

[6] Smith, *The Great Duty of Contentment*, 19.

[7] Ibid., 21.

survival strategy. Or, perhaps despite recognizing genuine bads in their circumstances, they nevertheless lower their sights and settle for less rather than striving for better. In Charles Griswold's words, "contentment seems to be the road to mediocrity"[8] and an enemy of appropriate striving. A disposition to contentment seems an unlikely candidate for a virtue.

Yet time spent around the chronically discontented who, to use the eighteenth-century language, continually "murmur and repine" against their condition, circumstances, and other people, naturally prompts a different thought: the chronically discontent seem criticizable, even when they respond to genuine bads in their circumstances. The problem is not just that the discontented, with their constant complaining and criticizing, are unpleasant to be around. Even if they control the outward manifestation of their discontent, there seems something deficient in being disposed to focus on what is flawed, inadequate, or disappointing. Nor is the problem that the discontented are mistaken in their assessments of what is flawed, inadequate, or disappointing. Often enough they are quite right. Indeed, their being right is part of what makes them difficult to be around; they invite us to become similarly discontent. The problem is that the discontented seem deficient in a capacity for grateful appreciation of what is good even in imperfect circumstances, intolerant of imperfection, or narrowly focused on their own welfare. (I argue later in this chapter that this is indeed often the case.) Most fundamentally, the chronically discontented may strike us as having gone wrong not by exaggerating how bad their circumstances are but in having *misplaced, or at least unnecessarily high, expectations about how good their circumstances must be in order to be good enough to be content with*. It is this thought that I pursue.

So, we have two main questions before us: "What are contentment and discontentment?" and "Is a disposition to contentment really a virtue—would it make us better people, not just bearers of enhanced well-being?"

TWO TARGETS OF CONTENTMENT

Eighteenth-century Christian moralists talked about two fundamentally different targets of contentment. It is important to be clear, before turning to our two main questions, what the target is of the contentment that is a candidate for a virtue. On the one hand, consider the contentment that many people believe they will have after death—complete and everlasting contentment—and that we fleetingly have in this life. For example, as you lie on the beach, listening to the waves, a warm breeze blowing over you and a margarita in your hand, you might exclaim, "Ah, I couldn't be more content!"

[8] Charles Griswold, "Happiness, Tranquillity, and Philosophy," *Critical Review* 10, no. 1 (1996): 1–32, 17.

The target of this contentment is *a perfectly good condition* containing no bads that could warrant discontent. Such contentment is largely out of our control. It is granted by God or serendipity. As such, it's not a likely candidate for a virtue.

Moreover, given the unlikelihood that our present condition is perfect, those who claim to be contented because their condition is perfectly good are likely to be victims of delusional thinking. Exactly this thought is at the center of Barbara Ehrenreich's *Bright-Sided: How the Relentless Promotion of Positive Thinking Has Undermined America.*[9] The cultural promotion of positive thinking, whether on self-policed breast cancer chat sites, in the new mega-churches, or in corporate culture, has gone hand in hand, she argues, with delusional thinking. Ehrenreich, herself having suffered from breast cancer, caustically observes the way that cancer victims are encouraged to avoid negative thinking. "In the most extreme characterization, breast cancer is not a problem at all, not even an annoyance—it is a 'gift' deserving the most heartfelt gratitude. One survivor turned author credits it with revelatory powers, writing in her book *The Gift of Cancer: A Call to Awakening* that 'cancer is your ticket to your real life. Cancer is your passport to the life you were truly meant to live.'"[10]

If contentment is, as Charles Griswold suggests, "a state of mind severed from an appraisal of the truth of the matter," then contentment cannot be a virtue.[11] The negative features you refuse to acknowledge in order to be content with a "perfect" condition are ones you should acknowledge. So, let us set aside contentment with a perfectly good condition.

The eighteenth-century Christian moralists focused instead on contentment with one's present earthly condition, whatever it happens to be. This is the contentment one might find even in the face of failure, painful infirmities, and in general, unsatisfied wants[12] where one recognizes the badness of one's condition and thus its imperfections. The target of contentment here is not a perfectly good condition, but a *good enough* condition. Because achieving contentment with an imperfect condition is a challenge, it looks to be a better candidate for virtue. Indeed, the eighteenth-century Christian moralists routinely offered St. Paul's affirmation, "I have learned, in whatsoever state I am, therewith to be content," as the model for such virtuous contentment.[13] Such contentment, some argued, better suits the reality of the human condition: "The present Life is so full of Uncertainty, Disappointment and Afflictions, that it is in vain to attempt making ourselves happy by bringing our outward Circumstances to be in

[9] Barbara Ehrenreich, *Bright-Sided: How the Relentless Promotion of Positive Thinking has Undermined America* (New York: Metropolitan Books, 2009).
[10] Ibid., 29.
[11] Griswold, "Happiness, Tranquillity, and Philosophy," 17.
[12] Smith, *The Great Duty of Contentment*, 37.
[13] Philippians 4: 11.

all Respects agreeable to our Wishes."[14] Given that pinning our hopes for contentment on our desires being perfectly satisfied is unlikely to meet with success, the only realistic option for achieving contentment is to "enjoy with a grateful Heart the natural Comforts and Satisfactions of Life"[15] and to "turn our View to every Consideration that may awaken a Sense of Gratitude in our Minds; and thus, by cultivating an active, thankful and cheerful Spirit, effectually debar the very Entrance of Discontent into our Bosoms."[16]

It is a disposition to contentment with imperfect conditions that I explore as a virtue.

WHAT ARE CONTENTMENT AND DISCONTENTMENT WITH IMPERFECT CONDITIONS?

Contentment and discontentment, I suggest:

1. Are dispositions to engage in counterfactual thinking about one's present condition.
2. Include a "good enough" (contentment) or "not good enough" (discontentment) judgment.
3. Depend on adopting a specific expectation frame about the degree of goodness one is "entitled" to expect and in relation to which one's present condition appears comparatively good, thus good enough . . . or not.
4. Are stances toward the evaluative facts.
5. Are practical or quasi-practical attitudes connected with an inclination to resistance (discontentment) or nonresistance (contentment) to the imperfections of our condition.
6. Are value-appreciating attitudes. In particular, contentment is a form of propositional gratitude.[17]

Counterfactual Thinking About the Present

Some emotional attitudes are, centrally, dispositions to engage in counterfactual or imaginative thinking. *Regret* is a disposition to think counterfactually about how things might have turned out otherwise in the past. *Hope* is a disposition to imagine possible futures and to prefer one of them. Contentment and discontentment with an imperfect present resemble regret and hope in this respect. The discontented are

---

[14] Leland, *Three Short Discourses on the Manner of Christ's Teachings*, 24.
[15] Ibid.
[16] Gentleman of Glasgow, *An Essay on Contentment*, 26.
[17] Propositional gratitude is gratitude *that* some good state of affairs occurred, and is contrasted with gratitude *to* some agent for a benefit the agent has conferred.

disposed to imagine how the temporal unfolding of events might have proceeded differently, producing a present condition that better satisfies their desires. The discontented home buyer imagines having ended up with a home with a better view ("If only the one down the street had been available!") or with a lower sales price ("If only home prices weren't inflated!"). Thus, the discontented think, "Things could have been better!" The contented, by contrast, imagine how the temporal unfolding of events might have proceeded differently, producing a present condition that does not satisfy their desires at all or satisfies them less well. The contented home buyer imagines homes that she looked at and could have ended up buying had her present, better home not been on the market. Thus the contented think, "Things could have been worse!"

To be disposed to this sort of counterfactual thinking does not mean that the contented and discontented always do entertain such thoughts. But they are at least disposed to acknowledge the relevance of particular sorts of counterfactual thoughts. The discontented, for example, readily accept others' observations to the effect, "Well, that could have turned out better for you!" and resist consoling observations to the effect that things could have turned out worse. For the contented, such consoling thoughts play an increasingly useful role in sustaining contentment the closer the situation gets to being just barely good enough, rather than plenty good enough.

The disposition to deploy counterfactual thinking distinguishes contentment from being pleased or glad, and discontentment from being displeased or unhappy. The contented's and discontented's evaluative assessments are comparative: "This is comparatively good. It could have been worse!" and "This is comparatively bad. It could have been better!" By contrast, being pleased, glad, displeased, or unhappy require only a positive or negative assessment of desire satisfaction: "I got what I wanted," and "I didn't get what I wanted."

The (Not-) Good-Enough Judgment

Fortified by the thought that things could have been worse, the contented view their condition as good enough. Fortified by the thought that things could have been better, the discontented view their condition as not good enough. But what makes a condition good enough? When is contentment with an imperfect condition warranted? The warrant for contentment cannot be the complete absence of genuine bads; this would be to assume that only a perfect condition warrants contentment. What we are looking for is an account not of perfect contentment but of contentment with imperfect conditions.

A tempting alternative thought is that there is, along the scale of value gradations, some qualitative degree that marks the boundary between what is good enough, despite there being higher possible qualitative degrees, and what is not good enough.

The good enough falls high enough on the scale. So, one need only tote up the goods and bads, arrive at an all-things-considered judgment of the degree of goodness, and check to see whether this reaches or falls short of the "good enough" mark. John Lachs takes this approach in his essay "Good Enough."[18] In his view, the good enough reaches the mark of the "clearly excellent," even if less than perfect.[19] Thus, the good enough is not simply what will do, or what is adequate, or what reaches a minimal level of acceptability.[20] Something is good enough, he claims, when it "simply [does] not need to be better than it [is]; it [is] plenty good and thus good enough."[21] Settling for the good enough in this sense permits one to have both high standards and to "dissolve the eternal dissatisfaction that permeates Western industrial society."[22]

The difficulty with this view is not only that it sets the mark for "good enough" too high to capture many quite ordinary cases of being reasonably contented with the good enough, but that it thinks there is one set mark. Instead, one wants to know "good enough in relation to what?" Lachs is interested in a good enough relative to having high standards without being unrealistically perfectionist. Satisficing offers a different measure: good enough in relation to finite cognitive and temporal resources. Both Lachs's high standards frame and the satisficing frame are expectation-setting frames: What degree of goodness ought one to expect if one has high standards? What degree of goodness ought one to expect under conditions of limited cognitive and temporal resources? As I detail in a moment, there are plenty of other yardsticks for measuring the good enough. So, the choice of "clearly excellent" as the mark of the good enough seems arbitrary.

Moreover, to search for a single qualitative degree that marks the boundary between the good enough and the not good enough is to assume that there is one, determinable fact of the matter about whether one's present condition is good enough or not. One might however think, as I do, that there is no such fact of the matter. Whether one's situation is good enough or not depends on the expectation frame one begins with: the good enough is as good as could be expected given a particular expectation frame. Thus, relative to some frames, your condition will be good enough; relative to other frames, the same condition will not be good enough.

Here is a little illustrative story: My father always ordered apple pie when my family ate out. He happened to have extremely high normative expectations about the quality of pie a restaurant should deliver. Those expectations were nearly always (severely) disappointed. His pie was never good enough. It could have been better. I, all too familiar

[18] John Lachs, "Good Enough," *Journal of Speculative Philosophy* 23, no. 1 (2009): 1–7.
[19] Ibid., 4.
[20] Ibid., 2.
[21] Ibid.
[22] Ibid., 7.

with this recurrent scene of discontent, sometimes thought to myself, "From a statistical point of view, mediocrity is what one might expect. Surely some of these pies are a cut above the statistical norm and better than one could expect!" We approached pies with different expectation frames, leading us to reach different good enough judgments.

Of course, you might think that in any given situation there is some one expectation frame you ought to be using. So, even if good enough is relative to the expectation frame, there is indeed one, determinable fact of the matter about whether your current condition—the current pie, for example—is good enough. That fact is to be discerned by identifying the one correct expectation frame. So, let's turn to expectation frames.

Expectation Frames

By "expectation frame" I mean an operating view of what we are, loosely speaking, "entitled" to expect in the way of the degree of goodness. It's an "operating" view in the sense that it determines where the bar for good enough is set, and thus whether goods or bads are salient and what the direction is that counterfactual thinking will take (could have been better, could have been worse). A high normative expectation frame like my father's or Lachs's is one possibility. An expectation frame based on statistical probability is another. The satisficing frame is yet another. And there are even more: what one has been led to expect on the basis of others' promises or guarantees; what befits one's status or role; what would be natural and normal even if not statistically normal; what a person with particular virtues, such as frugality, humility, or compassion, ought to expect; what someone of one's gender, class, profession, or talent should be able to expect; what, given the hand of luck in life, one should expect.

Return now to the pie. Was it good enough? In relation to what? The ideal or nearly ideal pie? The restaurant's promise of "the world's best pie"? The statistical norm for restaurant pies? Your grandmother's pies? What the global poor might expect to eat? None of these seems clearly the correct expectation frame. My father was not clearly wrong to base his expectations on his conception of excellent pies. Nor was I wrong to have expectations based on statistical probability. These are simply different bases for thinking one is entitled to expect a particular degree of goodness in restaurant pies. What he and I confronted was the option of choosing either one of the contentment-promoting expectation frames or one of the discontentment-promoting expectation frames. That there are a variety of deployable expectation frames doesn't mean that there is never something to be said for or against particular expectation frames. (Later, in taking up the question of whether a disposition to contentment is a virtue, I discuss both ineligible and morally criticizable expectation frames.)

A Stance Toward the Evaluative Facts

If contentment and discontentment depend on the particular expectation frame one uses to determine the good enough, this suggests that contentment and discontentment are themselves stances toward the evaluative facts of one's condition. Rather than being responsive solely to the evaluative facts, contentment and discontentment are ways of opting to regard the evaluative facts—as amounting to "good enough" in relation to this expectation frame or amounting to "not good enough" in relation to that frame.

Consider this temporal unfolding of events: it is 12:04 and I am waiting for my delayed flight out of New York City and am thinking I can still make my connection in Philadelphia and get home to Phoenix. At 12:05, my flight is canceled. I proceed to the airline's customer service desk and am rebooked through Charlotte on a flight that will still reach Phoenix the same day, but three hours later than originally planned and with a long layover in Charlotte.

One option is that I think contentedly to myself: "Whew! It could have been a lot worse. I could have been stuck overnight in the airport or a hotel with only dirty clothes in my suitcase. Good thing I only have carry-on luggage, so I don't have to worry that my luggage might not be rebooked on the same plane. Now I have more time to read the gripping novel I brought. Since I won't have time to grocery-shop and do laundry when I get home, I can just visit with the cats. And there will be plenty of time in Charlotte to find a nice lunch. I wonder if the other people on this canceled flight were so lucky?"

A second option is that I think discontentedly to myself: "Good grief! I'm getting home three hours later, and I won't be able to take care of grocery shopping and laundry tonight. Now I have three hours on uncomfortable seats in the Charlotte airport, trying to read with televisions blaring and other passengers talking on cellphones. I have to call my pet sitter and let her know I'll be late, and now I have to pay more for parking. And to top it off, I'm going to have a five-hour flight to Phoenix squished in a middle seat. What's wrong with airlines these days?"

The two me's know all the same facts about the good features of this unfolding of events, as well as the bad. As the first me is basking in the thought that she has escaped grocery shopping and doing laundry tonight, she's cognizant that this means these tasks will burden her workday tomorrow. As the second me is dreading five hours in that middle seat, she's aware that she'll have more hours than planned to read her gripping novel.

The facts, which are a mixed bag of goods and bads, do not by themselves decisively warrant being contented over being discontented, or being discontented over being contented. Instead, I seem presented with an option: it is up to me which expectation frame to employ and thus which stance I take toward the facts—being content with the present situation or being discontent with it. In the event, I happened to have employed a low-expectation frame governed by memories of sleeping on the airport floor and tracking down baggage that had gone off on a different flight, and by thoughts of the low odds of large numbers of passengers getting rebooked onto efficient alternative connections. Which kinds of frames we are disposed to adopt is open to cultivation. It is this fact that opens space for contentment to be a virtue.

In suggesting that contentment and discontentment are not dictated by the facts of the matter—in this case, an all-things-considered assessment of the goods and bads of one's present condition—I follow Adrienne Martin's analysis of hope and despair as stances that are not dictated by facts about the probability of the desired outcome's transpiring.[23]

Martin observes that two people who desire the same outcome can "both agree it is extraordinarily unlikely. One looks at the situation and says, 'I grant you it is *possible*, but the chance is only one in a thousand!' The other says, 'I grant you the chance is only one in a thousand, but it is *possible!*'"[24] The former despairs, the latter hopes. The difference between the two is not in their subjective probability assessment or in how much they desire the outcome, but in how they, in her words, "gestalt" the probability assessment: in terms of either the extreme unlikelihood of the outcome or of its possibility.[25] The hopeful person, focusing on possibility, treats the low probability as good enough to "license" activities related to the hoped-for outcome: "turning one's attention and thoughts—especially by constructing fantasies—to the outcome; feeling a positive sense of anticipation—feeling 'hopeful'—about it; and relying on it in one's plans—though only with a back-up plan."[26]

Contentment and discontentment have a similar structure. Two people who share the same subjective assessment of the goods and bads of the same present condition may regard those goods and bads as amounting to different things. Using an expectation frame within which the present outcome amounts to good enough licenses both reflecting on all the ways in which, counterfactually, things might have turned out worse as

---

[23] Adrienne M. Martin, *How We Hope: A Moral Psychology* (Princeton, NJ: Princeton University Press, 2014).
[24] Ibid., 45.
[25] Ibid., 23. Martin uses "gestalt" rather than "frame."
[26] Ibid., 69.

well as focusing appreciatively on the positive features of one's situation. It also provides the rationale for feeling appreciatively content with one's present condition.

A Quasi-Practical Attitude

R. Jay Wallace introduces the notion of a "quasi-practical attitude" in his analysis of regret.[27] Given that the circumstances occasioning regret are now in an unalterable past, deliberation cannot be focused on forming an intention to act now. Wallace suggests that regret is nevertheless a quasi-practical attitude insofar as reflection on what one would have done differently, could one return to the past, can yield conditional intentions for the future: this is what I would do were I in that situation again. In her analysis of hope, Victoria McGeer works out a different conception of quasi-practical attitudes: "although there may be nothing we can do now to bring about what we desire, our energy is still oriented toward the future, limitations notwithstanding. Our interests, our concerns, our desires, our passions, all of these continue to be engaged by what can be; hence, we lean into the future, ready to act when actions can do some good."[28]

Adrienne Martin works out yet a third conception of what a quasi-practical attitude might be. The activities licensed by hopeful and despairing stances may be largely or entirely internal, taking the form of fantasies about, for example, the hoped-for outcome, including imagining what one would do if the hoped-for future transpires.[29]

The general idea here is that emotional attitudes can have a practical dimension even when there are no present action options they could motivate and even when their rationales do not figure into deliberation about present action. That practical dimension includes the formation of conditional intentions, a preparedness to act were there an option to do so, and internal non-goal-oriented activities.

This notion of a quasi-practical attitude is useful in understanding discontent. Sometimes discontent is a straightforward practical attitude. That your present condition is not good enough—for example, you find yourself seated behind a large person who blocks your view of the movie screen—is a (defeasible) reason for framing and acting on the intention to change seats. Much discontent, however, is impotent. The temporal unfolding of events has produced a present condition that you are simply stuck with, as I was stuck with a less good, rebooked flight. In impotent discontent there are

[27] R. Jay Wallace, *The View from Here: On Affirmation, Attachment, and the Limits of Regret* (Oxford: Oxford University Press, 2013), 55–65.
[28] Victoria McGeer, "The Art of Good Hope," *Annals of the American Academy of Political and Social Sciences* 592 (March 2004): 110–127, 104.
[29] Martin, *How We Hope*, esp. 61–71.

no action options to deliberate about. But there are still quasi-practical dimensions to this attitude. The discontentment stance licenses dwelling in thought and imagination on the better, counterfactual unfolding of events; and this naturally invites thoughts about what you would have done if the better counterfactual present had obtained and on the fact that now you can't do those things. These may be frustrated actual intentions (in my plane example, intentions to grocery-shop and do laundry that night) or frustrated conditional intentions ("If I had a better income, I would . . . ; but since I don't have a better income, I can't . . . ").

All discontent, whether practical or quasi-practical, involves a refusal of the present, which is not good enough. Tamar Schapiro's Kantian account of inclination provides a useful way to understand that refusal. On her view, to have an inclination, say thirst, is to see objects in an imperatival mode—for example, to see water as to be drunk—and thus to experience inclination as issuing the imperative "Drink this!"[30] Similarly, the nonsatisfaction of desire might be said to involve seeing the imperfect situation in the imperatival mode—"Resist this!" The discontentment stance's not-good-enough judgment licenses acceding to this imperative. Because things are not good enough given the discontented's expectation frame, they ought to be resisted. The most effective way to comply with this demand is to change the world. When that's not possible and we are simply stuck with the not good enough, the "Resist this!" demand nevertheless persists. Resistance then takes other forms—complaining, blaming, ruminating about the bads, and imagining the counterfactual better. This leaning toward avenues of resistance is the restless mind of the discontented.

Similar points apply to contentment. Operating with an expectation frame within which imperfect conditions nevertheless appear good enough, the bads are unlikely to trigger a "Resist this!" inclination. Even if they do, the contentment stance licenses not acceding to this imperative: things are good enough. That one's condition is good enough is a (defeasible) reason for not forming and acting on intentions to alter one's present condition. Contentment is a practical attitude insofar as its constitutive good-enough judgment contributes to deliberation about when not to act.[31] Like discontent, however, contentment may often be a quasi-practical attitude, providing the rationale

---

[30] Tamar Schapiro, "The Nature of Inclination," *Ethics* 119 (2009): 229–256; and "Foregrounding Desire: A Defense of Kant's Incorporation Thesis," *Journal of Ethics* 15 (2011): 147–167.

[31] Deciding when not to act is important to rational practical activity, since not acting with respect to one feature of one's situation frees up time and resources, including cognitive resources, to act with respect to another. As Robert E. Goodin notes of settling for the good enough, "When settling for something we know or suspect to be suboptimal in this way, we typically do so simply to 'clear the decks' so we can focus on other matters for a time" (Goodin, *On Settling* [Princeton, NJ: Princeton University Press, 2012], 29).

for internal activities of gratefully appreciating the goods, and reflecting on how things might have gone worse.

Value Appreciation

The analysis of contentment offered so far—in terms of counterfactual thinking about how things could be worse, expectation frames, good-enough judgment, and a practical or quasi-practical attitude—is not complete. Where in all of this, one might ask, is the contentment, the positive affective attitude that is kin to being happy or pleased?[32] To see the problem, recall that the focus has been on contentment with imperfect conditions. Nothing about the imperfect situation precludes experiencing the inclinational imperative "Resist this!" even if one refuses to accede to that imperative because the present condition is good enough. Thus, much of the account provided so far seems consistent with begrudgingly contenting oneself with one's present condition, but not being content with it. What can be said about this aspect of contentment beyond observing that it is a positive affective attitude?

Let me suggest for now that contentment and discontentment are value-appreciating attitudes that go beyond the judgments "good enough" and "not good enough." The contented affectively appreciate the goodness of their present condition even if they may acknowledge its imperfections. The discontented affectively appreciate the badness of their present condition even if they may acknowledge that it is not wholly bad. As we will see, appreciation of the good is central to the disposition to contentment's being a virtue.

THE VIRTUE OF CONTENTMENT

Is a disposition to contentment—that is, a disposition to employ expectation frames that enable us to see our imperfect condition as good enough—a virtue? It's important to be clear that the question is not "Is a disposition to contentment, *no matter by what means*, a virtue?" There are, of course, all sorts of strategies for keeping imperfection out of sight and out of mind, and thus staving off discontent and engineering contentment. One can redescribe all bads as really goods (as some of the eighteenth-century moralists did). One can inflate the goods and downplay the bads. One can simply

---

[32] Writing on happiness, Charles Griswold points out that it is "a legitimate demand in a discussion of happiness . . . that the notion be explicitly linked up with some view of what it feels like to be happy" ("Happiness, Tranquillity and Philosophy," 12). It is equally a legitimate demand in a discussion of contentment that the notion be linked up with some view of what it feels like to be contented.

refuse to engage in counterfactual thinking so that the imperfections of one's present in relation to what might have been can't come into view. Or, one can gratefully dwell on the goods and studiously ignore the bads.[33] Such strategies (which look like efforts to find a "perfectly good" to be content with) would, sure enough, tend to have the effect of making us more rather than less content—but not content with imperfection.

If contentment with imperfection is a virtue, it does not fit a familiar model of virtue. We are used to thinking that virtuous attitudes are ones that hit the target, that get the evaluative facts right. Arrogance is a vice because it gets the evaluative facts wrong about one's own moral status in relation to others. Cowardice is a vice because it gets wrong the evaluative priority of one's own safety in relation to other goods. In the case of contentment, however, I've suggested that the evaluative facts do not by themselves determine what is good enough and thus a proper object of contentment. Once we pick an expectation frame, we can determine what is good enough. But it looks like there will generally be many reasonable expectation frames to choose from. Thus, if a disposition to contentment is a virtue and a disposition to discontentment is a vice, it is not because there is one correct target that contentment hits and discontentment misses. So, the argument for a virtue of contentment will have to take a different form.

I proceed in three steps. In the first two steps, my aim is to undercut a natural temptation to think that discontentment is generally a good thing: if conditions are imperfect, wouldn't it be a good thing to resist them? I begin by arguing that discontentment is sometimes the result of using morally *ineligible* expectation frames—ones that no one should ever use. I then argue that discontentment is sometimes the result of using *morally eligible* but nevertheless morally *criticizable* expectation frames. In the third step, I take up the positive argument for deploying contentment-promoting frames: a disposition to contentment is a corrective to a bias against appreciating the good.

Ineligible Expectation Frames

Many vices involve inflated normative expectations about what one is entitled to. Thus, a disposition to discontentment is often symptomatic of vice. The snobbish, socially proud, and arrogant have inflated views of their own value that distort their normative expectations about who should recognize them and what special attention and privileges they should receive. Those accustomed to power and spoiled by privilege may come unwarrantedly to think that things ought to go exactly as they wish them

---

[33] I don't mean to imply that keeping the imperfection of one's present situation out of view is always an unreasonable or a bad thing to do. My interest, however, is in a different question—namely, whether a general disposition to employ contentment-promoting expectation frames with respect to situations whose imperfections one doesn't try to evade noticing is a virtue.

to go. They take mere disappointment as sufficient to make their condition not good enough. The envious not only want no one to fare better than themselves but also may come to believe that no one ought to do so. So, too, the greedy may not only want more than what others receive but may also have a normative expectation that they ought to have more. Cultivating a disposition to employ contentment-promoting frames may be instrumental to overcoming vices that involve inflated normative expectations.

Criticizable Expectation Frames

Even when the discontented use morally eligible expectation frames—ones that are not inherently flawed—their choice of expectation frame may nevertheless be criticizable. The chronically discontented are often vulnerable to one of three criticisms: that they fail to use sufficiently enlarged expectation frames, that they ignore the role of luck in how things turn out, and that they are intolerant of imperfection.

Discontentment is often a product of failing to use sufficiently enlarged expectation frames. Eighteenth-century Christian moralists criticized the discontented for failing to use a sufficiently *temporally* enlarged frame. Limiting their view to an earthly life, the discontented frame expectations about the level of suffering they ought to be able to expect to be free of; and finding that their own lives don't meet those expectations, they judge their condition not good enough. But from a temporally enlarged perspective that includes earthly and eternal heavenly life, they ought not to expect to be free from even large amounts of earthly suffering, "[f]or, what are the momentary Pains and Afflictions of this Life, when compared with *the Glory which shall be revealed hereafter?*"[34]

In a similar but more secular vein, one might think that the discontented are often criticizable for failing to use sufficiently *socially* enlarged expectation frames. Limiting their view to their own social group, they frame socially comparative expectations (based on statistical frequency for the group, or group-based ideals of well-being) about the kinds and severity of bads they ought to be able to expect to be free of; and finding that their own lives don't meet those expectations, they judge their condition not good enough. But from an enlarged perspective of what lives are expectably like across all social strata, as well as globally, and of how dramatically worse off many persons are, they ought not to be discontent. In the face of global poverty, deprivation, and human rights insecurity, "murmuring and repining" about distinctly middle-class woes is criticizable. Maintaining the narrow, group-based expectation frame bespeaks dullness both to one's own privilege and to others' deprivations.

---

[34] Leland, *Three Short Discourses on Christ's Teaching*, 31.

A closely related point might be made about using lateral and upward social comparison frames under conditions of global environmental crisis. Determining what one ought to be able to expect in the way of satisfaction of consumption-related desires by looking to one's affluent peers, rather than to what would be globally fair to present and future humans and nonhumans, is morally criticizable. Maintaining an expectation frame calibrated to the lives of one's affluent peers bespeaks dullness to the consequences of high consumption and the importance of eco-injustice.[35]

The discontented are also often criticizable for using expectation frames that are insensitive to the role of luck in how one's present condition turns out. Contentment and discontentment, I have suggested, are stances taken toward the way that the temporal course of events has unfolded to yield an array of goods and bads with respect to some feature of one's present condition. Whatever that feature is—the pie delivered to one's table, one's income, the state of one's projects, one's health—it will be partly a matter of good or bad fortune that one's present condition is the way it is. Psychologists Maria Miceli and Cristiano Castelfranchi suggest that there is a common bias toward translating "the epistemic *should* into the deontic *ought*. That is, what in probabilistic terms, should happen, and I want to happen, turns into what is due, what I deserve and I am entitled to obtain."[36] If it does not obtain, it is not mere luck that it did not; rather, something has gone wrong. The result is resistance to accepting disappointments—in short, discontent. To the extent that this bias underlies discontent, the discontented are criticizable for being insufficiently sensitive to the role of luck in bad outcomes and for having unwarranted normative expectations about the extent to which they should be free from experiencing bad luck.

[35] Several writers, for example, have argued for interpretations of traditional virtues—frugality, temperance, simplicity—that are consistent with eco-justice (James A. Nash, "Toward the Revival and Reform of the Subversive Virtue: Frugality," *Annual of the Society of Christian Ethics* 15 [1995]: 137–160; Louke van Wensveen, "Attunement: An Ecological Spin on the Virtue of Temperance," *Philosophy in the Contemporary World* 8, no. 2 [2001]: 67–78; Joshua Colt Gambrell and Philip Cafaro, "The Virtue of Simplicity," *Journal of Agricultural and Environmental Ethics* 23 [2010]: 85–108). On their views, one ought (in my terms) to adopt an expectation frame with respect to consumption of material goods that is shaped by considerations of what a person ought to expect given the limits of the planet and the present and future needs of other species and global humanity. There is an interesting nineteenth-century literature that is critical of luxury consumption. See John Davidson, "Luxury and Extravagance," *International Journal of Ethics* 9, no. 1 (1898): 54–73; Henry Sidgwick, "Luxury," *International Journal of Ethics* 5 (1894): 1–16; and on the history of critiques of luxury consumption, Christopher Berry, *The Idea of Luxury: A Conceptual and Historical Investigation* (Cambridge: Cambridge University Press, 1994).

[36] Maria Miceli and Cristiano Castelfranchi, "Acceptance as a Positive Attitude," *Philosophical Explorations: An International Journal for the Philosophy of Mind and Action* 4, no. 2 (2001): 112–134, 117.

Finally, the discontented are often criticizable for their intolerance of imperfection. While there is nothing inherently objectionable about having high, including perfectionist, standards, there is something objectionable about deploying those standards against persons so that one ends up chronically discontent with one's fellows. Writing in the eighteenth century, Benjamin Bell argued that quarreling and discontent with other people has its source in unreasonably perfectionist expectations for what they ought to be like and do. "We must not expect too much of each other," he warns. "We must expect to find something disagreeable in the closest friends, and in the best of men, with which we should patiently bear. . . . At every trifle we must not scorn to take offense; otherwise we shall find enough to quarrel about as long as we live."[37] Making allowances for the imperfections of people and the burdens of their situation were important, he thought, to properly setting our normative expectations.[38] Parishioners, for example, should be careful not to take offense at their ministers for reproving vice, not preparing their sermons well enough, and presenting dry and lifeless sermons. "People should consider that the *best* of ministers are *but ministers* at their best; that they are subject to weakness and infirmities, in common with other men."[39] While Bell's concern was with the quarreling and unjustified censure that springs from the discontented's perfectionist expectations, less perfectionist expectations also open the door for appreciating the good in our imperfect fellows.

Contentment as Virtue of Appreciation

These reflections on discontentment yield only a limited defense of contentment. Contentment is preferable to the discontent prompted by vicious and morally criticizable expectations. But there will be lots of everyday circumstances where content and discontent seem equally appropriate options.[40] Recall me and my father on the subject of restaurant pies or the two me's in the airport. When discontentment manifests neither a vice nor a morally criticizable attitude, what reason is there to seek contentment instead?

In her pluralistic account of virtues, Christine Swanton proposes that a virtue is a trait "whose possession tends to enable, facilitate, make natural, the possessor's promoting,

---

[37] Benjamin Bell, *The Nature and Importance of a Pure Peace* (Windsor: Alden Spooner, 1792), 14–15.

[38] I'm inclined to think intolerant perfectionism toward oneself is also criticizable. But this is a more contentious view, which I will not defend, though I later comment on the acceptability of contentment with one's own moral imperfection.

[39] Bell, *The Nature and Importance of a Pure Peace,* 10–11.

[40] In the last section, I take up cases where discontent seems not only the preferable but also the required option.

expressing, honoring and appreciating value; or enhancing, expressing, honoring or appreciating valuable objects or states of affairs which are valuable."[41] Not all virtues exhibit all four "profiles" of virtue. Compassion, for example, tends toward promotion of others' well-being; humility is not aimed at promoting anything, but both expresses and honors others' equal or greater standing. Other virtues are strongly connected with simply appreciating value. Gratitude to benefactors, for example, involves a deep appreciation of the value of the benefactor's good will displayed in the benefit rendered or attempted. Swanton mentions connoisseurship as a virtue of appreciation. And one might think that aesthetic sensibility and the capacity to appreciate the wonders of nature are also virtues of appreciation, even if not moral virtues. The capacity to appreciate what is special, delightful, and interesting in particular individuals—a capacity connected with being able to love and cherish individuals —might also be thought to be a virtue of appreciation.

If there are virtues of appreciation, as seems likely, then contentment is a candidate for such a virtue. Contentment closely resembles propositional gratitude—gratitude *that* something occurred. In focusing on the goods that would have been absent in a different counterfactual unfolding of events, the contented appreciate the goodness of their present condition. They appreciate their good fortune in having events unfold as they did, when they might have unfolded for the worse.

But why think this sort of value appreciation is an excellence, a virtue? Connoisseurship, aesthetic sensibility, appreciating the value of another's good will, and appreciating an individual's unique value all involve appreciating what we might call marked, or significant, values. Appreciating the good (enough) fortune of receiving a decent if unexceptional piece of pie doesn't involve appreciating anything of marked value. Indeed, the sorts of goods the contented appreciate are often quite quotidian. And it's not just that these seem trivial values by comparison to, say, the beauty of artworks or awesomeness of nature. It's that there is no apparent difficulty requiring a refined skill for value appreciation in doing so. So, what could be excellent about appreciating everyday goods? It cannot be just that the capacity to appreciate value in all its guises is a kind of excellence. The discontented also appreciate value by being keenly mindful of the bads in their present situation.

Not all virtues of appreciation, however, are virtues because they depend on refined capacities to appreciate value. Consider gratitude to benefactors. It takes no refined skill to detect and appreciate a benefactor's good will. Yet we often don't appreciate what others do for us. The problem isn't lack of valuational skill but, rather, a tendency not to notice the effort and cost that went into rendering a benefit. What makes gratitude a virtue is, in part, that a grateful disposition corrects a tendency not to attend

---

[41] Christine Swanton, "Profiles of the Virtues," *Pacific Philosophical Quarterly* 76, no. 1 (1995): 47–72, 50.

to the benefactor but, instead, simply to enjoy the benefit. In short, if we assume that some virtues are primarily virtues of appreciation, and that Philippa Foot hit upon a characteristic feature of virtue when she proposed that virtues "are *corrective*, each one standing at a point at which there is some temptation to be resisted or deficiency of motivation to be made good,"[42] then a disposition to use expectation frames that enable appreciation of goods in one's present condition would be a virtue if it corrects a prevalent tendency to overlook, discount, or minimize those goods.[43]

A variety of factors contribute to just such a tendency. To begin, features connected with our being evaluators and doers work against our even noticing the goods in our present condition. As doers, monitoring failures, obstacles, and setbacks is typically more relevant to achieving our practical aims than is attending to how things are going according to plan.[44] Failures, obstacles, and setbacks call for resetting ends or means, while the smooth sailing of our plans can be safely disattended. In addition, to be an evaluator is to think in scalar terms about value, a scale whose endpoint is perfection. For any present good or present balance of goods over bads, we can always imagine what would be better. There is thus a bias built into being an evaluator toward imagining the better that could have been, and thus toward the counterfactual thinking that supports discontent.

Perhaps more obviously, we live in a competitive and consumer culture that relentlessly encourages the pursuit of more and better, as well as the thought that whatever we have now is not good enough. The marketing of consumer goods and services depends heavily on advertising aimed at persuading consumers that whatever they presently have isn't good enough and should be replaced with bigger, better, more luxurious items. Indeed, it is part of the dynamism of luxury goods that yesterday's luxury becomes today's commonplace, as ever greater qualitative refinements of existing goods continuously enter the market.[45] The result of this dynamism is to encourage disattention to and minimization of present goods and to continuously push the good enough out of the present and into an aspirational future.

Our culture is also increasingly concerned with ratings—rating your purchases on Amazon.com, rating visits to websites, rating services, rating your sex life, rating

---

[42] Philippa Foot, "Virtues and Vices," in *Virtues and Vices: And Other Essays in Moral Philosophy* (Berkeley: University of California Press, 1978), 8.

[43] In arguing for a virtue of living well that she calls "perspective," Valerie Tiberius similarly makes use of Foot's conception of the virtues as correctives to argue that part of the instrumental value of the virtue of perspective lies in its enabling us to appreciate goods that we tend to overlook (Tiberius, *The Reflective Life: Living Wisely With Our Limits* [New York: Oxford University Press, 2014], 103–104).

[44] Thanks to Carmen Pavel for this point about our nature as doers.

[45] Berry, *The Idea of Luxury*, esp. chap. 1.

restaurants, rating your Netflix rentals. Requests to rate focus our attention less on what's good about our purchases and experiences and more on the importance of five-star items and the deficiency of anything less. You're perfectly content with your new shoes, but now you have to rate them and it's obvious they're not five-star shoes: they're not as good as they could have been. Meritocratic workplaces can be particularly intense fora for rating. The average academic spends an enormous amount of time rating—rating papers, manuscripts, job candidates, students, prize candidates, programs—where the aim is to find the very best, by comparison to which the less than best are not good (enough).

One of the most tempting expectation frames for determining what counts as good enough, and one that consumer marketing relies on, is generated through social comparison. We are naturally social beings, and presumably also naturally status-conscious beings. In evaluating what one ought to be able to expect, and thus what counts as good enough, it is natural to look laterally at social peers. Are most of them doing better?[46] It is also natural to engage in upward social comparison with those who have better jobs, better salaries, better homes, more status, buffer bodies, more stylish clothes, and better vacations. Those with better and more set the standard not only for aspiration but also for contentment with one's present condition. Contentment thus gets endlessly deferred to a future present where one will have the more and the better, as one's present condition appears never quite good enough by comparison to one's social betters.

If contentment qualifies as a virtue of appreciation because it corrects a bias not to notice the good in imperfect situations, then contentment will be in large part a *situated* virtue. Although some of the bias that a disposition to contentment corrects for is built into our very nature as doers, evaluators, and status-conscious beings, a substantial portion of that bias is culturally produced.

OBJECTIONABLE CONTENTMENT

You may be thinking at this point, "This is all well and good, but surely contentment sometimes is not a good thing, and then people ought to be encouraged to be discontent."

Here is one reason for thinking so: sometimes what enables people to be content is that they expect too little. They use normatively distorted expectation frames. So, for example, just as one might criticize the arrogant for using an expectation frame that

---

[46] Looking to social inferiors who are largely faring worse will not, one might suspect, be very informative about what one ought to be able to expect. That social inferiors typically fare worse might only go to show that they have *even more* cause for discontentment, not that one has reason to be content with one's comparatively better lot.

no one should use, so one might criticize those who have internalized their socially subordinate status for using a normatively distorted frame that no one should use. Some adaptive preferences, for example, depend on wrongly diminished normative expectations: women, the poor, and lower castes may believe they ought not to expect to be free from deprivation and abuse, and so ought not regard their condition as not good enough.[47] This suggests an important qualification. If a disposition to employ contentment-promoting expectation frames is to be a virtue, it will have to be restricted to morally eligible expectation frames. Just as the superiorizing expectation frame of the arrogant is morally ineligible, so will be morally inferiorizing expectation frames.

There is no particular oddity in suggesting that a disposition to contentment is a virtue, despite the possibility of contentment's sometimes being objectionable. Here, it is useful to consider analogies between contentment and other trait names for virtues, such as humility, pride, honesty, courage, and industry. All these traits can take nonvirtuous forms. It is "proper," "appropriate," or "due" humility, pride, and so forth that are the virtues. Thus, what cases of misguided contentment show is not that a disposition to contentment is not a virtue but, rather, that this trait, to adopt Foot's words, does not always "operate as a virtue."[48]

But now you might have this thought: "With respect to moral perfection and to justice, the only morally eligible expectation frames are those of ideally correct conduct and ideal social justice, or something very close." It's one thing to recommend a disposition to contentment with imperfect satisfaction of desires for material goods, excellent restaurant pies, lively sermons, and unproblematic airline travel. It is quite another thing to recommend a disposition to contentment with our own or others' moral imperfection or with social injustice. In these latter cases, one ought always to be discontented. I suspect that the impulse to insist that only a very high or perfectionist expectation frame will do in these cases derives, in part, from confusing *standards* for what persons' moral character and actions and the justice of social arrangements ought to be like—standards that determine what demands we are entitled to make of ourselves, others, and social institutions, and what counts as a moral imperfection— with *expectation frames* that govern our emotional attitudes toward how the temporal unfolding of events has actually turned out.

As in the case of pies, one eligible moral expectation frame is perfection. But as in the case of pies, there are other eligible expectation frames; for example, what one might expect given the statistical norm for moral performance or what one might

---

[47] Not all adaptive preferences depend on an inferiorizing expectation frame. The expectation frame connected with an adaptive preference might instead be calibrated to what one can normally or statistically expect under conditions like this—i.e., to a morally eligible expectation frame.
[48] Foot, "Virtues and Vices," 16–17.

expect in the way of progress toward social justice given our particular past. Consider this example: the Supreme Court ruling in *Obergefell v. Hodges* marked a significant step forward toward a more socially just world for lesbians and gays, but we are still a far cry from ideal social justice. One option is to adopt an expectation frame based on the standard of ideal social justice: the present is not good enough; one is discontented. Another option is to adopt an expectation frame based on what, statistically, one might expect given the slow pace that social transformation normally takes (after all, it took women one hundred years to get the right to vote!): the present is good enough; one is content with how the temporal unfolding of events has proceeded so far. It will not do here to object, "But then you're contented with social injustice, with the failure to set adequate social policies, with others' continued moral misbehavior, and perhaps with your own failures of sufficient activism. And what sense does it make to be content with *that*?" This is to misdescribe the object of contentment, which is not the bad but, rather, with the good enough on some expectation frame despite the presence of these kinds of bads.[49]

Having distinguished the standard that enables you to recognize imperfection from the expectation frame that governs your assessment of whether the degree of imperfection is nevertheless good enough (or not), you might now have this thought: "Wouldn't it always be better to employ an expectation frame that promotes discontentment with moral imperfection and social injustice? Wouldn't a disposition to contentment be the enemy of appropriate striving?" Contentment, I suggested earlier, is a practical attitude not because it provides us with a reason to improve imperfect conditions but precisely because it provides us with a reason not to. It is precisely this feature of contentment that has led some to insist that contentment is a bad thing.

I'm inclined to think this concern is misplaced. Those who criticize contentment as the enemy of appropriate striving assume that contentment with one's present condition is incompatible with being motivated to improve one's condition. But this isn't true. Consider the beginning student who is delighted to receive a B on her paper and perfectly content with this grade. The paper is her first effort at philosophy and she's done as well as or better than she expected. She is moved neither to bemoan the grade nor to argue with the grader. But she nevertheless might exclaim, "Next time, I'll work harder and do even better!" To be content with one's present condition sometimes just means being satisfied with how the temporal unfolding of events has proceeded so far.

---

[49] It also will not do to object, "Why not instead just be content with the good features and discontent with the bad and thus avoid contentment with the imperfect altogether?" The goodness and badness of different features are themselves *scalar* properties. So, one will have to decide how good is good enough to be content with and how bad is bad enough to be discontent with— which takes us back to the unavoidability of selecting an expectation frame in relation to which the imperfectly good is good enough and the imperfectly bad is not.

Thus, although contentment's good-enough judgment is a reason not to strive to alter the present, one should keep in mind that conditions that are good enough now may only be good enough under the assumption that they are not enduring conditions.

More important, two questions need to be kept quite distinct: First, "What should the ends of my practical activity be, and what should I do given those ends?" Second, "What attitude should I have toward the imperfect present?" That the imperfect present is good enough given one's expectation frame provides *a* reason not to alter it. It does not necessarily provide a *decisive* reason. Consider the two me's in the airport. The contented me finds her rebooked flight good enough given her modest expectation frame for airline service. That's *a* reason for not trying, once she arrives in Charlotte, to find an earlier flight. The question of what to do, however, is not to be decided by looking only at one's reasons for contentment. Given the original plan to travel efficiently so as to do laundry and grocery-shop that evening, there are prudential reasons to try to secure an improved flight connection.

In ordinary language, we sometimes do use "discontented" to refer to any instance of taking ourselves to have sufficient reason to try to improve our condition; and we sometimes do use "contented" to refer only to instances of taking ourselves to have sufficient reason not to try to improve our condition. If this is what one means by "contented," a disposition to contentment would indeed be an enemy of appropriate striving. I have not been trying to capture that usage of "contented" but, rather, what I hope is an equally familiar notion of contentment as an emotional attitude connected with good-enough judgments, a disposition to counterfactual thinking, value appreciation, and a practical attitude. It is this emotional attitude that I take the eighteenth-century Christian moralists to have recommended as a duty and a virtue, and that I am proposing is a virtue. Focusing on contentment as an emotional attitude, rather than a state of taking oneself to have sufficient reason not to act, makes it possible to see that the kinds of reasons that are relevant to answering the question, "Ought I to adopt an expectation frame that enables appreciation of the goods in my imperfect present condition?" are not identical with the kinds of reasons that are relevant to answering the question, "What ought I to do given the imperfection of the present?" Suppose, for example, you are a woman working at an academic institution where there are significant disparities in the salaries of female faculty and those of comparable male faculty. What you ought to do given those inequities and your being positioned to do something about them is to act so as to produce gender equity in faculty salaries. But this does not answer the question of what attitude to have toward those inequities. I have argued that the privileged (as academics are) are criticizable for employing socially comparative expectation frames narrowly focused on their similarly privileged peers, and for "murmuring and repining" about the woes local to the privileged. The appropriate expectation frame is a socially enlarged one from whose vantage point it is reasonable to be gratefully appreciative of the goods in one's present imperfect condition—goods unavailable to the vast majority of workers.

Finally, one might think that a disposition to contentment is not the right corrective where one's own moral imperfection or social injustice that affects others is concerned, and thus no virtue. Too often we deploy expectation frames that enable contentment with our own moral imperfections and with unjust social arrangements from which others, but not ourselves, suffer. Here, a disposition to discontentment is needed to correct a bias against noticing the bad. The best expectation frame for that purpose is moral perfection and ideal justice. Perhaps that's right, but I suspect that, at least for social injustice, encouraging use of a high or ideal expectation frame is not the right corrective. That is because the problem is not a failure to use a sufficiently demanding expectation frame but, instead, in a distortion of the evaluative facts by inflating the goods accessible to the downtrodden, redescribing bads as deserved suffering that the downtrodden bring upon themselves, or simply assuming (out of ignorance of what the lives of the downtrodden are in fact like) that their lives resemble our more fortunate own. Consider William Paley's 1793 tract, *Reasons for Contentment; Addressed to the Labouring Part of the Public.*[50] In it, he aimed to persuade the laboring class that not being wealthy, far from imposing a hardship, enabled the laboring class to enjoy a life offering manifold sources of contentment unavailable to the wealthy.

> When compared with the life of the rich, [the life of the laboring class] is better in these important respects. It supplies employment, it promotes activity. It keeps the body in better health, the mind more engaged, and of course, more quiet. It is more sensible of ease, more susceptible of pleasure. It is attended with greater alacrity of spirits, a more constant chearfulness and serenity of temper. It affords easier and more certain methods of sending children into the world in situations suited to their habits and expectations. It is free from many heavy anxieties which rich men feel; it is fraught with many sources of delight which they want.[51]

Distorting the evaluative facts into a delusionally rosy picture of poverty and an equally deluded magnification of the wealthy's "smallest inconvenience . . . into calamities,"[52] Paley makes the poor laborer's life appear good enough relative to a variety of

[50] William Paley, Archdeacon of Carlisle, *Reasons for Contentment; Addressed to the Labouring Part of the Public* (Dublin: J. Millken, 1793).

[51] Ibid., 21–22.

[52] A Poor Labourer, *A Letter to William Paley, M.S., Archdeacon of Carlisle, from a Poor Labourer, in Answer to his Reason for Contentment Addressed to the Labouring Part of the British Public* (London: J. Ridgway, 1793), 14.

demanding expectation frames: what the wealthy might reasonably expect, what might be expected of a satisfying and well-lived life, and even what might be expected on high standards of social justice. Had Paley gotten the evaluative facts right, he would have seen that the avenues open to the poor for finding contentment and appreciating what goods there are in their lives are constricted to a narrow band of expectation frames. That itself is a measure of social injustice. The false contentment that Paley instead seeks to engineer by distorting the evaluative facts is indeed an enemy to appropriate striving, since those distorted facts interfere with correctly answering, "What ought I to do given the imperfection of the present?"

In sum, my aim in recommending contentment as a virtue was not to suggest that we should never be discontented on particular occasions, nor even less that we should cease striving to improve imperfect conditions. It was, instead, to draw attention to the importance of cultivating a disposition to contentment as a corrective to our biases against, and the vice-induced obstacles to, gratefully appreciating the goods in our almost always imperfect present conditions.

Conclusion

This has been a book about doing valuable time. We have a life's worth of time to get through, and as evaluators we care both that we actively expend our time in valuable ways and that what we are presented with in time is valuable. This has also been a book about the different ways we as evaluators connect and disconnect ourselves from our present and future.

One of the most important ways we do valuable time is by living meaningfully. In thinking about what living meaningfully consists in and is like, I have suggested that we give up a number of initially attractive and commonplace ways of thinking about meaningful living. Most important, I argued that if we have to choose among different senses in which we talk about "meaningful lives" in ordinary language, it is best to give up talk about meaningful lives as significant or humanly excellent lives. It is, of course, still important to think about what a significant or humanly excellent life would be, and doing so is *relevant* to leading a meaningful life. This is because one sort of reason we have for choosing the ends we do is what I called reasons-for-anyone to regard a life as choiceworthy. And those reasons-for-anyone will often be reasons for thinking that a pursuit is significant or a humanly excellent thing to do. But because we have plenty of alternative vocabulary for talking about the agent-independent goodness of a life ("significant," "flourishing," "humanly excellent") but really no alternative vocabulary for capturing the significance of a life to the agent herself, I recommended a more subjectivist conception of meaningful living that I called the normative outlook conception: meaningful living consists in spending one's life's time on ends that you take yourself, in your best judgment, to have reason to value and thus to use yourself up on. In selecting ends, we consider not just reasons-for-anyone but also reasons-for-the initiated and reasons-for-me. The normative outlook conception of meaningfulness, because it attends to these different types of reasons that factor into selecting ends, is able to capture in a non–ad hoc way both the relevance to meaningful living of thoughts about what (the agent thinks) is agent-independently good and the intuition that the constituents of a meaningful life must be ones that the agent herself cares about.

I have also suggested that we give up the idea that the meaningfulness of lives is to be assessed entirely by looking at the characterizing features of life—what a life is about. Again, doing so is *relevant* to assessing the meaning of a life. But it's also important to look at actual time expenditures. We need to ask ourselves, as Friedan's housewife did, "Ye Gods, what do I do with my time?" Some of the ends we expend our life's time on come with substantial quantities of entailed time expenditures and sometimes also filler and norm-required time expenditures. As a result, a life that appears meaningful at the temporally global level where we look at long-term activities (like mothering or being a professor) may appear much less meaningful when we pay attention to what's going on at the temporally local level, where we look at what we are actually doing with our time.

In part because commitments to time-extended activities almost inevitably come with lots of entailed time expenditures, either on instrumental means or constitutive activities that we may not value for their own sake, I also suggested that we detach ourselves from the idea that meaningful living requires making commitments. In committing ourselves, we set the bar very high for reconsidering our ends, treating new negative information, obstacles, and setbacks as "to be dealt with" rather than as reasons to reconsider. I have argued that locking in the future this way is not essential to meaningful living, although locking in the future may certainly be *attractive* because it makes the future familiar.

I have also argued that we should not expect that a meaningful life won't be a boring life. Indeed, for a variety of reasons the pursuit of a meaningful life may itself generate boredom. The ends we most value using ourselves up on may come with lots of temporal costs. Like Friedan's housewife, we may end up expending most of our time on entailed activities that we don't value for their own sake, that don't engage our capacities as agent evaluators, and that thus bore us. Even primary time expenditures can be boring either because we have reached the point of value satiety or, in the worst case, because the meaningful pursuit has stalled so that our efforts end up being just more of the same, going nowhere.

One theme of the book, which I summarized in the introduction, concerns the difficulties inherent in living life as a temporal evaluator: the vulnerabilities to demoralization, estrangement, boredom, loss of basal hopefulness, discontentment, and meaninglessness at the temporally local level. Some of these difficulties have to do with basic facts of our lives. For example, our finitude means that we typically have to choose between time-consuming, highly valued pursuits and the many less-valued pursuits that the time-consuming ones crowd out. And the sheer quantity of time we have to fill can exceed the resources of even the most inventive agent, resulting in boredom. Some of these difficulties also have to do with external circumstances, as is the case when exposure to disastrous misfortune or habituation to failed pursuits undermines one's ability to sustain basal hopefulness about the future and thus motivation to endeavor on. Some of these difficulties have to do with specific features of our culture. The strong distinction we draw between work and leisure, and with it the normative requirement not to work during leisure time, increases the likelihood that leisure time will bore us. In addition, culturally encouraged upward social comparisons, consumer aspirations for the ever better, and attention to ratings encourage discontentment. Some of the difficulties, however, result from our being strong evaluators. Having high standards for what we are willing to take an interest in is a setup for value disappointment and boredom; and having high normative expectations for what the temporal unfolding of events will deliver is a setup for discontent.

Throughout the book, I have suggested that our lives as evaluators are shaped in important ways by the personal, the nonrational, and optional styles. Defending a subjectivist account of meaningfulness has been central to that project. Drawing attention to the role that reasons-for-me, and to a lesser extent reasons-for-the initiated, plays in selecting a normative outlook was even more central. The most important nonrational element emphasized in this book is our phenomenological idea of the future. We are temporal agents not just because we frame intentions or make commitments, construct plans, and have desires *for* the future but also because we live under an idea *of* the future whose content is only partially previsaged and much of which is not open to reflective awareness. Our being motivated to lead the life of an agent at all or to continue on in pursuits that are, or prove to be, unlikely to succeed is not fully explicable in terms of our motivating reasons. Basal hopefulness and a phenomenological idea of the determinate future as one containing success typically "second" our motivating reasons. That reasons have motivating force also depends not just on our having a normative outlook but also on our not being estranged from that outlook, as those suffering depression sometimes are.

Our lives as evaluators are obviously shaped by the decisions we make about whether to merely intend, provisionally plan, or fully commit to various pursuits. Where to set the bar for reconsideration is part of the deliberative process itself. We ask ourselves, for example, whether the pursuit is valuable enough to risk unredeemed costs if it fails. But I have also suggested that the attraction to commitments rather than to provisional plans is also a matter of personal style. It is connected with both a "prizing" normative style and a temporal style that involve preferring a familiar future over the less predictable futures of provisional planners.

Personal style also enters into the management of the temporal pursuit of value in a finite life. Our ends typically exceed what can actually be pursued within the constraints of a finite life, so a decision will have to be made about whether to pursue time-consuming ends that crowd out things of lesser value or to abandon the time-consuming end so more of our normative outlook can be realized. Which option we go for—to be maximizers, investing our time in the highly valued but time-consuming end, or to be pluralizers, investing our time in many less-time-consuming ends—I have suggested, is at least partly a matter of personal time-management style. The boredom and discontent we experience as evaluators is also, in part, a matter of optional style. Snobs, I suggested, are not wrong to have high standards for what they are willing to take an interest in; nor are those with lower standards for what they are willing to take an interest in wrong to have those lower standards. But high versus low standards for the quality of what we are willing to take an interest in has consequences for how vulnerable we will be to being bored.

Finally, although I argued in the last chapter that a disposition to contentment is a virtue, I did not argue that discontentment with the imperfect is unwarranted. Whether we are content or discontent with the present that emerges in the temporal unfolding of events is a function of native or cultivated dispositions to use lower versus higher expectation frames for what can be reasonably expected.

Bibliography

Achebe, Chinua. *Things Fall Apart*. New York: Anchor Books, 1959.

Arpaly, Nomy. *Unprincipled Virtue: An Enquiry into Moral Agency*. New York: Oxford University Press, 2003.

Arpaly, Nomy. "Comment." In *Meaning in Life and Why It Matters*, by Susan Wolf, 85–91. Princeton, NJ: Princeton University Press, 2010.

Audi, Robert. "Intrinsic Value and Meaningful Life." *Philosophical* Papers 34 (November 2005): 331–355.

Baier, Annette. "Demoralization, Trust, and the Virtues." In *Setting the Moral Compass: Essays by Women Philosophers*, edited by Cheshire Calhoun, 176–188. New York: Oxford University Press, 2004.

Barbalet, J. M. "Boredom and Social Meaning." *British Journal of Sociology* 50, no. 4 (December 1999): 631–646.

Bargdill, Richard W. "The Study of Life Boredom." *Journal of Phenomenological Psychology* 31, no. 2 (2000): 188–219.

Beck, Aaron T. "A Cognitivist Analysis of Depression." In *The Nature of Melancholy*, edited by Jennifer Radden, 317–323. Oxford: Oxford University Press, 2002.

Beck, Aaron T., and Arlene Weissman. "The Measurement of Pessimism: The Hopelessness Scale." *Journal of Consulting and Clinical Psychology* 42, no. 6 (1974): 861–865.

Bell, Benjamin. *The Nature and Importance of a Pure Peace*. Windsor: Alden Spooner, 1792.

Bernstein, Haskell E. "Boredom and the Ready-Made Life." *Social Research* 42 (Autumn 1975): 512–537.

Berry, Christopher. *The Idea of Luxury: A Conceptual and Historical Investigation*. Cambridge: Cambridge University Press, 1994.

Betzler, Monika. "Sources of Practical Conflicts and Reasons for Regret." In *Practical Conflicts: New Philosophical Essays*, edited by Peter Baumann and Monika Betzler, 197–222. Cambridge: Cambridge University Press, 2004.

Bratman, Michael E. *Intention, Plans, and Practical Reason*. Cambridge, MA: Harvard University Press, 1987.

Bratman, Michael E. *Faces of Intention: Selected Essays on Intention and Agency*. Cambridge: Cambridge University Press, 1999.

Bratman, Michael E. "Reflection, Planning and Temporally Extended Agency." *Philosophical Review* 109 (2000): 35–61.

Bratman, Michael E. "Valuing and the Will." *Nous* 34, Supplement 14 (2000): 249–265.

Bratman, Michael E. "A Thoughtful and Reasonable Stability: A Comment on Harry Frankfurt's 2004 Tanner Lectures." In *Taking Ourselves Seriously, and Getting it Right*, by Harry G. Frankfurt, 77–99. Stanford, CA: Stanford University Press, 2006.

Brewer, Tal. "Savoring Time: Desire, Pleasure, and Wholehearted Activity." *Ethical Theory and Moral Practice* 6 (2003): 143–160.

Brison, Susan J. *Aftermath: Violence and the Remaking of a Self.* Princeton, NJ: Princeton University Press, 2002.

Brissett, Dennis, and Robert P. Snow. "Boredom: Where the Future Isn't." *Symbolic Interaction* 16, no. 3 (1993): 237–256.

Buss, Sarah, and Lee Overton, eds. *Contours of Agency: Essays on Themes by Harry Frankfurt.* Cambridge, MA: MIT Press, 2002.

Calhoun, Cheshire. "Standing for Something." *Journal of Philosophy* 92 (1995): 235–260.

Coetzee, J. M. *Disgrace.* New York: Viking, 1999.

Csikszentmihalyi, Mihalyi. *Beyond Boredom and Anxiety: The Experience of Play in Work and Games.* San Francisco, CA: Jossey-Bass, 1975.

Cunningham, Michael. *The Hours.* New York: Farrar, Straus and Giroux, 1998.

Darwall, Stephen. *Impartial Reason.* Ithaca, NY: Cornell University Press, 1983.

Davidson, John. "Luxury and Extravagance." *International Journal of Ethics* 9, no. 1 (1898): 54–73.

Day, J. P. "Hope." *American Philosophical Quarterly* 6 (1969): 89–102.

Deigh, John. "Reason and Motivation." In *The Sources of Moral Agency: Essays in Moral Psychology and Freudian Theory*, 133–159. Cambridge: Cambridge University Press, 1996.

DesAutels, Peggy, and Margaret Urban Walker, eds. *Moral Psychology: Feminist Ethics and Social Theory.* Lanham, MD: Rowman & Littlefield, 2004.

Dillon, Robin. "Self-Respect: Moral, Emotional, Political." *Ethics* 107, no. 2 (1997): 226–249.

Downie, R. S. "Hope." *Philosophy and Phenomenological Research* 24 (1963): 248–251.

Ehrenreich, Barbara. *Bright-Sided: How the Relentless Promotion of Positive Thinking has Undermined America.* New York: Metropolitan Books, 2009.

Esman, Aaron H. "Some Reflections on Boredom." *Journal of the American Psychoanalytic Association* 27, no. 2 (1979): 423–439.

Fenichel, Otto. "On the Psychology of Boredom." In *The Collected Papers of Otto Fenichel*, 1st Series, 292–302. New York: W.W. Norton, 1953.

Foot, Philippa. "Virtues and Vices." In *Virtues and Vices: And Other Essays in Moral Philosophy.* Berkeley: University of California Press, 1978.

Frankfurt, Harry G. *The Importance of What We Care About: Philosophical Essays.* Cambridge: Cambridge University Press, 1988.

Frankfurt, Harry G. *Necessity, Volition, and Love.* Cambridge: Cambridge University Press, 1999.

Frankfurt, Harry G. "On the Usefulness of Final Ends." In *Necessity, Volition, and Love*, 82–94. Cambridge: Cambridge University Press, 1999.

Frankfurt, Harry G. "Volitional Necessities." In *Free Will*, 2nd ed., edited by Gary Watson, 88–122. Oxford Readings in Philosophy. Oxford: Oxford University Press, 2003.

Frankfurt, Harry G. *The Reasons of Love.* Princeton, NJ: Princeton University Press, 2004.

Frankfurt, Harry G. *Taking Ourselves Seriously, and Getting it Right.* Preface by Debra Satz. Stanford, CA: Stanford University Press, 2006.

Friedan, Betty. *The Feminine Mystique.* New York: Dell, 1964.

Gambrell, Joshua Colt, and Philip Cafaro. "The Virtue of Simplicity." *Journal of Agricultural and Environmental Ethics* 23 (2010): 85–108.

Gentleman of Glasgow. *An Essay on Contentment. In Which this Important Subject Is Treated after a New Manner.* London: J. Davison, 1749.

Gini, Al. *The Importance of Being Lazy: In Praise of Play, Leisure, and Vacations.* New York: Routledge, 2003.

Goodin, Robert E. *On Settling.* Princeton, NJ: Princeton University Press, 2012.

Goodstein, Elizabeth S. *Experience Without Qualities: Boredom and Modernity.* Stanford, CA: Stanford University Press, 2005.

Griswold, Charles. "Happiness, Tranquillity, and Philosophy." *Critical Review* 10, no. 1 (1996): 1–32.

Haslanger, Sally. "Gender and Race: (What) Are They? (What) Do We Want Them to Be?" *Nous* 34 (March 2000): 31–55.

Haslanger, Sally. *Resisting Reality: Social Construction and Social Critique.* New York: Oxford University Press, 2012.

Haworth, John T. *Work, Leisure, and Well-Being.* New York: Routledge, 1997.

Healy, Sean Desmond. *Boredom, Self, and Culture.* Cranbury, NJ: Fairleigh Dickinson University Press, 1984.

Hurka, Thomas. "The Well-Rounded Life." *Journal of Philosophy* 84 (1987): 727–746.

Jack, Dana Crowley. *Silencing the Self: Women and Depression.* Cambridge, MA: Harvard University Press, 1991.

Jones, Karen. "Trust and Terror." In *Moral Psychology: Feminist Ethics and Social Theory*, edited by Peggy DesAutels and Margaret Urban Walker, 3–18. Lanham, MD: Rowman & Littlefield, 2004.

Jones, Karen. "How to Change the Past." In *Practical Identity and Narrative Agency*, edited by Catriona MacKenzie and Kim Atkins, 269–287. New York: Routledge, 2008.

Kekes, John. "The Informed Will and the Meaning of Life." *Philosophy and Phenomenological Research* 47 (September 1986): 75–90.

Koethe, John. "Comment." In *Meaning in Life and Why it Matters* by Susan Wolf, 67–74. Princeton, NJ: Princeton University Press, 2010.

Kolodiejchuk, Brian, ed. and comm. *Mother Teresa, Come Be My Light: The Private Writings of the "Saint of Calcutta."* New York: Doubleday, 2007.

Korsgaard, Christine. "Personal Identity and the Unity of Agency: A Kantian Response to Parfit." *Philosophy and Public Affairs* 18, no. 2 (Spring 1989): 101–132.

Korsgaard, Christine. *Creating the Kingdom of Ends.* Cambridge, MA: Harvard University Press, 1996.

Korsgaard, Christine. *The Sources of Normativity.* Cambridge: Cambridge University Press, 1996.

Korsgaard, Christine. "Self-Constitution in the Ethics of Plato and Kant." *Journal of Ethics* 3, no. 1 (1999): 1–29.

Kovach, Vanya, and John Fitzpatrick. "Resolutions." *Australasian Journal of Philosophy* 77, no. 2 (1999): 161–173.

Lachs, John. "Good Enough." *Journal of Speculative Philosophy* 23, no. 1 (2009): 1–7.

Larmore, Charles. "The Idea of a Life Plan." *Social Philosophy and Policy* 16, no. 1 (1999): 96–112.

Leer, Jonathan. *Radical Hope: Ethics in the Face of Cultural Destruction.* Cambridge, MA: Harvard University Press, 2008.

Leland, John, John Rogers, and Thomas Amory. *Three Short Discourses on the Manner of Christ's Teaching, the Fear of God, and Christian Contentment*, abridged from Leland, Rogers, and Amory by a member of the Society for Promoting Christian Knowledge. Newark: S. and I. Ridge, circa 1800.

Lewinsky, Hilde. "Boredom." *British Journal of Educational Psychology* 13 (1943): 147–152.

Lyumbomirsky, Sonya. "Why Are Some People Happier Than Others? The Role of Cognitive and Motivational Processes in Well-Being." *American Psychologist* 56, no. 3 (2001): 239–249.

MacIntyre, Alastair. *After Virtue: A Study in Moral Theory*, 2nd ed. Notre Dame, IN: University of Notre Dame Press, 1984.

Mannell, Roger C., Jiri Zuzanek, and Reed Larson. "Leisure States and 'Flow' Experiences: Testing Perceived Freedom and Intrinsic Motivation Hypothesis." *Journal of Leisure Research* 20 no. 4 (1988): 289–304.

Martin, Adrienne M. *How We Hope: A Moral Psychology*. Princeton, NJ: Princeton University Press, 2014.

Martin, Mike. "Love's Constancy." *Philosophy* 68, no. 263 (1993): 63–77.

Marya, Schechtman. "Diversity in Unity: Practical Unity and Personal Boundaries." *Synthese* 162 (2008): 405–423.

McGeer, Victoria. "The Art of Good Hope." *Annals of the American Academy of Political and Social Sciences* 592 (2004): 100–127.

McMurtry, Larry. "From *Walter Benjamin at the Dairy Queen*." In *Unholy Ghost: Writers on Depression*, edited by Casey Nell, 67–74. New York: Perennial, 2002.

Metz, Thaddeus. "Utilitarianism and the Meaning of Life." *Utilitas* 15, no. 1 (2003): 50–70.

Metz, Thaddeus. "The Meaningful and the Worthwhile: Clarifying the Relationships." *Philosophical Forum* 43 (2012): 435–448.

Metz, Thaddeus. *Meaning in Life: An Analytic Study*. New York: Oxford University Press, 2013.

Miceli, Maria, and Cristiano Castelfranchi. "Acceptance as a Positive Attitude." *Philosophical Explorations: An International Journal for the Philosophy of Mind and Action* 4, no. 2 (2001): 112–134.

Millgram, Elijah. "On Being Bored Out of Your Mind." *Proceedings of the Aristotelian Society* 104 (January 2004): 165–186.

Moran, Richard. "Frankfurt on Identification: Ambiguities of Activity in Mental Life." In *Contours of Agency: Essays on Themes by Harry Frankfurt*, edited by Sarah Buss and Lee Overton, 189–217. Cambridge, MA: MIT Press, 2002.

Musharbash, Yasmine. "Boredom, Time, and Modernity: An Example from Aboriginal Australia." *American Anthropologist* 109, no. 2 (2007): 307–317.

Nash, James A. "Toward the Revival and Reform of the Subversive Virtue: Frugality." *Annual of the Society of Christian Ethics* 15 (1995): 137–160.

Neu, Jerome. "Boring from Within: Endogenous versus Reactive Boredom." In *A Tear is an Intellectual Thing: The Meanings of Emotion*, 95–107. New York: Oxford University Press, 2000.

Nussbaum, Martha C. "Love and the Individual: Romantic Rightness and Platonic Aspiration." In *Reconstructing Individualism: Autonomy, Individuality, and the Self in Western Thought*, edited by Arnold I. Davidson, Thomas C. Heller, Morton Sosna, David E. Wellbery, and Ann Swindler, 253–277. Stanford, CA: Stanford University Press, 1986.

Paley, William, Archdeacon of Carlisle, *Reasons for Contentment; Addressed to the Labouring Part of the Public*. Dublin: J. Millken, 1793.

Peterson, Christopher, Steven F. Maier, and Martin E. P. Seligman. *Learned Helplessness: A Theory for the Age of Personal Control*. New York: Oxford University Press, 1993.

Pettit, Philip. "Hope and Its Place in Mind." *Annals of the American Academy of Political and Social Sciences* 592 (2004): 152–165.

Poor Labourer, A. *A Letter to William Paley, M.S., Archdeacon of Carlisle, from a Poor Labourer, in Answer to his Reason for Contentment Addressed to the Labouring Part of the British Public*. London: J. Ridgway, 1793.

Portmore, Douglas W. "Welfare, Achievement, and Self-Sacrifice." *Journal of Ethics and Social Philosophy* 2, no. 2 (2007): 1–28.

Ratcliffe, Matthew. "What Is It to Lose Hope?" *Phenomenology and the Cognitive Sciences* 12, no. 4 (2013): 597–614.

Ratcliffe, Matthew, Mark Ruddell, and Benedict Smith. "What Is a 'Sense of Foreshortened Future'? A Phenomenological Study of Trauma, Trust, and Time." *Frontiers in Psychology* 5 (September 17, 2014). doi: 10.3389/fpsyg.2014.01026

Rosati, Connie S. "Mortality, Agency, and Regret." In *New Trends in Philosophy: Moral Psychology*, edited by Sergio Tenenbaum, 231–260. Poznan Studies in the Philosophy of the Sciences and the Humanities, vol. 94. New York: Rodopi, 2007.

Schauber, Nancy. "Integrity, Commitment and the Concept of a Person." *American Philosophical Quarterly* 33 (January 1996): 119–129.

Schechtman, Marya. "Self-Expression and Self-Control." In *The Self?* edited by Galen Strawson, 45–62. Malden, MA: Blackwell, 2005.

Schechtman, Marya. "Diversity in Unity: Practical Unity and Personal Boundaries." *Synthese* 162 (2008): 405–423.

Schmidtz, David. "The Meanings of Life." In *Life, Death, and Meaning: Key Philosophical Readings on the Big Questions*, 2nd ed., edited by David Benatar, 93–114. Lanham, MD: Rowman & Littlefield, 2010.

Seligman, Martin E. P. *Helplessness: On Depression, Development, and Death.* San Francisco: W.H. Freeman, 1975.

Shapiro, Tamar. "The Nature of Inclination." *Ethics* 119 (2009): 229–256.

Shapiro, Tamar. "Foregrounding Desire: A Defense of Kant's Incorporation Thesis." *Journal of Ethics* 15 (2011): 147–167.

Sidgewick, Henry. "Luxury." *International Journal of Ethics* 5 (1894): 1–16.

Simonds, Susan L. *Depression and Women: An Integrative Treatment Approach.* New York: Springer, 2001.

Smith, Rev. Mr. *The Great Duty of Contentment and Resignation to the Will of God.* London: self-published, 1777.

Snow, Nancy E. "Hope as an Intellectual Virtue." In *Virtues in Action: New Essays in Applied Virtue Ethics*, edited by Michael W. Austin, 152–170. New York: Palgrave MacMillan, 2013.

Solomon, Robert C. *The Passions: Emotions and the Meaning of Life.* Indianapolis: Hackett, 1993.

Spacks, Patricia Meyer. *Boredom: The Literary History of a State of Mind.* Chicago: University of Chicago Press, 1995.

Sparks, Elizabeth. "Depression and Schizophrenia in Women: The Intersection of Gender, Race/Ethnicity, and Class." In *Rethinking Mental Health and Disorder: Feminist Perspectives*, edited by Mary Ballou and Laura S. Brown, 279–305. New York: Guilford Press, 2002.

Starkey, Charles. "Meaning and Affect." *The Pluralist* 1, no. 2 (2006): 88–103.

Strawson, Galen. "Against Narrativity." In *The Self?* 63–86. Malden, MA: Blackwell, 2005.

Strawson, Galen, ed. *The Self?* Malden, MA: Blackwell, 2005.

Stocker, Michael. "Affectivity and Self-Concern: The Assumed Psychology in Aristotle's Ethics." *Pacific Philosophical Quarterly* 64 (1983): 211–229.

Svendsen, Lars. *A Philosophy of Boredom.* Translated by John Irons. London: Reaktion, 2005.

Swanton, Christine. "Profiles of the Virtues." *Pacific Philosophical Quarterly* 76, no. 1 (1995): 47–72.

Taylor, Richard. *Good and Evil.* Amherst, NY: Prometheus Books, 2000.

Tiberius, Valerie. "Value Commitments and the Balanced Life." *Utilitas* 17, no. 1 (March 2005): 24–45.

Tiberius, Valerie. *The Reflective Life: Living Wisely With Our Limits.* New York: Oxford University Press, 2014.

van Hooft, Stanley. "Commitment and the Bond of Love." *Australasian Journal of Philosophy* 74, no. 3 (1996): 454–466.

Velleman, J. David. "The Possibility of Practical Reason." *Ethics* 106 (1996): 694–726.

Velleman, J. David. *The Possibility of Practical Reason*. Oxford: Oxford University Press, 2000.

Velleman, J. David. "Identification and Identity." In *Contours of Agency: Essays on Themes by Harry Frankfurt*, edited by Sarah Buss and Lee Overton, 227–244. Cambridge, MA: MIT Press, 2002.

Velleman, J. David. *Self to Self: Selected Essays*. Cambridge: Cambridge University Press, 2005.

Walker, Margaret Urban. *Moral Understandings: A Feminist Study in Ethics*, 2nd ed. New York: Oxford University Press, 2007.

Walker, Margaret Urban. "Hope(s) After Genocide." In *The Uproar of Emotions: Genocide Studies after the Emotional Turn*, edited by Thomas Brudholm and Johannes Lang. New York: Cambridge University Press, forthcoming.

Wallace, R. Jay. *The View From Here: On Affirmation, Attachment, and the Limits of Regret*. Oxford: Oxford University Press, 2013.

Watson, Gary. "Free Agency." *Journal of Philosophy* 72 (1975): 205–220.

Watson, Gary. "Volitional Necessities." In *Agency and Answerability: Selected Essays*, 129–159. Oxford: Oxford University Press, 2004.

Webster, William. *The New Art of Contentment; contained in an Essay upon Philippians IV: 11*. London: J. Everingham and T. Reynolds, 1754.

Wensveen, Louke van. "Attunement: An Ecological Spin on the Virtue of Temperance." *Philosophy in the Contemporary World* 8, no. 2 (2001): 67–78.

Williams, Bernard. "Integrity." In *Utilitarianism: For and Against*, by J. J. C. Smart and Bernard Williams, 108–117. Cambridge: Cambridge University Press, 1973.

Williams, Bernard. *Problems of the Self: Philosophical Papers 1956-1972*. Cambridge: Cambridge University Press, 1973.

Williams, Bernard. *Moral Luck: Philosophyical Papers 1973-1980*. Cambridge: Cambridge University Press, 1981.

Wiggins, David. "Truth, Invention, and the Meaning of Life." *Proceedings of the British Academy* 62 (1977): 331–378.

Winokur, Jon, ed. *Ennui to Go: The Art of Boredom*. Seattle, WA: Sasquatch Books, 2005.

Wollheim, Richard. "Ourselves and Our Future." In *How Many Questions? Essays in Honor of Sidney Morganbesser*, edited by Leigh Cauman, Roberet Schwartz, and Charles Parson, 366–383. Indianapolis, IN: Hackett, 1983.

Wollheim, Richard. *The Thread of Life*. Cambridge, MA: Harvard University Press, 1984.

Wolf, Susan. *Meaning in Life and Why It Matters*. Princeton, NJ: Princeton University Press, 2010.

Wolf, Susan. "Happiness and Meaning: Two Aspects of the Good Life." *Social Philosophy & Policy* 14, no. 1 (1997): 207–225.

Wolf, Susan. "Meaning and Morality." *Proceedings of the Aristotelian Society*, New Series, 97 (1997): 299–315.

Wolf, Susan. "The True, the Good, and the Lovable: Frankfurt's Avoidance of Objectivity." In *Contours of Agency: Essays on Themes by Harry Frankfurt*, edited by Sarah Buss and Lee Overton, 227–244. Cambridge, MA: MIT Press, 2002.

Wolf, Susan. "Meanings of Lives." In *The Variety of Values: Essays on Morality, Meaning & Love*, 89–106. New York: Oxford University Press, 2015.

Wong, Wai-hung "Meaningfulness and Identities." *Ethical Theory and Moral Practice* 11 (2008): 123–148.

Index

motivating interest in the future
  creaturely, 47
  global, 50–52 (*see also* agency,
    background frames of; basal
    hopefulness)
  and valuing attitudes, 49–50
motivating reasons, 82–83, 85
  defeat of (*see* agency, internal defeat of)
  in depression, 61, 85
  and emotions, 83
  "seconding" of, 75, 86, 88–89

narrative unity. *See* life, narrative unity of
normative constraint, 132–135
normative delinquencies, 119, 121–122, 128.
    See also normative constraint
normative outlook, 35–36, 52, 105. *See also*
    leading a life, broad sense of
  defectively held, 58–60
  estrangement from (*see* estrangement)
  maximizing approach to, 38
  and meaningful living (*see* conception of
    meaningfulness, normative outlook)
  misidentification of, 60–61
  pluralizing approach to, 38
  and valuing attitudes (*see* valuing attitude)
normative style. *See* prizing

Paley, William, 168–169
paralysis of the will, 65
Paul, Saint, 148
Pettit, Philip, 70, 79, 80–82, 84, 86
plans
  inability to rely on, 64–66
  and planning idea of the future (*see*
    future, planning idea of)
  precautionary or backup, 78n27,
    80, 81–82
  provisional (*see* commitment, different
    from provisional plans and mere
    intentions)
  reconsideration (*see* intention,
    reconsideration bar for)
  setbacks and obstacles to, 1, 6, 15, 69,
    75–76, 80, 82–84, 140, 163, 171
Portmore, Douglas W., 76n23

positive thinking, 148, 157–158. *See also*
    hope, "as-if"; hope, optimistic
previsaged future, 8–9, 50, 72, 116
prizing, 112–114
probability assessment. *See* hope, and
    probability assessment

quasi-practical attitude. *See* contentment, as
    quasi-practical attitude

Ratcliffe, Matthew, 74
reasons-for-anyone, 33–34, 39, 44, 106
reasons-for-the-initiated, 34, 39
reasons-for-me, 35, 39, 40, 108
redeemed costs, 76–77. *See also*
    unredeemed costs
regret, 62n34, 70n7, 78, 149, 155
Rosati, Connie S., 99

Schapiro, Tamar, 156
Schechtman, Marya, 103
Seligman, Martin E. P., 65
Snow, Nancy, 84
Snow, Robert P., 130, 135
Spacks, Patricia Meyer, 125, 144
Svendsen, Lars, 123, 127
Swanton, Christine, 161–162

Taylor, Richard, 47–48
temporal attitudes, 1, 70n7, 136, 149–150.
    See also future-oriented attitudes
temporal costs, 6, 33, 37–38, 118, 171
temporal meaning, 129–130, 132,
    141–142
  vs. evaluative meaning, 128–129
temporal style, 112–114, 140. *See also* time
    expenditure, temporal management
    style of
temporally oriented beings, 1–2, 7–8, 32, 85,
    88, 145, 172
Things Fall Apart, 68–69, 73–74
time expenditure, 13–18, 118, 171
  entailed, 15–17, 111, 118
  filler, 15
  and meaningful living, 17–18, 32–33,
    37–39, 44–45, 108, 171
  norm-required, 17